Level 2

Integrated Chinese

中文聽說讀寫

Traditional and Simplified Textbook

Yuehua Liu and Tao-chung Yao
Yaohua Shi and Nyan-ping Bi

Cheng & Tsui Company

First edition 1997
2005 Printing

Cheng & Tsui Company
25 West Street
Boston, MA 02111-1213 USA

Library of Congress Catalog Card Number: 97-068900

Traditional and Simplified Character Edition
ISBN 0-88727-275-4

Companion workbooks, teacher's manual and audio tapes are also available from the publisher.

Printed in the United States of America

前　言

　　我們為本書命名為《中文聽說讀寫》，因為這套教材的目的是全面訓練學生的聽、說、讀、寫能力。這一任務是由課文、語法、句型練習(或詞語練習)和學生手冊共同承擔的。

　　在本教材的編寫過程中我們一直遵循結構與功能相結合的原則。學一種語言，不學發音、語法、詞匯是不可想像的。我們十分重視語法、句型、重點詞語的教學，不但一年級有語法註釋，二年級仍然有語法註釋。二年級的語法教學是在一年級的基礎上，在深度與廣度上更加進一步的循環，並增加了相似語法現象的比較。我們解釋語法時儘可能做到簡明實用，避免過多的語法術語，使學生容易懂，容易掌握。我們在語法注釋中特別著重用法的講解。

　　學習語言的目的是為了能運用這種語言，所以我們在教好學生漢語基本結構的基礎上，力求在培養學生的交際能力上下功夫。這體現在：我們的課文力求接近學生的生活，使學生學了就能用；二年級的課文涉及學校、家庭、社會生活以及中國文化等很多方面，一方面可以使學生學到很多有用的詞語，另一方面可以引起學生說話、討論的興趣。學生手冊的閱讀部分，有一些真實材料，目的是使學生儘早接近中國的實際生活。在口語練習部分，提供很多接近實際生活的話題供教學參考。

　　我們畢竟教的是中文，所以絲毫不能忽視中國文化知識的介紹。我們儘量把文化背景知識的傳授寫於語言教學之中。本書副課文的內容不少是有關中國情況的，在聽力閱讀材料中，更能體現這一點。

　　本書的學生手冊內容比較豐富，除了聽力閱讀練習以外，還有語法、重點詞語練習，翻譯練習等，形式力求多樣，力求與課文密切配合。學生手冊是本教材不可分割的一部分。但由於各個學校的課時不同，學生的背景不同，學生手冊中的練習可以酌情選擇使用。

　　本書的教師手冊目前與學生手冊的內容基本相同，只是提供了練習答案，並附有中文語法注釋，供教師參考。今後我們將逐漸充實教師手冊的內容，比如提出教學建議，課堂活動，題庫等等。

　　《中文聽說讀寫》是一個教材系列，包括兩套，供一、二年級使用。本書的編寫計劃是1993年夏在印地安那大學暑期中文學校開始制定的，1993年秋天到1994春天花了七、八個月的時間編寫出初稿，1994年暑假開始在印第安那大學暑期學校試用。1994年秋，University of Massachusetts at

Amherst , Amherst College , Mount Holyoke College，首先試用這一套教材，在試用過程中給提出我們很多寶貴。意見和建議。其後，又先後有Washington University in St. Louis, University of Winsconsin at Madision, San Diego State University, University of Iowa, University of Notre Dame 等二十多所學校試用，給予我們很大的支持。在這里我們要感謝曾經給我們提過很多建議並大力推薦本教材的鄧守信、Alvin Cohen、藍樺、滕小平、何寶璋、柯傳仁、張正聲、吳鳳濤、鄭文君等諸位老師。在教材編寫過程中，印第安那大學暑期學校的賈志傑、沈靜、郭愛華老師給予我們很多具體幫助。我們也要感謝項佳因同學為我們畫了許多插圖，Margot Lenhart, Karen McCabe 幫助修改英文，Debbie Struemph 曾給予我們大力支持，在此我們一併表示感謝。

　　最後我們還應該感謝張光天女士、張澤蒼先生、潘永慶女士，感謝他們四年來給予我們的無私支持和幫助。

編者

1997年8月

PREFACE

We named this set of instructional materials *Integrated Chinese* out of the belief that a holistic approach is the best way to develop students' listening, speaking, reading, and writing skills. The textbooks, their companion workbooks and teacher's manuals are all designed to achieve that purpose.

The ultimate goal of learning a new language is to develop the ability to communicate in that language. Without neglecting basic structures, we strive to develop students' communicative skills by incorporating topics that are of interest to them: campus and family life, social issues, aspects of Chinese culture, etc. The hope is that students will be sufficiently engaged by the subjects and be motivated to quickly apply their newly-acquired vocabulary and grammatical structures in conversation. The workbooks provide many such topics for oral practice.

While we emphasize the communicative functions, we attempt to give equal weight to linguistic structures. We believe that to master a foreign language one must study phonetics and grammar as well as vocabulary. Therefore, we devote much attention to teaching grammar, sentence patterns, and important phrases and expressions. Our grammar notes go beyond merely describing discrete grammatical phenomena; instead, we try to situate them in their appropriate contexts and emphasize their usage. In *Integrated Chinese, Level Two*, we try to expand the student's understanding of Chinese grammar further by highlighting similar or easily confused structures.

To teach Chinese language is also to teach Chinese culture. Because most of the dialogues in *Integrated Chinese* are set in the United States, we use the listening and reading exercises to acquaint students with aspects of Chinese culture. In the second half of *Integrated Chinese, Level Two*, for example, we include a paragraph about contemporary China after each dialogue.

The workbooks are an essential part of *Integrated Chinese*. A great variety of materials designed to develop students' listening, speaking, reading, and writing skills are included: pattern drills, grammar and translation exercises, oral practice, writing practice, reading exercises, etc. Because no two language programs are alike, instructors need not assign all the exercises, nor use them in the same order as they appear in the books. There is flexibility in their application.

At present, the teacher's manual contain all the exercises in the student workbooks, workbook answer keys and grammar notes in Chinese. In time, we plan to add pedagogical suggestions, classroom activities and a test bank.

Despite our best intentions and efforts, we realize that there is room for improvement. The sheer scale of the project also means that mistakes are occasionally overlooked. Feedback on any aspect of *Integrated Chinese* will be much appreciated.

ACKNOWLEDGMENTS

The project of compiling a series of new Chinese language teaching materials was initiated in the summer of 1993 at the East Asian Summer Languages Institute (EASLI) at Indiana University. The first draft took about eight months to complete. It was truly a collaborative effort, with two teams of teachers simultaneously working on two sets of textbooks, student workbooks and teacher's manuals. Several of our colleagues contributed to both sets of materials. Professor Liangyan Ge, for instance, wrote four lessons for *Integrated Chinese, Level Two*. The entire series was adopted on a trial basis at the EASLI Chinese School in the summer of 1994. In the fall of 1994, our colleagues at the University of Massachusetts at Amherst, Amherst College and Mount Holyoke College graciously offered to field test *Integrated Chinese*. Subsequently, it was adopted at more than twenty universities and colleges around the country, including Washington University in St. Louis, University of Wisconsin at Madison, San Diego State University, University of Iowa and University of Notre Dame. We are deeply grateful to our colleagues at these institutions for their encouragement and careful critique.

Space does not allow us to thank each and every one of the teachers and colleagues whose support and wisdom sustained us throughout the compilation and revision process. However, we would like to express our appreciation to Professor Shou-hsin Teng for recommending *Integrated Chinese* to our colleagues when it was still in its infancy. Our gratitude also goes to Professors Alice Cheang, Alvin Cohen, Baozhang He, Chuanren Ke, Hua Lan, Xiaoping Teng, Fengtao Wu, Hongming Zhang and Zhengsheng Zhang for their vote of confidence and invaluable suggestions.

At EASLI, Mr. Zhijie Jia, Ms. Jing Shen, and Ms. Aihua Guo were exceedingly generous with their time and expertise. Ms. Margot Lenhart and Ms. Karen McCabe fine-tuned our English. Ms. Debbine Struemph showed great patience with our numerous requests for favors. To all of them, we would like to acknowledge our gratitude.

We are also deeply indebted to Ms. Jiayin Xiang. The illustrations, which she drew to our specifications, are now an indispensable part of *Integrated Chinese, Level Two*.

Finally, we would like to thank Ms. K. T. Yao, Mr. Tes-Tsang Chang and Ms. Pan Yongqing for their understanding and unfailing support throughout the four years of compiling and revising *Integrated Chinese*.

Table of Abbreviations

adj	*adjective*
adv	*adverb*
av	*auxiliary verb*
ce	*common expression*
col	*colloquialism*
conj	*conjunction*
exe	*exclamation*
interj	*interjection*
m	*measure word*
n	*noun*
np	*noun phrase*
nu	*numerals*
p	*particle*
pr	*pronoun*
prep	*preposition*
ono	*onomatopoeic*
qp	*question particle*
qpr	*question pronoun*
t	*time word*
v	*verb*
vc	*verb plus complement*
vo	*verb plus object*
*	*vocabulary items which first appeared in integrated Chinese, Level One*

The Integrated Family

本書人物

Table of Contents

Lesson One: 開學 1

    Vocabulary 5

    Grammar Notes: 7

        the Dynamic Particle 了;

        the "是...的" Construction;

        除了...以外, 還...;

        再說...

    Words and Expressions 14

Lesson Two: 宿舍 17

    Vocabulary 21

    Grammar Notes: 23

        Word Order in Chinese (I);

        Existential Sentences;

        比較; 得很; 那麼; 恐怕

    Words and Expressions 30

Lesson Three: 飯館 35

    Vocabulary 41

    Grammar Notes: 44

        About "topics;" Adverbial and 地;

        一+V; 原來;

        極了; 又...又...;

        多/少 + V (+ NU + M + N)

    Words and Expressions 50

Lesson Four: 買東西 55

    Vocabulary 61

    Grammar Notes: 64

        the Position of Time Phrases;

        無論...都...;

        於是; 真;

        Adj./V + 是 + Adj. /V, 可是/ 但是

        難道; Reduplication of Verbs

    Words and Expressions 72

Lesson Five: 選專業 78

    Vocabulary 81

Grammar Notes: 84
只是/就是；對他來說 (to him)；
至於；要麼...要麼...；
另外；Resultative Complements (I)；
再、又、还 Compared

Words and Expressions 92

Lesson Six: 租房子 95

Vocabulary 101

Grammar Notes: 103
Descriptive Complements with 得；
...以後 Compared with ...的時候；
...的話；最...不過(沒有)了；
Directional Complements (I)；
Chinese Numeric Series

Words and Expressions 110

Lesson Seven: 男朋友 113

Vocabulary 119

Grammar Notes: 122
...,才；先...再...；
...上；V來V去；
Directional Complements (II): (indicating result)
出(來) (indicating result)；
...以後 and ....以來 Compared；

Words and Expressions 127

Lesson Eight: 電影和電視的影響 131

Vocabulary 135

Grammar Notes: 138
Distinguishing among 的、地、得；
一邊...，一邊...；
就是...也... (even if ...still...)；
反而；難免；rhetorical questions

Words andExpressions 145

Lesson Nine: 旅行 149

Vocabulary 155

Grammar Notes: 158
過(indicating experience)；
過(indicating completion)；
除非；哪兒...哪兒...

既然...就...；然後；
Word Order in Chinese (II)

Words and Expressions 166

Lesson Ten: 在郵局 171

Vocabulary 175

Grammar Notes: 180

V著V著；Resultative Complements (II);
把 Structure; Attributives and 的；
一向 and 一直

Words and Expressions 189

Lesson Eleven: 一封信 193

Vocabulary 197

Grammar Notes: 200

"幾天來"；才 and 就 compared;
"好不容易"；再三；
the prepositions 跟、向、對 compared；
了 after a verb and 了 at the end of a sentence；

Words and Expressions 206

Lesson Twelve: 中國的節日 209

Vocabulary 215

Grammar Notes: 217

Potential Complements;
"戴著玩"；the Indefinite Use of
the Interrogative Pronoun 什麼；
Cohesion

Words and Expressions 225

Lesson Thirteen: 談體育 229

Vocabulary 235

Grammar Notes: 238

連...也/都；反正；
(成千)上(萬)；(有益)於；
Ways of Making Comparisons;
Written Style

Words and Expressions 243

Lesson Fourteen: 家庭 247

Vocabulary 253

Grammar Notes: 255
    Directional Complements (III): (indicating state);
    Potential Complement V + 不/得+了;
    要(應該);
    下來 (indicating result)
    Topics (II)

Words and Expressions 261

Lesson Fifteen: 男女平等 265

Vocabulary 271

Grammar Notes: 275
    同樣 and 一樣;
    隨著...;在...方面;
    甚至; Sentence Structure and
    Word Order in Chinese (III)

Words and Expressions 279

Lesson Sixteen: 健康與保險 283

Vocabulary 289

Grammar Notes: 292
    Multiple Attributives;
    是 Indicating Emphasis or Confirmation;
    V + 不/得 起;
    Modal Verb 會;
    畢竟(到底、究竟);
    Using 不如 to Make Comparisons;
    Reduplication of Measure Words

Words and Expressions 300

Lesson Seventeen: 教育 305

Vocabulary 311

Grammar Notes: 315
    很不以爲然; 簡直;
    V+壞了; 適合 and 合適;
    被 Structure; 從來

Words and Expressions 319

Lesson Eighteen: 槍枝與犯罪 325

Vocabulary
Grammar Notes:
    槍走了火; the Adverb 正;
    the Conjunction 並; 等(等)

Words and Expressions 337

Lesson Nineteen: 動物與人 341

    Vocabulary 347

    Grammar Notes: 350

        為了 and 因為; the adverb 可;
        (死)於; 其中; 而

    Words and Expressions 354

Lesson Twenty: 環境保護 357

    Vocabulary 361

    Grammar Notes: 363

        怎麼 and 為什麼;
        (好)多了 and (好)得多
        ...吧, ...吧...;
        往往 and 常常

    Words and Expressions 368

Index to Vocabulary 372

第一課　開學

一・課文

　　暑假結束了，學校就要開學了。學生從各個地方回到了學校。張天明是一年級的學生，家在波士頓，離這裏很遠。他是自己一個人坐飛機來的。辦完了註冊手續，他來到了新生宿舍。

張天明：　人怎麼這麼多？
柯　林：　你是新生嗎？
張天明：　是，我是。你呢？

第一课 开学

一·课文

　　暑假结束了，学校就要开学了。学生从各个地方回到了学校。张天明是一年级的学生，家在波士顿，离这里很远。他是自己一个人坐飞机来的。办完了注册手续，他来到了新生宿舍。

张天明：　人怎么这么多？

柯　林：　你是新生吗？

张天明：　是，我是。你呢？

柯　林：　我是老生，在這兒幫新生搬東西。你是中國人吧？

張天明：　我祖籍是中國，可是我是在美國出生、在美國長大的。

柯　林：　請問，你的中文名字是…

張天明：　我姓張，弓長張，也就是一張紙的張，名字是天明，天氣的天，明天的明。

柯　林：　我正在學中文，我的中文名字叫柯林。你手續都辦完了嗎？

張天明：　辦完了。你住在哪兒？也住在這兒嗎？

柯　林：　不，這是新生宿舍，我住在校外。

張天明：　住在校內好，還是住在校外好？

柯　林：　有的人喜歡住學校宿舍，覺得方便、安全。有的人喜歡住在校外，覺得省錢。我住在校外，除了為了省錢以外，還為了自由，再說，住在校內也不見得方便。

張天明：　是嗎？那我也搬到校外好嗎？

柯　林：　你剛來，在學校住對你有好處，可以適應一下大學生活。過些時候如果想搬家，就找我，我幫你找房子。

張天明：　好，謝謝。我離開家的時候，媽媽告訴我："在家靠父母，出門靠朋友"。她說得很有道理。以後請你多幫忙。

柯　林：　沒問題。哎，前邊沒有人了，你可以搬了。我幫你提行李，走吧。

張天明：　好，謝謝。

柯　林：　我是老生，在这儿帮新生搬东西。你是中国人吧？

张天明：　我祖籍是中国，可是我是在美国出生、在美国长大的。

柯　林：　请问，你的中文名字是...

张天明：　我姓张，弓长张，也就是一张纸的张，名字是天明，天气的天，明天的明。

柯　林：　我正在学中文，我的中文名字叫柯林。你手续都办完了吗？

张天明：　办完了。你住在哪儿？也住在这儿吗？

柯　林：　不，这是新生宿舍，我住在校外。

张天明：　住在校内好，还是住在校外好？

柯　林：　有的人喜欢住学校宿舍，觉得方便、安全。有的人喜欢住在校外，觉得省钱。我住在校外，除了为了省钱以外，还为了自由，再说，住在校内也不见得方便。

张天明：　是吗？那我也搬到校外好吗？

柯　林：　你刚来，在学校住对你有好处，可以适应一下大学生活。过些时候如果想搬家，就找我，我帮你找房子。

张天明：　好，谢谢。我离开家的时候，妈妈告诉我："在家靠父母，出门靠朋友"。她说得很有道理。以后请你多帮忙。

柯　林：　没问题。哎，前边没有人了，你可以搬了。我帮你提行李，走吧。

张天明：　好，谢谢。

二·生詞表

開學	开学	vo	kāi xué	new semester begins
暑假*		n	shǔjià	summer vacation
結束	结束	v	jiéshù	end
各*		pr	gè	each; every
年級*	年级	n	niánjí	grade; year
坐*		v	zuò	sit; travel by
飛機*	飞机	n	fēijī	airplane
辦*	办	v	bàn	do; handle
註冊	注册	v	zhùcè	register; matriculate
手續	手续	n	shǒuxù	procedure
新生		n	xīnshēng	new student
老生		n	lǎoshēng	returning student; lit. old student
搬*		vc	bān	move
祖籍		n	zǔjí	ancestral home
出生		v	chūshēng	be born
長大	长大	vc	zhǎng dà	grow up
弓		n	gōng	bow
長*	长	adj	cháng	long
校外			xiào wài	off-campus
校内			xiào nèi	on-campus
方便*		adj	fāngbiàn	convenient

住在城裏買東西很方便。

**我想問您一個問題，您
現在方便嗎？**

安全		adj	ānquán	safe
				這個地方很安全。
				我們宿舍的安全問題很大。
省錢	省钱	vo	shěng qián	save money; economical
自由		adj	zìyóu	free
再說	再说	conj	zàishuō	besides
不見得	不见得		bú jiàn de	not necessarily
好處	好处	n	hǎochù	advantage
				聽錄音對學中文有好處。
				坐飛機的好處是很快。
適應	适应	v	shìyìng	adapt
				我們來美國，對美國的天氣還不適應。
				你適應大學的生活了嗎？
搬家		vo	bān jiā	move (house)
離開	离开	vc	lí kāi	leave
靠		v	kào	depend
				一個人應該靠自己，不應該常常靠別人幫助。
				我不會開車，去什麼地方都靠你了。
出門*	出门	v	chū mén	be away from home; go out
道理		n	dàolǐ	reason; sense
前邊	前边		qiánbian	in front
行李*		n	xíngli	luggage

專名 Proper Nouns

張天明	张天明		Zhāng Tiānmíng a masculine name

| 波士頓 | 波士頓 | Bōshìdùn | Boston |
| 柯林 | | Kē Lín | a masculine name |

難寫的字：

機 續 搬 籍 離 邊

三·語法註釋 Grammar Notes

1. The dynamic particle "了"：

The dynamic particle "了" signifies realization or completion. It can appear either after a verb or at the end of a sentence. It suggests that at a certain time something occurred, or an action was completed or a certain change took place. There is usually a time phrase in the sentence.

(1) 昨天上午我看了一個電影。

昨天上午我看了一个电影。

Yesterday morning I saw a movie.

(2) 去年我媽媽去了一次北京，在那兒住了很長時間。

去年我妈妈去了一次北京，在那儿住了很长时间。

Last year my mother went to Beijing, and stayed there for a long time.

(3) A：這本書你看了嗎？

这本书你看了吗？

Have you read this book?

B：看了。

看了

Yes, I have.

If there is an object involved, and if that object is modified by an attributive, "了" should be put immediately after the verb, unless the sentence is embedded in a longer piece of discourse with a "了" at the end. The object could be modified by a measure word, which is usually the case, as in the first clause of (1) and (2), or by an adjective or a noun, as in the second clause of (2).

(4) 四月了，天氣慢慢暖和了。

四月了，天气慢慢暖和了。

It's April. The weather has begun to warm up.

(5) 我原來想今天晚上看電影，可是明天要考試，所以不看了。

我原来想今天晚上看电影，可是明天要考试，所以不看了。

I originally planned to see a movie tonight, but I have an exam tomorrow, so I'm not going.

(6) A：你昨天做什麼了？

你昨天做什么了？

What did you do yesterday?

B：看電影了。

看电影了。

I saw a movie.

Sometimes there is no time phrase in the sentence. The time implied is "just now" or "up till now:"

(7) A：你吃飯了嗎？

你吃饭了吗？

Have you eaten?

B：吃了。

吃了。

Yes, I have.

A：花了多少錢？

花了多少钱？

How much money did you spend?

B：十塊錢。

十块钱。

Ten dollars.

Sometimes there is no time phrase in a sentence with "了." In this kind of sentence there are generally two verbal phrases. The time of action is a relative one. For instance,

(8) 他下了課就來了。

他下了课就来了。

He came right after the class.

(9) 我吃了飯就去。

我吃了饭就去。

I'll go right after lunch.

In (8) the time of "來" is "下了課" i.e., after the class. In (9) the time of "去" is "吃了飯," i.e., after lunch..

2. The " 是...的... " Construction:

When the occurrence of an action or an event is known to both the listener and the speaker, one must use the "是...的 ..." construction to indicate the time, place, manner, or purpose of the occurrence or the agent of the action. "是" is optional.

(1) A：王老師來了嗎？

王老师来了吗？

Did Wang Laoshi come?

B：來了。

来了。

Yes, he did.

A：（是）什麼時候來的？

（是）什么时候来的？

When did he come?

B：昨天晚上來的。

昨天晚上来的。

Yesterday evening.

A：（是）跟誰一起來的？

（是）跟谁一起来的？

Whom did he come with?

B：是跟他姐姐一起來的。

是跟他姐姐一起来的。

With his sister.

A：是坐飛機來的還是開車來的？

是坐飞机来的还是开车来的？

Did they come here by plane or by car?

B：開車來的。

开车来的。

By car.

(2) 張天明是在波士頓出生的。

张天明是在波士顿出生的。

Zhang Tianming was born in Boston.

(The question of birthplace presupposes birth.)

(3) A：你是大學生嗎？

你是大学生吗？

Are you an undergrad?

B：不，我是研究生。

不，我是研究生。

No, I am a graduate student.

A：你是在哪兒上的大學？

你是在哪儿上的大学？

Where did you go to college?

B：在波士頓大學。

在波士頓大学。

Boston University.

To recapitulate, when it is a known fact that an action already took place, to inquire about or explain the time or place of the action, one should use "是...的...." instead of "了."

3. "除了...以外，還...":

"除了...以外，還..." is an inclusive pattern. The English equivalent is "in addition to."

(1) 他除了學中文以外，還學法文。

他除了学中文以外，还学法文。

(＝他學中文，也學法文。)

(＝他学中文，也学法文。)

Besides Chinese, he also studies French.

(i.e, "He studies both Chinese and French.")

(2) 我的同學除了小王以外，還有小林去過中國。

我的同学除了小王以外，还有小林去过中国。

(＝小王和小林都去過中國。)

(＝小王和小林都去过中国。)

In our class, besides Xiao Wang, Xiao Lin has also been to China.

(i.e., "Both Xiao Wang and Xiao Lin have been to China.")

(3) 我晚上除了看書以外，還常常看電視。

我晚上除了看书以外，还常常看电视。

(＝＝我晚上常常看書，也常常看電影。)

(＝＝我晚上常常看书，也常常看电影。)

Besides reading, I also often watch TV in the evening.

(i.e, "I often read and watch TV in the evening.")

On the contrary, "除了...以外, 都..." is an exclusive pattern. The English equivalent is "except for:"

(4) 除了小柯以外，我的同學都去過中國。

除了小柯以外，我的同学都去过中国。

(＝＝小柯沒去過中國。)

(＝＝小柯没去过中国。)

Except for Xiao Ke, all of my classmates have been to China

(i.e., "Xiao Ke has not been to China.")

(5) 除了看書以外，晚上什麼事我都做。

除了看书以外，晚上什么事我都做。

(＝＝我晚上不喜歡看書。)

(＝＝我晚上不喜欢看书。)

Except for reading, I'll do anything in thc evening.

(i.e., "I don't like to read in the evening.")

4. " 再說 "：

"再說" is used to provide additional reasons:

(1) 你別走了，天太晚了，再說我們要說的事還沒說完
呢。

你別走了，天太晚了，再説我們要説的事還没説完
呢。

Please stay. It's too late. Besides, we haven't finished discussing the things that
we need to discuss.

(2) 我不想學日文，日文太難，再説對我的專業也没有好
處。

我不想学日文，日文太难，再说对我的专业也没有好
处。

I don't want to study Japanese. Japanese is too difficult. Besides, it
doesn't do any good for my major.

(3) 她不應該跟那個人結婚，那個人不太聰明，再説對她
也不是太好。

她不应该跟那个人结婚，那个人不太聪明，再说对她
也不是太好。

She shouldn't marry that guy. He is not very bright. Besides, he is not very
nice to her.

Note that "而且" also means "furthermore," but it is not used to explain reasons only:

(4) 我現在不但上英文，而且還上中文。

我现在不但上英文，而且还上中文。

Now besides English, I'm also taking Chinese.

(5) 他姐姐不但很聰明，而且很漂亮。

他姐姐不但很聪明，而且很漂亮。

His sister is not only bright but also pretty.

In (1), (2), (3) "再説" is interchangeable with "而且," but in (4) and (5)"而且" is not
interchangeable with "再説."

四·詞語練習

1. " 有的...，有的... " (some...some...):

Example: 有的人喜歡住學校宿舍，覺得方便、安全，有的人
喜歡住校外，覺得省錢。

有的人喜欢住学校宿舍，觉得方便、安全，有的人
喜欢住校外，觉得省钱。

(1) 我的同學，_____住在學校的宿舍裏，_____住在家裏。

我的同学，_____住在学校的宿舍里，_____住在家里。

(2) 我買的書，有的是_____的，有的是_____的。

我买的书，有的是_____的，有的是_____的。

(3) 他的朋友，有的是_____，有的是_____。

他的朋友，有的是_____，有的是_____。

2. " 覺得 " (與 " 認為 " 比較)(覺得 vs. 認為)(feel):

Example: 有的人喜歡住學校宿舍，覺得方便、安全，有的人
喜歡住校外，覺得省錢。

有的人喜欢住学校宿舍，觉得方便、安全，有的人
喜欢住校外，觉得省钱。

(1) 你_____這部電影好不好？

你_____这部电影好不好？

(2) 我覺得你的想法_____。

我觉得你的想法_____。

(3) 我覺得波士頓這個地方 _____。

我觉得波士顿这个地方 _____。

When expressing an opinion, one could use "覺得," which is less formal than "認為."

3. "**不見得**" (not necessarily):

> Example: 再說，住校內也不見得方便。
>
> 再说，住校内也不见得方便。

(1) 我認爲吃牛肉＿＿＿＿＿＿對身體沒有好處。

我认为吃牛肉＿＿＿＿＿＿对身体没有好处。

(2) 日本汽車不見得比＿＿＿＿＿＿貴。

日本汽车不见得比＿＿＿＿＿＿贵。

(3) 中文不見得比日文＿＿＿＿＿＿。

中文不见得比日文＿＿＿＿＿＿。

4. "**對...有好處**" (good for...):

> Example: 你剛來，在學校住一段時間對你有好處。
>
> 你刚来，在学校住一段时间对你有好处。

(1) 多聽多說對＿＿＿＿＿＿有好處。

多听多说对＿＿＿＿＿＿有好处。

(2) 少喝酒對＿＿＿＿＿有好處。

少喝酒对＿＿＿＿＿有好处。

(3) 汽車太多對＿＿＿＿＿＿沒有好處。

汽车太多对＿＿＿＿＿＿没有好处。

五・看圖說話

第二課　宿　舍

一・課文

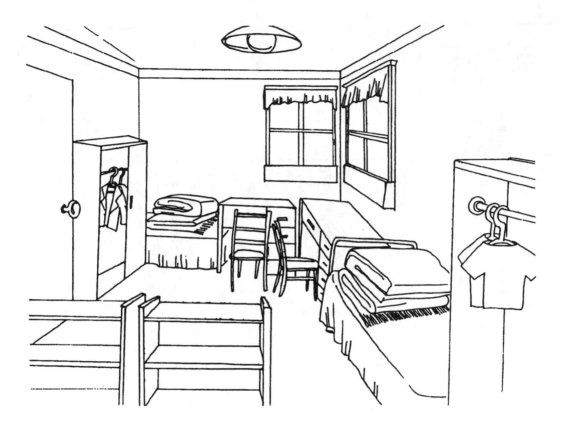

　　張天明宿舍的房間不太大，住兩個人。他的同屋叫約翰，是前天從華盛頓來的，對學校已經比較熟悉了。

　　房間裏有一些家俱。靠窗戶擺著兩張書桌，每張桌子的前邊有一把椅子。書桌的旁邊是床，床上有被子和毯子。床前有兩個衣櫃，櫃子裏掛著一些衣服。門旁邊放著兩個書架，書架還是空的。

第二课 宿 舍

一. 课 文

张天明宿舍的房间不太大，住两个人。他的同屋叫约翰，是前天从华盛顿来的，对学校已经比较熟悉了。

房间里有一些家具。靠窗户摆着两张书桌，每张桌子的前边有一把椅子。书桌的旁边是床，床上有被子和毯子。床前有两个衣柜，柜子里挂着一些衣服。门旁边放着两个书架，书架还是空的。

張天明： 約翰，真熱！房間裏沒有空調嗎？

約　翰： 沒有。聽說這棟樓設備比較舊，廁所、浴室也比較小。

張天明： 那住這兒恐怕很不方便吧？

約　翰： 不，我來了兩天了，覺得很方便。餐廳就在樓下，餐廳旁邊有一個小商店，賣日用品和文具。教室離這兒不遠，走路差不多五、六分鐘。

張天明： 洗衣服方便嗎？

約　翰： 方便得很。我們這層樓有三台洗衣機和三台烘乾機。

張天明： 這兒吵不吵？

約　翰： 不，這兒離大馬路很遠，很安靜。

張天明： 聽說學校餐廳的飯一般都不太好。這兒的呢？

約　翰： 你猜對了，餐廳的飯真的不怎麼樣。我來這兒以後，剛吃了一天就沒有胃口了。

張天明： 真的？那怎麼辦？

約　翰： 你別著急。我聽說附近有很多飯館，還有一家中國餐館呢。

張天明： 我覺得美國的中國餐館，好吃的不多。

約　翰： 那也不見得。聽老生說，那家中國餐館的菜很地道。

張天明： 真的嗎？那麼過幾天你帶我去那兒看看，好嗎？

約　翰： 好，沒問題。

张天明：　约翰，真热！房间里没有空调吗？

约　翰：　没有。听说这栋楼设备比较旧，厕所、浴室也比
　　　　　较小。

张天明：　那住这儿恐怕很不方便吧？

约　翰：　不，我来了两天了，觉得很方便。餐厅就在楼下，
　　　　　餐厅旁边还有一个小商店，卖日用品和文具。教室离
　　　　　这儿不远，走路差不多五、六分钟。

张天明：　洗衣服方便吗？

约　翰：　方便得很。我们这层楼有三台洗衣机和三台烘干机。

张天明：　这儿吵不吵？

约　翰：　不，这儿离大马路很远，很安静。

张天明：　听说学校餐厅的饭一般都不太好。这儿的呢？

约　翰：　你猜对了，餐厅的饭真的不怎么样。我来这儿以後，
　　　　　刚吃了一天就没胃口了。

张天明：　真的？那怎么办？

约　翰：　你别着急。我听说附近有很多饭馆，还有一家中国
　　　　　餐馆呢。

张天明：　我觉得美国的中国餐馆，好吃的不多。

约　翰：　那也不见得。听老生说，那家中国餐馆的菜很地道。

张天明：　真的吗？那么过几天你带我去那儿看看，好吗？

约　翰：　好，没问题。

二·生詞表

同屋		n	tóngwū	roommate
前天		t	qiántian	the day before yesterday
熟悉		adj	shúxi	familiar

我剛來，對這兒還
不太熟悉。

你不是高中生了，應該熟悉
一下大學老師怎麼上課。

家俱*	家具	n	jiājù	furniture
靠(窗戶)		v	kào	next to; near
窗戶		n	chuānghu	window
擺	摆	v	bǎi	put; place
床		n	chuáng	bed
被子		n	bèizi	comforter; quilt
毯子		n	tǎnzi	blanket
衣櫃	衣柜	n	yīguì	wardrobe
櫃子	柜子	n	guìzi	cabinet; cupboard
掛	挂	v	guà	hang
書架*	书架	n	shūjià	bookshelf
空		adj	kōng	empty
空調	空调	n	kōngtiáo	air-conditioning
棟	栋	m	dòng	measure word for buildings
設備	设备	n	shèbèi	facilities
舊	旧	adj	jiù	(of things) old
廁所*	厕所	n	cèsuǒ	restroom

浴室		n	yùshì	bathroom
恐怕		adv	kǒngpà	I'm afraid
餐廳*	餐厅	n	cāntīng	cafeteria
樓下	楼下		lóu xià	downstairs
商店		n	shāngdiàn	shop
日用品		n	rìyòngpǐn	daily household necessities
文具		n	wénjù	writing supplies; stationery
層	层	m	céng	measure word for floors
台		m	tái	measure word for machines
洗衣機	洗衣机	n	xǐyī jī	washing machine
烘乾機	烘干机	n	hōnggān jī	drier
吵*		adj	chǎo	noisy
馬路	马路	n	mǎlù	road
安靜*	安静	adj	ānjìng	quiet

我們的宿舍很安靜。
安靜點兒，弟弟在睡覺。

一般		adv	yìbān	generally
聽說*	听说		tīngshuō	be told; hear of
猜對了	猜对了	vc	cāi duì le	guessed correctly

你猜今天的舞會誰會來？
我猜不著。

胃口		n	wèikǒu	appetite
真的		adv	zhēnde	really; truly
著急	着急	v	zháojí	worry; feel anxious

聽說妹妹病了，我很著急。
別著急，她的病會好的。

| 餐館 | 餐馆 | n | cānguǎr | restaurant |

地道		adj	dìdào	authentic

他說的北京話很地道。

這是地道的中國菜。

過幾天	过几天		guò jǐ tiān	in a few days
帶	带	v	dài	take somebody along

媽媽常常帶我去公園玩兒。

專名 Proper Nouns

約翰	约翰	Yuēhàn	John
華盛頓	华盛顿	Huáshèngdùn	Washington

難寫的字：

窗 擺 櫃 舊 餐 廳

三·語法註釋 Grammar Notes

1. Word Order in Chinese (I) :

In Chinese, if the predicate is a verb, the structure of a sentence can be very complex. The question then arises as to how to structure the sentence. The usual word order in Chinese is: Subject--Verb—Object. For instance,

我　打　球了。

我　打　球了。

I　　played　ball.

If the subject or the object is modified by an attributive signifying possession, quantity, etc., the attributive should precede the modified. In the following sentences, the attributives appear in parentheses.

(1)（我的）（小）妹妹買了（一本）（很有意思的）書。

　　（我的）（小）妹妹买了（一本）（很有意思的）书。

(My) (little) sister bought (a) (very interesting) book.

(2) 我很喜歡（媽媽給我寄來的）衣服。

　　我很喜欢（妈妈给我寄来的）衣服。

I really like the clothes (that my mother sent me).

(3) 這就是（我以前住的）地方。

　　这就是（我以前住的）地方。

This is the place (where I used to live).

If there is an adverbial signifying the time, place, co-agent, or manner of an action, it should precede the verb. One could also put the time and place before the subject. In the following sentences the adverbials appear in brackets.

(4) 我們<昨天>去了（一個）（很遠的）地方。

　　我们<昨天>去了（一个）（很远的）地方。

<Yesterday> we went to (a) (far-away) place.

(5) 他<在房間裏><慢慢地>走著。

　　他<在房间里><慢慢地>走着。

He was pacing <slowly > <in the room.>

(6) <明天>我要<跟一個朋友><從學校>開車去南方旅行。

　　<明天>我要<跟一个朋友><从学校>开车去南方旅行。

<Tomorrow> I'm going to drive <from school> to the south <with a friend.>

It should be noted that attributives and adverbials always appear before the words they modify. However, verbs are very often followed by complements indicating the results of the actions. For example,

(7) 我<剛才>寫[錯]了（一個)字。

　　我<刚才>写[错]了（一个)字。

I wrote a character [wrong] <just now>.

(8) 請你坐[下]。

请你坐[下]。

Please sit [down].

The above is a brief description of the basic word order in Chinese. Many factors can affect the word order in Chinese. We will be touching upon these factors later on.

2. Existential Sentences:

The word order of an existential sentence is somewhat different from that of the typical Chinese sentence. The structure of existential sentences is as follows: place word + verb + (了/著 +) numerals + noun. Existential sentences indicate that something exists at a certain place. For instance, "桌子上放著一本書 (there is a book lying on the desk)," "門前有一棵樹 (there is a tree in front of the door)," "房後是一片綠地 (behind the house there is a green space)." There are three kinds of verbs in existential sentences: "有," "是," and verbs signifying bodily movements:

(1) 黑板上有一些字。

黑板上有一些字。

There are a few characters on the blackboard.

(2) 桌子上是一本書。

桌子上是一本书。

There's a book on the desk.

(3) 書架上放著三本書。

书架上放着三本书。

There are three books on the bookshelf.

(4) 床上坐著一個人。

床上坐着一个人。

There's someone sitting on the bed.

When denoting existence, "有" and "是" differ from each other in that "是" suggests that there is only one object at that place, unlike "有." Compare:

(5) 桌子上有一本書，一個本子，一張報和一些紙。

桌子上有一本书，一个本子，一张报和一些纸。

There's a book, a notebook, a newspaper, and several pieces of paper on the desk.

(6) A：你看，桌子上放著什麼？

你看，桌子上放着什么？

Look, what's on the desk?

B：桌子上是書。

桌子上是书。

That's a book on the desk.

(7) 我們學校的前面是一條馬路，後面是一個公園。

我们学校的前面是一条马路，后面是一个公园。

In front of our school is a road. Behind it there is a park.

Existential sentences are used to describe places or people's appearance. (1) through (7) describe places. Here are examples of existential sentences that describe people:

(8) 這時從前面走來一個人，他頭上戴著一頂紅帽子，身上穿著一件運動衫，腳上穿著一雙運動鞋。

这时从前面走来一个人，他头上戴着一顶红帽子，身上穿着一件运动衫，脚上穿着一双运动鞋。

At that moment a guy came in from the front. He was wearing a red cap, a sweatshirt, and a pair of sneakers.

(9) 那個女孩手裏拿著一封信。

那个女孩手里拿着一封信。

That girl is holding a letter in her hand.

3. "比較":

The word "比較" is not the equivalent of the comparative degree in English.

(1) 這本書比較貴，你別買了。

這本书比较贵，你别买了。

This book is rather expensive. Don't buy it.

(2) 我比較矮，才五尺四，不能打籃球。

我比较矮，才五尺四，不能打篮球。

I am rather short. I'm only five four. I can't play basketball.

(3) 今天比較冷，你多穿點衣服吧。

今天比较冷，你多穿点衣服吧。

It's rather cold today. You'd better put on more clothes.

(4) A: 你喜歡看什麼電影？

你喜欢看什麽电影？

What kind of movie do you like?

B: 我比較喜歡看中國電影。

我比较喜欢看中国电影。

I rather like Chinese movies.

Note the following sentences:

(1) A：你的病怎麼樣了？

你的病怎么样了？

How's your illness?

B：好一點兒了。(incorrect：比較好。)

好一点儿了。

It's better.

(2) 我很高，我哥哥更高。

我很高，我哥哥更高。

I'm very tall. My elder brother is even taller

(incorrect: 我很高,我哥哥比較高。)

4. "（方便）得很"：

"得很" can be used after adjectives and verbs that denote psychological activities to suggest an extreme degree:

(1) 外面冷得很，別出去了。

外面冷得很，別出去了。

It's really cold out there. Don't go out.

(2) 那所學校學費貴得很。

那所学校学费贵得很。

Tuition is really high at that school.

(3) 我們的學校大得很。

我们的学校大得很。

Our school is really big.

(4) 離開家一個多月了，張天明想家得很。

离开家一个多月了，张天明想家得很。

Zhang Tianming really missed home.

"冷得很" is colder than "很冷."

5. "那（麼）"：

"那（麼）" connects a sentence with the previous one. The second sentence denotes a conclusion or judgement derived from the preceding sentence. One can simply say "那" instead of "那麼." For instance,

28

(1) A：晚上去看電影好嗎？

晚上去看电影好吗？

Shall we go and see a movie tonight?

B：可是今天晚上我沒有空兒。

可是今天晚上我没有空儿。

But I don't have time tonight.

A：那（麼）就明天吧。

那（么）就明天吧。

Tomorrow then.

B：好吧。

好吧。

OK.

(2) A：媽媽，我不喜歡當醫生。

妈妈，我不喜欢当医生。

Mom, I don't want to be a doctor.

B：那（麼）學電腦怎麼樣？

那（么）学电脑怎么样？

How about being a computer scientist then?

A：我也沒有興趣。

我也没有兴趣。

I am not interested in that, either.

B：那就什麼都不學，在家裏當家庭主婦吧。

那就什么都不学，在家里当家庭主妇吧。

Then don't study anything. Stay at home and be a housewife.

A：看您說的！

看您说的！

Mom!

6. " 恐怕 " (I'm afraid) :

The adverb "恐怕" is used to express the speaker's assessment of a situation. For instance,

(1) 住這兒恐怕很不方便吧？

住这儿恐怕很不方便吧？

It's not very convenient to live here, right?

(2) 下雨了，恐怕我們不能打球了。

下雨了，恐怕我们不能打球了。

It's raining. I'm afraid we can't play ball.

(3) 十一點了，現在給他打電話恐怕太晚了。

十一点了，现在给他打电话恐怕太晚了。

It's eleven o'clock. I'm afraid it's too late to call him now.

(4) 窗戶外有一條路，這兒恐怕很吵吧？

窗户外有一条路，这儿恐怕很吵吧？

There's a road outside the window. It's very noisy here, right?

Note: One does not usually say "我恐怕." For instance, one does not usually say, "我恐怕他不能去," "我恐怕你會不高興." If one says, "我恐怕不能去了," what one really means is "（我）恐怕我不能去了 (I'm afraid I won't be able to go);" one can also say, "他恐怕不能去了" meaning "（我）恐怕他不能去了 (I'm afraid he won't be able to go)."

四·詞語練習

1. " 一般 "(generally speaking):

Example: 我還聽說學校餐廳的飯一般都不太好。

　　　　　我还听说学校餐厅的饭一般都不太好。

(1) 我們_____早上八點起床。

我们_____早上八点起床。

(2) 他週末一般都_____去吃飯。（到飯館）

他周末一般都_____去吃饭。（到饭馆）

(3) 學生一般都沒_____汽車。（有很貴的）

学生一般都没_____汽车。（有很贵的）

2. " 差不多 "(about; roughly):

Example: 教室離這兒不遠，走路差不多五、六分鐘。

教室离这儿不远，走路差不多五、六分钟。

(1) A: 這件衣服多少錢？

這件衣服多少钱？

B: 差不多_____。（一百塊）

差不多_____。（一百块）

(2) 電影八點開始，現在差不多_____了，快走吧。
（七點五十）

电影八点开始，现在差不多_____了，快走吧。
（七点五十）

(3) 我差不多_____給媽媽打一次電話。（一個星期）

我差不多_____给妈妈打一次电话。（一个星期）

3. " 聽說... (hear; hear of):

Example: 聽說這棟樓設備比較舊，廁所、浴室也比較小。

听说这栋楼设备比较旧，厕所、浴室也比较小。

(1) A:_____校外的房子比學校宿舍便宜，是嗎？

_____校外的房子比学校宿舍便宜，是吗？

B: 我看不見得。

我看不見得。

(2) ＿＿＿＿明天中文課不考試了，真的嗎？

　　＿＿＿＿明天中文课不考试了，真的吗？

(3) ＿＿＿＿學校旁邊的那家中國飯館不錯，你去過嗎？

　　＿＿＿＿学校旁边的那家中国饭馆不错，你去过吗？

4. " 不怎麼樣 " (not that great; just so so):

　　Example: 餐廳的飯真的不怎麼樣。

　　　　　　餐厅的饭真的不怎么样。

(1) 這個圖書館不怎麼樣，書＿＿＿＿＿＿＿＿。

　　这个图书馆不怎么样，书＿＿＿＿＿＿＿＿。

(2) 這個校園不怎麼樣，＿＿＿＿＿＿＿＿＿＿。

　　这个校园不怎么样，＿＿＿＿＿＿＿＿＿。

(3) 張天明妹妹的＿＿＿＿＿＿＿＿＿不怎麼樣。

　　张天明妹妹的＿＿＿＿＿＿＿＿＿不怎么样。

五・看圖說話

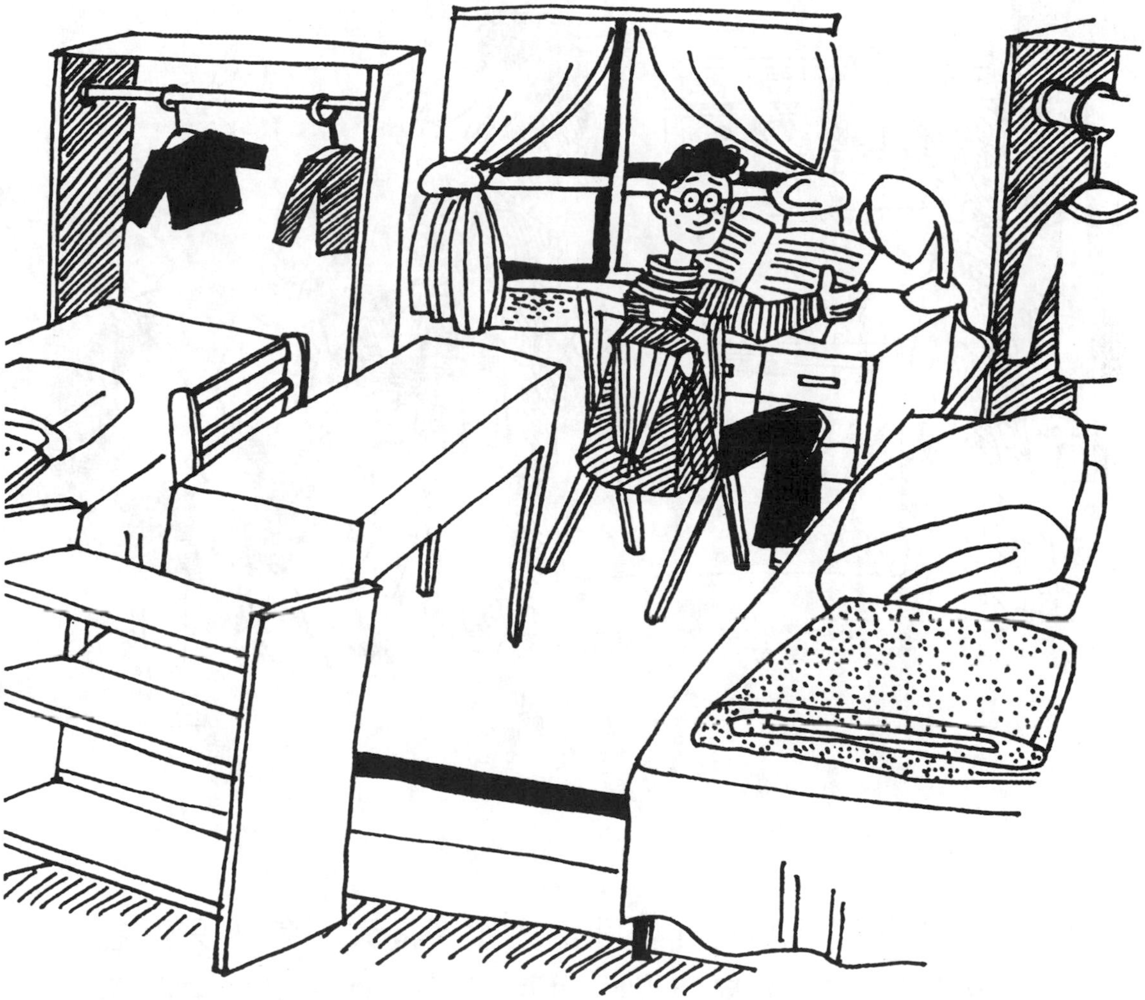

第三課 在飯館

一・課 文

　　開學已經兩個多星期了，因爲太忙，張天明每天只好在學校的餐廳吃飯。很長時間沒吃中國飯了，他很想去中國飯館吃一頓。今天是週末，再說功課也不多，他就打了個電話給柯林，問他想不想一起去中國城吃飯。柯林聽了很高興地說，他的女朋友林雪梅正好也想吃中國飯，他讓張天明在宿舍門口等，他開車來接他。

第三课　在饭馆

一·课文

　　开学已经两个多星期了，因为太忙，张天明每天只好在学校的餐厅吃饭。很长时间没吃中国饭了，他很想去中国饭馆吃一顿。今天是周末，再说功课也不多，他就打了个电话给柯林，问他想不想一起去中国城吃饭。柯林听了很高兴地说，他的女朋友林雪梅正好也想吃中国饭，他让张天明在宿舍门口等，他开车来接他。

一刻鐘以後，柯林的汽車到了。張天明往車裏一看，柯林的女朋友原來是個中國女孩，長得很漂亮。十分鐘以後，他們三個人到了柯林常去的一家中國飯館。

服務員：　柯先生，你好！好久不見了。幾位？
柯　林：　小陳，你好。三個人，不吸煙。
服務員：　好，請跟我來。

*　　　　　*　　　　　*

服務員：　這是菜單。
柯　林：　謝謝。小張，你想吃點什麼？
張天明：　你是這兒的常客。這個飯館什麼菜最拿手？
林雪梅：　這兒魚做得很好，特別是清蒸魚，味道好極了。
柯　林：　芥蘭牛肉也不錯，又嫩又香。
林雪梅：　再叫一個湯吧。
柯　林：　這兒的菠菜豆腐湯很好，叫一個好不好？
張天明：　好，好。再要個什麼？
柯　林：　我看再來一個素菜吧。
服務員：　現在可以點菜了嗎？
柯　林：　可以了。一個清蒸魚，一個芥蘭牛肉，一個菠菜豆腐湯。今天你們有什麼新鮮的青菜？
服務員：　小白菜怎麼樣？
柯　林：　可以。小陳，麻煩跟老闆說少放點鹽，別放味精。
服務員：　好。菜馬上來。

*　　　　　*　　　　　*

　　　一刻钟以后，柯林的汽车到了。张天明往车里一看，柯林的女朋友原来是个中国女孩，长得很漂亮。十分钟后他们三个人到了柯林常去的一家中国饭馆。

服务员：　柯先生，你好！好久不见了。几位？
柯　林：　小陈，你好。三个人，不吸烟。
服务员：　好，请跟我来。

　　　　　　　　　＊　　　　　　＊　　　　　　＊

服务员：　这是菜单。
柯　林：　谢谢。小张，你想吃点什么？
张天明：　你是这儿的常客。这个饭馆什么菜最拿手？
林雪梅：　这儿鱼做得很好，特别是清蒸鱼，味道好极了。
柯　林：　芥兰牛肉也不错，又嫩又香。
林雪梅：　再叫一个汤吧。
柯　林：　这儿的菠菜豆腐汤很好，叫一个好不好？
张天明：　好，好。再要个什么？
柯　林：　我看再来一个素菜吧。
服务员：　现在可以点菜了吗？
柯　林：　可以了，一个清蒸鱼，一个芥兰牛肉，一个菠菜豆腐汤。今天你们有什么新鲜的青菜？
服务员：　小白菜怎么样？
柯　林：　可以。小陈，麻烦跟老板说少放点盐，别放味精。
服务员：　好。菜马上来。

　　　　　　　　　＊　　　　　　＊　　　　　　＊

柯　林： 有一個美國記者寫文章說中國菜卡路里多，對健康並沒有好處。你們有什麼看法？

林雪梅： 我認為那個記者的說法太片面。中國菜總的來說，是對身體健康有好處的。也許有的菜油多一些，這就要看你會不會點菜了。我們今天點的菜，除了牛肉以外，都很清淡。

張天明： 我同意小林的看法。柯林，你還沒說你的看法呢。

柯　林： 其實，那個記者的看法我也不同意，要不然，今天我就不會帶你們到這兒來。哎，我們的菜來了。

柯　林：　有一个美国记者写文章说中国菜卡路里多，对健康并没有好处。你们有什么看法？

林雪梅：　我认为那个记者的说法太片面。中国菜总的来说，是对身体健康有好处的。也许有的菜油多一些，这就要看你会不会点菜了。我们今天点的菜，除了牛肉以外，都很清淡。

张天明：　我同意小林的看法。柯林，你还没说你的看法呢。

柯　林：　其实，那个记者的看法我也不同意，要不然，今天我就不会带你们到这儿来。哎，我们的菜来了。

二 · 生 詞 表

只好		adv	zhǐhǎo	have to; be forced to
頓*	顿	m	dùn	measure word for meals
週末*	周末	n	zhōumò	weekend
功課*	功课	n	gōngkè	homework
中國城*	中国城	n	Zhōngguó chéng	Chinatown
正好		adv	zhènghǎo	as it turns out; by chance

我今天正好有時間，我跟你去買衣服吧。

我去找他的時候，他正好要出門。

門口*	门口		ménkǒu	doorway; entrance
接*		v	jiē	pick up (somebody)
一刻鐘	一刻钟	t	yí kè zhōng	a quarter (of an hour)
原來		adv	yuánlái	as it turns out
女孩		n	nǚhái	a young woman; a girl
長得*	长得	v	zhǎng de	(of a person's physical appearance) look; grow

我弟弟長得很高。

她長得跟她媽媽差不多。

漂亮*		adj	piàoliang	pretty
吸煙	吸烟	vo	xīyān	smoke
跟		v	gēn	follow
菜單	菜单	n	càidān	menu
常客		n	chángkè	frequent patron; regular
拿手		adj	náshǒu	good at; adept

清蒸		v	qīngzhēng	steam (food without heavy
魚	鱼	n	yú	fish
味道		n	wèidao	taste
芥蘭	芥兰	n	jièlán	Chinese broccoli
牛肉		n	niúròu	beef
嫩		adj	nèn	tender
香		adj	xiāng	nice smelling
叫(菜)		v	jiào (cài)	order (food)
湯	汤	n	tāng	soup
菠菜		n	bōcài	spinach
豆腐		n	dòufu	bean curd
素菜		n	sùcài	vegetable dishes
點*	点	v	diǎn	order (food)
新鮮*	新鲜	adj	xīnxiān	fresh
青菜		n	qīngcài	green leafy vegetables
小白菜		n	xiǎo báicài	small Chinese cabbage
麻煩*	麻烦	adj	máfan	troublesome

做中國菜很麻煩。
麻煩你告訴老師我病了，
不能去上課了。

老板		n	lǎobǎn	boss; owner
少		adj	shǎo	(of quantity) little
鹽	盐	n	yán	salt
味精*		n	wèijīng	MSG

馬上	马上	adv	mǎshàng	immediately; right away

你的火車是三點的，你得馬上走。

你等我一下，我馬上回來。

記者	记者	n	jìzhě	reporter
文章		n	wénzhāng	article
卡路里		n/m	kǎlùlǐ	calorie
健康*		adj/n	jiànkāng	healthy; health

我身體很健康。

他的健康越來越糟糕。

看法		n	kànfǎ	point of view
認為	认为	v	rènwéi	consider; think
說法	说法	n	shuōfǎ	way of saying a thing; statement
片面		adj	piànmiàn	one-sided
總的來說	总的来说		zǒng de lái shuō	on the whole
也許	也许	adv	yěxǔ	perhaps
油		n/adj	yóu	oil; oily
會		av	huì	be good at
清淡		adj	qīngdàn	light; bland
同意		v	tóngyì	agree

我同意她的看法。

你的看法我不同意。

其實	其实	adv	qíshí	actually
要不然*		conj	yàobùrán	otherwise

專名 Proper Nouns

林雪梅	Lín Xuěméi	a feminine name
小陳	Xiǎo Chén	"little" Chen

難寫的字：

三·語法註釋 Grammar Notes

1. About "topics":

If someone, something or some event has already been mentioned, in other words, if it is no longer new information to the speaker or the interlocutor, then it should appear at the beginning of a sentence. The positioning of known information at the beginning of a sentence is an important characteristic of Chinese. For instance,

(1) 其實，<u>那個記者的看法</u>我也不同意.。（第三課）

其实，<u>那个记者的看法</u>我也不同意.。（第三课）

Actually, I don't agree with <u>that reporter's view</u>, either. (Lesson Three)

(2) <u>他剛才告訴我的那件事</u>我早就聽說了。

<u>他刚才告诉我的那件事</u>我早就听说了。

I had already heard <u>what he just told me</u>.

(3) 你<u>手續</u>都辦完了嗎？

你<u>手续</u>都办完了吗？

Have you completed all <u>the formalities</u>?

(4) <u>這兒魚</u>做得很好。

<u>这儿鱼</u>做得很好。

<u>Their fish</u> is pretty good.

This type of topic + comment structure differs from the usual word order in Chinese. In (1) if "那個記者的看法" were not known information, the word order would be, "我給你們介紹一下一個記者對中國菜的看法，好嗎?" which would be a typical "Subject + Verb + Object" type of sentence. Similarly, if the "topic" in (2) were not known information, the sentence would read, "我聽說了一件事, ...那件事他早就告訴我了."

Known information also means information that has already been mentioned or things that are taken for granted, such as eating, sleeping, or students going to classes, doing homework, etc. For instance,

(5) 功課你做完了嗎？

功课你做完了吗？

Have you finished your homework?

(6) 飯要慢慢吃，吃得太快對身體不好。

饭要慢慢吃，吃得太快对身体不好。

Eat slowly. It is not good for you to eat too quickly.

When we say the usual word order in Chinese is "Subject + Verb +Object," we are talking about an isolated sentence. In actual practice, many factors can affect word order.

2. Adverbials and "地":

Some adverbials signify the manner of an action or the accompanying state. In this situation, one should usually use "地."

(1) 他慢慢地走進了教室。

他慢慢地走进了教室。

He slowly walked into the classroom.

(2) 我用力地把桌子搬起來。

我用力地把桌子搬起来。

Straining myself, I lifted the table.

(3) 看見了我，妹妹很高興地問："姐姐，你跟我玩球，好嗎？"

看見了我，妹妹很高興地問：“姐姐，你跟我玩球，好嗎？”

When she saw me, my younger sister happily asked, "Could you please play ball with me?"

3. " — +V " :

"—" plus a verb (usually monosyllabic) suggests a brief action:

(1) 外面有人叫我，我開門一看，是送信的。

外面有人叫我，我开门一看，是送信的。

There was someone calling my name. I opened the door and took a look. It was the mailman.

(2) 他把書往桌子上一扔，很快地跑了出去。

他把书往桌子上一扔，很快地跑了出去。

He threw the book onto the desk and quickly ran out.

When "—" is used in this way, there sometimes follows a sentence denoting the result of the action. "就" is used to link the two actions.

(2) 這個句子很容易，他一看就懂。

这个句子很容易，他一看就懂。

This sentence was really easy to understand. He got it right away.

(3) 你的聲音我很熟，一聽就知道是你。

你的声音我很熟，一听就知道是你。

Your voice is familiar to me. The minute I heard you I knew it was you.

(4) 他病了，一看書就頭疼。

他病了，一看书就头疼。

He's sick. The sight of books is enough to give him a headache.

4. "原來":

"原來" has two meanings:

A. "in the past, before a change occurred"

(1) 他原來學中文，後來改學電腦了。

他原来学中文，后来改学电脑了。

Originally, he studied Chinese. Then he switched to computer science.

(2) 我原來不認識他，上大學以後在一起上課，才認識了。

我原来不认识他，上大学以后在一起上课，才认识了。

I didn't know him before. At college we went to the same classes. That's how we came to know each other.

(3) 我的中學老師還是原來的樣子，一點都沒變。

我的中学老师还是原来的样子，一点都没变。

My high school teacher looks the same. He hasn't changed a bit.

(4) 你還住在原來的宿舍嗎？

你还住在原来的宿舍吗？

Do you still live in the same dorm?

B. It is used upon the discovery of new information. It implies sudden realization:

(1) 我早就聽說有一個重要人物要來，原來就是你呀。

我早就听说有一个重要人物要来，原来就是你呀。

I heard that a big shot was coming. So it was you!

(2) 房間裏冷得很，原來暖氣壞了。

房间里冷得很，原来暖气坏了。

The room was really cold. It turned out that the heating system was not working.

(3) 我覺得好像在哪兒見過你，原來你是我的同學的姐姐。

我觉得好像在哪儿见过你，原来你是我的同学的姐姐。

I was thinking that I had seen you somewhere. [I didn't realize that] you're my classmate's sister.

47

5. "極了" :

"極了" is used after adjectives or verbs that denote psychological activities to suggest an extreme degree:

(1) 我聽媽媽說暑假帶我去中國旅行，高興極了。

我听妈妈说暑假带我去中国旅行，高兴极了。

When I heard my mother say that she would take me on a trip to China during the summer vacation, I was really happy.

(2) 妹妹說她離開家以後，想家想極了。

妹妹说她离开家以后，想家想极了。

My sister said she was really homesick after she left home.

(3) 這本書好極了，你應該看看。

这本书好极了，你应该看看。

This book is really good. You should read it.

(4) 那個地方遠極了，你別去了。

那个地方远极了，你别去了。

That place is really far away. Don't go.

6. "又...又..." :

The "又 adj/verb 又 adj/verb" pattern can be used to indicate two concurrent situations or actions:

(1) 他的女朋友又聰明又漂亮。

他的女朋友又聪明又漂亮。

His girlfriend is both bright and beautiful.

(2) 今年夏天天氣真不好，又熱又悶。

今年夏天天气真不好，又热又闷。

The weather is really lousy this summer. It's hot and stuffy.

(3) 孩子們又跑又跳，玩得十分高興。

孩子们又跑又跳，玩得十分高兴。

The kids ran and jumped. They had a good time.

(4) 那個小孩又哭又鬧，我們一點辦法也沒有。

那个小孩又哭又闹，我们一点办法也没有。

That child cried and fussed. We couldn't do a thing.

Note that when two adjectives are used in this way, they must be unidirectional, i.e., both complimentary or both pejorative. Furthermore, the adjectives must be related in meaning. For instance, when describing people, we often say, "clever and pretty;" "tall and thin;" "short and overweight." "The weather is hot and stuffy" or "cold and humid." When verbs are used, the actions denoted must be concurrent. For example, "say" and "laugh;" "cry and yell;" "hit and scold," etc. We will find that the usage, "也…也…," requires some kind of context. The adjectives that "也" introduces should have already been mentioned.

A：你幫我找一個工作好嗎？

你帮我找一个工作好吗？

Can you find me a job?

B：好啊，你要找什麼樣的工作？

好啊，你要找什么样的工作？

Sure. What kind of job are you looking for?

A：我要找一個又不累錢又多的工作。

我要找一个又不累钱又多的工作。

I'd like to find a job that pays well, and one that's not too exhausting.

B：我知道有一個醫院有工作，也不累，錢也多，可是對身體不太好。你願意去嗎？

我知道有一个医院有工作，也不累，钱也多，可是对身体不太好。你愿意去吗？

I know there is a position at a hospital. It is not too exhausting, and it pays well, but it wouldn't be good for your health. Would you be willing to work there?

7. "多/少" + V (+ NU+M+N)

In imperative sentences, one should say, "多買一點東西, 多吃一點, 多寫兩遍, 少看幾本, 少看電視, 上課少説英文," NOT "買多一點東西..., 看少幾本書..."

四‧詞語練習

1. "特別是" (especially):

Example: 這兒魚做得很好, 特別是清蒸魚, 味道好極了。

這儿鱼做得很好, 特别是清蒸鱼, 味道好极了。

(1) 他喜歡看電影, 特別是＿＿＿＿＿電影。

他喜欢看电影, 特别是＿＿＿＿＿电影。

(2) 她不喜歡運動, 特別是＿＿＿＿＿＿＿＿。

她不喜欢运动, 特别是＿＿＿＿＿＿＿＿。

(3) 日文很難, 特別是日文＿＿＿＿＿＿＿＿。

日文很难, 特别是日文＿＿＿＿＿＿＿＿。

2. "並" (not really):

Example: 有一個美國記者寫文章説中國菜卡路里多, 對健康並沒有好處。

有一个美国记者写文章说中国菜卡路里多, 对健康并没有好处。

(1) 人們都説這兒的天氣好, 我覺得這兒的天氣並不好。

人们都说这儿的天气好, 我觉得这儿的天气并不好。

(2) 我認為中文並不難。

我认为中文并不难。

(3) 你們説這個購物中心東西貴, 其實並不貴。

你们说这个购物中心东西贵, 其实并不贵。

3. " 總的來說 " (generally speaking):

Example: 中國菜總的來說，是對人體健康有好處的。

(1) 總的來説，美國西南部的天氣＿＿＿＿＿＿＿＿。

總的來说，美国西南部的天气＿＿＿＿＿＿＿。

(2) 這本書總的來説還是＿＿＿＿＿＿＿的，雖然長了些。

这本书总的来说还是＿＿＿＿＿＿＿的，虽然长了些。

(3) 這個飯館的菜總的來説很不錯，雖然油＿＿＿＿＿＿＿。

这个饭馆的菜总的来说很不错，虽然油＿＿＿＿＿＿。

4. " 這（就）要看 . . .（了）" (It depends on ...):

Example: 有的菜油是多一些，這就要看你會不會點菜了。

有的菜油是多一些，这就要看你会不会点菜了。

(1) 學生：明天的考試難不難？

學生：明天的考试难不难？

老師：這就要看你準備得＿＿＿＿＿＿了。

老师：这就要看你准备得＿＿＿＿＿＿了。

(2) A：這個電影有意思嗎？

这个电影有意思吗？

B：這就要看你喜歡＿＿＿＿＿＿電影了。

这就要看你喜欢＿＿＿＿＿＿电影了。

(3) A：我們明天還去公園玩嗎？

我们明天还去公园玩吗？

B：這就要看天氣＿＿＿＿＿＿了。

这就要看天气＿＿＿＿＿＿了。

五·看圖說話

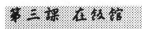

5. " 其實 " (actually):

　　Example: 其實，那個記者的看法我也不同意。

　　　　　　其实，那个记者的看法我也不同意。

　　(1) 你們都說那個學校不好，其實那個學校＿＿＿＿＿＿。

　　　　你们都说那个学校不好，其实那个学校＿＿＿＿＿＿。

　　(2) 柯林的女朋友其實＿＿＿＿＿＿。

　　　　柯林的女朋友其实＿＿＿＿＿＿。

　　(3) 那個法國飯館其實＿＿＿＿＿＿。

　　　　那个法国饭馆其实＿＿＿＿＿＿。

6. " （要）不然 " (otherwise):

　　Example: 其實，那個記者的看法我也不同意，要不然，今天
　　　　　　我就不會帶你們到這兒來。

　　　　　　其实，那个记者的看法我也不同意，要不然，今天
　　　　　　我就不会带你们到这儿来。

　　(1) 菜裏少放些油，（要）不然他們＿＿＿＿＿。

　　　　菜里少放些油，（要）不然他们＿＿＿＿＿。

　　(2) 你們別這麼客氣，（要）不然我們下次不＿＿＿＿了。

　　　　你们别这么客气，（要）不然我们下次不＿＿＿＿了。

　　(3) 你別這麼說，（要）不然她會＿＿＿＿＿的。

　　　　你别这么说，（要）不然她会＿＿＿＿＿的。

第四課　買東西

一‧課文

　　從飯館出來，張天明想起來應該買一些穿的和用的東西。他從家裏來的時候，媽媽給他買了幾件衣服，像 T 恤衫、毛衣、牛仔褲等等，可是他覺得無論是樣子還是顏色都不太好，而且也不是名牌。另外他還需要買洗衣粉、牙膏、香皂、衛生紙等日用品以及喝水的杯子、浴巾什麼的，於是他就請柯林帶他去買東西。正好林雪梅也想買一些化妝品，他們就一起開車來到附近一家最大的購物中心。

第四课　买东西

一·课文

　　从饭馆出来，张天明想起来应该买一些穿的和用的东西。他从家里来的时候，妈妈给他买了几件衣服，像T恤衫、毛衣、牛仔裤等等，可是他觉得无论是样子还是颜色都不太好，而且也不是名牌。另外他还需要买洗衣粉、牙膏、香皂、卫生纸等日用品以及喝水的杯子、浴巾什么的。于是他就请柯林带他去买东西。正好林雪梅也想买一些化妆品，他们就一起开车来到附近一家最大的购物中心。

柯　　林：　你要買什麼衣服？

張天明：　我想買一套運動服。

柯　　林：　這邊兒就是。你看看這一套，樣子、大小、長短、厚薄都合適，而且減價，打八折，價錢不貴。

張天明：　顏色也不錯。多少錢？什麼牌子的？

林雪梅：　四十塊。這個牌子沒聽說過。不過是純棉的。

張天明：　那不行，我想買阿迪達斯的。

柯　　林：　那件好像是阿迪達斯的。哎呀，三百多塊，真貴！

張天明：　買東西，我只買好的，名牌的，要不然就不買。因為名牌的衣服質量好。有的衣服便宜是便宜，可是牌子不好，穿一、兩次就不想穿了，只好再買一件。這樣兩件衣服花的錢比買一件名牌的更多。

林雪梅：　我同意小張的看法。

柯　　林：　買衣服只圖便宜當然不好，但是也不要太挑剔，非買名牌的不可。我買衣服的標準，第一是穿著舒服，第二是物美價廉，是什麼牌子的，我不在乎。穿衣服是為了自己，也不是為了給別人看。

林雪梅：　我不同意你的看法。

張天明：　對。我也不同意。難道你喜歡看小林穿不好看的衣服嗎？

柯　　林：　好，好，好。我不跟你們爭論了。雪梅，我陪你去化妝品那邊看看。

張天明：　你們去吧，我先去付錢，過一會兒去找你們，我還得去買一些日用品。

柯　　林：　好吧，我們一會兒見。

（張天明去付錢）

柯　　林：　你要买什么衣服？

张天明：　我想买一套运动服。

柯　　林：　这边儿就是。你看看这一套，样子、大小、长短、厚
　　　　　　薄都合适，而且减价，打八折，价钱不贵。

张天明：　颜色也不错。多少钱？什么牌子的？

林雪梅：　四十块。这个牌子没听说过。不过是纯棉的。

张天明：　那不行，我想买阿迪达斯的。

柯　　林：　那件好像是阿迪达斯的。哎呀，三百多块，真贵！

张天明：　买东西，我只买好的，名牌的，要不然就不买。因为
　　　　　　名牌的衣服质量好。有的衣服便宜是便宜，可是牌子
　　　　　　不好，穿一、两次就不想穿了，只好再买一件。这样
　　　　　　两件衣服花的钱比买一件名牌的更多。

林雪梅：　我同意小张的看法。

柯　　林：　买衣服只图便宜当然不好，但是也不要太挑剔，非买
　　　　　　名牌的不可。我买衣服的标准，第一是穿着舒服，第
　　　　　　二是物美价廉，是什么牌子的，我不在乎。穿衣服
　　　　　　是为了自己，也不是为了给别人看。

林雪梅：　我不同意你的看法。

张天明：　对。我也不同意。难道你喜欢看小林穿不好看的衣服
　　　　　　吗？

柯　　林：　好，好，好。我不跟你们争论了。雪梅，我陪你去化
　　　　　　妆品那边看看。

张天明：　你们去吧，我先去付钱，过一会儿去找你们，我还得
　　　　　　去买一些日用品。

柯　　林：　好吧，我们一会儿见。

（张天明去付钱）

售貨員： 先生，付現金，還是用信用卡？

張天明： 信用卡。

售貨員： 先生，加上稅一共是三百八十六塊四。

張天明： 這個州的稅怎麼這麼重？百分之八點七五。

售貨員： 是的，請你在這兒簽個字。……這是您的收據，
謝謝。

售货员：　先生，付现金，还是用信用卡？

张天明：　信用卡。

售货员：　先生，加上税一共是三百八十六块四。

张天明：　这个州的税怎么这么重？百分之八点七五。

售货员：　是的，请你在这儿签个字。……这是您的收据，
　　　　　谢谢。

二·生詞表

想起來		vc	xiǎng qǐ lai	realize; occur to
穿*		v	chuān	wear
衣服*		n	yīfu	clothes
T恤衫		n	tìxùshān	T shirt
毛衣		n	máoyī	woolen sweater
牛仔褲	牛仔裤	n	niúzǎikù	jeans; lit. cowboy pants
等等			děngděng	etc.
無論	无论	conj	wúlùn	whether it be
樣子	样子	n	yàngzi	style
名牌		n	míngpái	famous brand; name brand
需要		v/n	xūyào	need
洗衣粉		n	xǐyī fěn	laundry detergent
牙膏		n	yágāo	toothpaste
香皂		n	xiāngzào	perfumed soap
衛生紙	卫生纸	n	wèishēngzhǐ	toilet paper
以及		conj	yǐjí	(formal) and
杯子		n	bēizi	cup
浴巾		n	yùjīn	bath towel
於是	于是	conj	yúshì	so; therefore
化妝品*	化妆品	n	huàzhuāngpǐn	cosmetic products
購物中心	购物中心	n	gòuwù zhōngxīn	shopping center
套*		m	tào	suit; set
運動服*	运动服	n	yùndòng fú	sportswear; sports clothes

大小		n	dàxiǎo	size
長短	长短	n	chángduǎn	length
厚薄		n	hòubó	thickness
合適*	合适	adj	héshì	suitable

這件衣服太長，你穿不合適。

減價	减价	vo	jiǎnjià	discount; sale
打折		vo	dǎ zhé	discount
價錢	价钱	n	jiàqián	price
牌子		n	páizi	brand
純棉的	纯棉的		chúnmián	pure cotton
行*		col	xíng	will work; will do
好像*	好像	adv	hǎoxiàng	as if
哎呀		exc	āiyā	(an exclamation indicating suprise) gosh; oh

質量	质量	n	zhìliàng	quality
圖	图	v	tú	seek; pursue

他做事只圖自己高興，不在乎別人怎麼想。

挑剔		adj	tiāoti	fastidious; picky

他買東西很挑剔。

你不要太挑剔，這個房間已經很不錯了。

非...不可*			fēi...bùkě	have to be
標準	标准	n	biāozhǔn	standard; criterion
物美價廉	物美价廉		wù měi jià lián	attractive goods at affordable prices

在乎		v	zàihu	mind; care

你的車不見了，你怎麼一點
都不在乎？

他很在乎別人對他的
看法。

難道	难道	adv	nándào	(introducing a rhetorical question) Do you mean to say?
好看		adj	hǎokàn	nice looking; attractive
爭論	争论	v	zhēnglùn	argue
陪		v	péi	accompany; go with someone

我不太舒服，你陪我去醫院
好嗎？

這個孩子的媽出去了，你陪
陪他好嗎？

付錢	付钱	vo	fù qián	pay bills
現金*	现金	n	xiànjīn	cash
信用卡*		n	xìnyòng kǎ	credit card
稅		n	shuì	tax
州		n	zhōu	state
百分之			bǎifēn zhī	percent
簽字	签字	vo	qiān zì	sign one's name
收據	收据	n	shōujù	receipt

專名 Proper Noun

阿迪達斯	阿迪达斯		Ādídásī	Adidas

難寫的字：

膏 衛 薄 圖 廉 論 據

三‧語法註釋 Grammar Notes

1. The Postion of Time Phrases:

There are two kinds of time phrases. The first kind signifies points in time, such as "today," "Monday," "1996," "three days ago," "the time when...." The second kind has to do with duration, such as "one hour," "three days," "two years." Adverbials that signify points in time are placed at the beginning of a sentence or before the verb, as you already know. In this lesson, we will concentrate on adverbials that have to do with durations of time. These adverbials indicate the duration of an action or a state. For instance,

(1) 我來了兩天了，覺得很方便。（第二課）

我来了两天了，觉得很方便。（第二课）

I have been here for two days. I find it very convenient (to live here). (***Lesson Two***)

(2) 開學已經兩個多星期了。（第三課）

开学已经两个多星期了。（第三课）

School has been in session for two weeks now. (***Lesson Three***)

(3) 我昨天做功課做了兩個小時。

我昨天做功课做了两个小时。

I spent two hours doing my homework yesterday.

(4) 你學中文學了多長時間？

你學中文學了多長時間？

How long have you been studying Chinese?

Phrases that signify durations of time are usually placed after verbs. In this type of sentence, the verbs involved all have to do with actions that can last, such as "學," "做," "寫," "走," etc. If there is an object after the verb, one must repeat the verb before stating the duration of the action. Cf. (2) and (3). If the actions cannot last by their nature, such as "來/ come," "結婚/ get married," "畢業/ graduate," "死/ die," then one does not repeat the verbs. Cf. (1).

If those phrases that normally signify durations of time do not denote the durations of actions, as when they are preceded by a word of negation, or if the phrases have to do with the frequency of an action, such as "一天吃三次/ eat three times a day," "三天來一次/ come every three days," they are placed before the verbs:

(5) 我一個星期沒有看見他了。

我一个星期没有看见他了。

I haven't seen him for a week.

(6) 很長時間沒吃中國飯了，他很想去中國飯館吃一頓。
（第三課）

很长时间没吃中国饭了，他很想去中国饭馆吃一顿。
（第三课）

He hasn't had Chinese food for a long time. He really wants to have a good meal in a Chinese restaurant.

(7) 這種藥一天吃三次。

这种药一天吃三次。

Take this medicine three times a day.

2. "無論... ，都... "：

"無論" signifies that the result will remain the same under any condition or circumstance. It must be used together with an indefinite interrogative pronoun or an alternative compound. For example,

(1) 明天無論誰請客我都不去。

　　明天无论谁请客我都不去。

　　No matter who's paying tomorrow, I'm not going.

　　("誰" is an indefinite interrogative pronoun.)

(2) 今天學校裏無論什麼地方我都去過了，太累了。

　　今天学校里无论什么地方我都去过了，太累了。

　　I went everywhere today. I'm exhausted.

　　("什麼地方" "whichever place" is indefinite.)

(3) 我們已經決定明天去買東西，你無論同意不同意都得跟
　　我們去。

　　我们已经决定明天去买东西，你无论同意不同意都得跟
　　我们去。

　　We've already decided to go shopping tomorrow. Whether you agree or not,
　　you have to go with us.

　　("同意不同意" is an alternative compound.)

(4) 他無論在家裏還是在學校，總是看書，很少看見他玩。

　　他无论在家裏还是在学校，总是看书，很少看见他玩。

　　Whether he's at home or at school, he's always reading. [You] seldom see him
　　play [relax].

　　("在家裏還是在學校" is an alternative compound.)

3. "於是"：

　　The conjunction "於是" connects two clauses. The second clause usually denotes a new situation or action which is consequent on the situation or action mentioned in the first clause. For instance,

(1) 我給他打了很多次電話都沒有人接，於是就寫了一封
信。

我给他打了很多次电话都没有人接，于是就写了一封
信。

I called him many times, but nobody answered, so I wrote him a letter.

(2) 晚飯後，他去一家購物中心買運動鞋，那裏沒有他喜
歡的，於是又開車去了另一個購物中心。

晚饭后，他去一家购物中心买运动鞋，那里没有他喜
欢的，于是又开车去了另一个购物中心。

After dinner he went to the shopping center to get a pair of sneakers. They
didn't have what he liked, so he drove to another shopping center.

(3) 本來週末孩子們要去爬山，沒想到星期六早上下雨了，
於是他們就不去了。

本来周末孩子们要去爬山，没想到星期六早上下雨了，
於是他们就不去了。

The kids were going to go mountain-climbing over the weekend, but it rained
on Saturday morning, so they didn't go.

(4) 小明在書店看見一本新書，他很喜歡，於是就買下來
了。

小明在书店看见一本新书，他很喜欢，于是就买下来
了。

Xiao Ming saw a new book at the bookstore. He liked it very much, so he
bought it.

NB: Although "於是" also indicates result, it differs from "所以." "於是" must be
preceded by a clause indicating a cause, but the causal relationship is not very strong. In
the examples above, "於是" cannot be replaced by "所以;" "於是" often introduces an
action or change. "所以" is not so limited. For example,

(1) 這次考試，因爲我沒有準備，所以考得很不好。

这次考试，因为我没有准备，所以考得很不好。

I didn't prepare for the exam, so I didn't do very well.

(2) 上海人多車多，所以開車很容易緊張。

上海人多车多，所以开车很容易紧张。

There are too many people and cars in Shanghai, so it's easy to get nervous when you drive.

(3) 天要下雨，所以非常悶。
天要下雨，所以非常闷。

It's going to rain. That's why it's so muggy.

In these sentences, "於是" cannot be substituted for "所以." In (1), although the first clause indicates a circumstance, the second clause does not involve an action or change. (2) and (3) are the same.

4. "真":

"真" lends emphasis to the tone of voice. It is used before adjectives and verbs that denote psychological activities:

(1) 今天真冷，穿三件毛衣都不行。

今天真冷，穿三件毛衣都不行。

It's really cold today. You could be wearing three sweaters, and you still would be cold.

(2) 你們老師給的功課真多，你做了三個鐘頭了還沒做完。

你们老师给的功课真多，你做了三个钟头了还没做完。

Your teacher really assigned a lot of homework. You've been at it for three hours, and you still haven't finished it.

(3) 你真聰明，這麼難的字也會寫。

你真聪明，这么难的字也会写。

You're really smart! Such a difficult character, and you know how to write it!

It should be noted that unlike "很, 十分, 特別", "真" does not suggest an extreme degree. It is used to indicate an affirmative or emphatic tone of voice. It does not provide new information. Therefore avoid using "真" in ordinary descriptive sentences. For instance,

(4)A：喂，小張，你聽天氣預報了嗎？明天的天氣怎麼樣？

喂，小张，你听天气预报了吗？明天的天气怎么样？

Xiao Zhang, did you listen to the weather forecast? What's the weather going to be like tomorrow?

B：天氣預報說明天的天氣會到二十度，很冷。

天气预报说明天的天气会到二十度，很冷。

According to the weather forecast, [the temperature] will be twenty degrees tomorrow. Really cold!

It is incorrect to say: "天氣預報說明天的天氣會到二十度, 真冷."

"真" can sometimes mean "truly, honestly." It is often followed by the particle "的." For instance,

(5)我真的不想去看電影。

我真的不想去看电影。

I honestly don't want to go to the movies.

(6)A：畢業以後我想去賣東西。

毕业以后我想去卖东西。

After graduation I'd like to be a salesman.

B：你真這麼想嗎？

你真这么想吗？

You honestly want to do that?

5. "adj./V+是+adj./V，可是/但是..."：

This structure is equivalent to "although...(yet)."

(1)A：我決定學文學了。

我决定学文学了。

I've decided to study literature.

B：學文學好是好，可是找工作不太容易吧？

學文學好是好，可是找工作不太容易吧？

Studying literature is not bad, but isn't it rather difficult to find a job [with such a degree]?

(2) A：這件衣服太貴了，別買！

這件衣服太贵了，别买！

This jacket is too expensive. Don't buy it.

B：這件衣服貴是貴，可是牌子好。

这件衣服贵是贵，可是牌子好。

It *is* expensive, but it's a good brand.

(3) A：明天的晚會你去不去？

明天的晚会你去不去？

Are you going to the party tomorrow?

B：我去是去，不過可能晚一點。

我去是去，不过可能晚一点。

Yes, I'm going, but I'm probably going to be a bit late.

(4) A：你不吃肉嗎？

你不吃肉吗？

Do you eat meat?

B：我吃是吃，可是吃得很少。

我吃是吃，可是吃得很少。

Yes, I do, but very little of it.

6.「難道」：

「難道」 is used in rhetorical questions. It lends force to the tone of voice. For instance,

(1) 這麼容易的題，難道你還不會做嗎？

这么容易的题，难道你还不会做吗？

This is such a simple question. Don't tell me you don't know how to answer it.

(2) 他來美國十年了，難道他連一句英文都不會說？

他来美国十年了，难道他连一句英文都不会说？

Do you mean to say that he has been in the States for ten years and cannot even speak a word of English?

(3) 這件事不是他做的，難道是你做的？

这件事不是他做的，难道是你做的？

If he didn't do this, are you telling me that you did it?

NB: "難道" can be used before or after the subject. Because "難道" is used in rhetorical questions, the questions have to be Yes/No questions. For instance, one cannot say: "這件事情不是你，難道是誰?" or "你難道去不去?" etc.

Note also that rhetorical questions require some kind of context. Therefore one cannot use "難道" out of the blue.

7. Reduplication of Verbs :

Reduplicated verbs are used in imperative sentences to soften the tone of voice. For example,

(1) 我陪你去化妝品那邊看看。（第四課）

我陪你去化妆品那边看看。（第四課）

I'll go to the cosmetic department with you. (*Lesson Four*)

(2) 你看看我寫得對不對？

你看看我写得对不对？

Please take a look and see if I wrote it correctly.

(3) 你好好跟他說說，叫他不要不高興了。

你好好跟他说说，叫他不要不高兴了。

Please talk to him. Tell him to stop being angry.

"一下" has the same effect:

    (1) 你們不認識，我來介紹一下。

       你们不认识，我来介绍一下。

       You guys don't know each other. Let me introduce you.

    (2) 你看一下我寫得對不對？

       你看一下我写得对不对？

       Please see if I wrote it correctly.

    (3) 等一下，晚飯還沒好。

       等一下，晚饭还没好。

       Wait a second, dinner is not ready yet.

四·詞語練習

1. " 另外 " (besides):

Example: 另外還應該買喝水的杯子。

         另外还应该买喝水的杯子。

    (1) 你不舒服，應該_____，另外再多喝點水。

       你不舒服，应该_____，另外再多喝点水。

    (2) 明天小王和小張會來，另外_____。

       明天小王和小张会来，另外_____。

    (3) 明天考試，你們要準備第三課的生詞，另外還要

       _____。

       明天考试，你们要准备第三课的生词，另外还要

       _____。

2. "...什麼的" (...etc.):

> Example: 另外他還需要買洗衣粉、牙膏、香皂、衛生紙等日
> 用品以及喝水的杯子、浴巾什麼的。
>
> 另外他还需要买洗衣粉、牙膏、香皂、卫生纸等日
> 用品以及喝水的杯子、浴巾什么的。

(1) 媽媽晚上請客，做了很多菜。有＿＿＿＿＿＿＿＿＿＿。

　　妈妈晚上请客，做了很多菜。有＿＿＿＿＿＿＿＿＿＿。

(2) 明天是週末，我們應該＿＿＿＿＿＿＿＿。

　　明天是周末，我们应该＿＿＿＿＿＿＿＿。

(3) 昨天他過生日，朋友送了很多禮物，有＿＿＿＿＿＿＿＿＿＿。

　　昨天他过生日，朋友送了很多礼物，有＿＿＿＿＿＿＿＿＿＿。

3. "大小、厚薄..." (size, thickness, etc.):

> Example: 你看看這一套，樣子、大小、長短、厚薄都合適，
> 而且減價，打八折，價錢不貴。
>
> 你看看这一套，样子、大小、长短、厚薄都合适，
> 而且减价，打八折，价钱不贵。

(1) 這件衣服＿＿＿＿＿＿正合適。

　　这件衣服＿＿＿＿＿＿正合适。

(2) 你寫的文章＿＿＿＿＿＿正好。

　　你写的文章＿＿＿＿＿＿正好。

(3) 我穿衣服＿＿＿＿＿＿沒關係，便宜就行。

　　我穿衣服＿＿＿＿＿＿没关系，便宜就行。

4. "打折" (discount):

> Example:...而且減價，打八折，價錢不貴。
>
> 　　...而且减价，打八折，价钱不贵。

(1) 這個週末很多東西都＿＿＿＿＿＿，我們去買吧。

这个周末很多东西都＿＿＿＿＿＿，我们去买吧。

(2) 這件衣服原來八十塊，現在打八折，是＿＿＿＿＿＿錢。

这件衣服原来八十块，现在打八折，是＿＿＿＿＿＿钱。

(3) 我買了一本書，打五折，二十五塊錢，不打折是
＿＿＿＿＿＿＿錢。

我买了一本书，打五折，二十五块钱，不打折是
＿＿＿＿＿＿＿钱。

5. "**要不然**" (otherwise):

Example: 買東西，我只買好的，名牌的，要不然就不買。

买东西，我只买好的，名牌的，要不然就不买。

(1) 明天看電影你得來接我，＿＿＿＿＿＿我就不去。

明天看电影你得来接我，＿＿＿＿＿＿我就不去。

(2) 十分鐘以後就上課了，快走吧，要不然就＿＿＿＿＿＿了。

十分钟以后就上课了，快走吧，要不然就＿＿＿＿＿＿了。

(3) 明天是你的女朋友的生日，你應該給她買一件禮物，
要不然 ＿＿＿＿＿＿＿＿＿＿ 了。

明天是你的女朋友的生日，你应该给她买一件礼物，
要不然 ＿＿＿＿＿＿＿＿＿＿ 了。

6. "**非...不可**" (insist on):

Example: 買衣服只圖便宜當然不好，但是也不要太挑剔，
非買名牌不可。

买衣服只图便宜当然不好，但是也不要太挑剔，
非买名牌不可。

(1) 看電視的時候，姐姐想要看電影，弟弟非要看
　　＿＿＿＿不可。

　　看电视的时候，姐姐想要看电影，弟弟非要看
　　＿＿＿＿不可。

(2) 爸爸叫他明年去中國，他非要＿＿＿＿＿不可。

　　爸爸叫他明年去中国，他非要＿＿＿＿＿不可。

(3) 我說那件衣服太貴，又不太好，可是她非＿＿＿＿不可。

　　我说那件衣服太贵，又不太好，可是她非＿＿＿＿不可。

五・看圖說話

第五課　選　專　業

一・課　文

　　張天明這個學期選了四門課：東亞史、統計學、美國文學
和中文。除了中文以外，其他的課雖然很有意思，也學到了不
少東西，只是都得花很多時間準備，有點受不了。因爲張天明
的父母在家常常說中文，所以一年級的中文課，對他來說，聽
和說很容易，就是寫漢字太難，一個字得反復練習才能記住。
　　這個學期已經過了一大半了，馬上又得爲下學期註冊了。
後天張天明要去見他的指導教授，討論下學期選課的事。他覺
得應該找李哲聊聊，聽聽他的想法。

第五课　选专业

一·课文

　　张天明这个学期选了四门课：东亚史、统计学、美国文学和中文。除了中文以外，其他的课虽然很有意思，也学到了不少东西，只是都得花很多时间准备，有点受不了。因为张天明的父母在家常常说中文，所以一年级的中文课，对他来说，听和说很容易，就是写汉字太难，一个字得反复练习才能记住。

　　这个学期已经过了一大半了，马上又得为下学期注册了。後天张天明要去见他的指导教授，讨论下学期选课的事。他觉得应该找李哲聊聊，听听他的想法。

張天明： 怎麼樣，下學期的課你選好了嗎？

李　哲： 還沒呢。你呢？

張天明： 我肯定要選中文，至於另外兩門課選什麼，還不知道。你還得再上幾門課才能畢業？

李　哲： 我還得上三門課。我想拿雙學位，再選一門物理課，另外再選兩門電腦系的課，學分就夠了。

張天明： 你畢業以後打算做什麼呢？

李　哲： 我想念研究所*，要麼是工學院，要麼是管理學院。你想選什麼專業？

張天明： 我想學文學。可是我媽媽說，學文科將來不容易找工作，而且賺錢也少，她讓我念醫學院。但是，我最不願意當醫生，整天跟病人打交道，多沒意思。

李　哲： 唉，我的父母跟你的父母差不多。其實，我最喜歡的是哲學，因為我喜歡想問題。西方人一般不太管孩子選什麼專業，比我們自由。

張天明： 你想申請哪些學校？

李　哲： 我想申請離家比較近的學校，這樣我就可以搬回家去住，把房租跟飯錢省下來。

張天明： 不過在家裏住太不自由了。

李　哲： 是嗎？那我再考慮考慮。

張天明： 也許你可以先找個地方實習一下，有點工作經驗，這樣對你寫履歷有好處，將來申請學校、找工作都可以提一提。

李　哲： 我明天去找指導教授的時候，再聽聽他的意見。

張天明： 明天我也要去找指導教授。希望他們能給咱們一些好的建議。

张天明：怎么样，下学期的课你选好了吗？

李　哲：还没呢。你呢？

张天明：我肯定要选中文，至于另外两门课选什么，还不知道。你还得再上几门课才能毕业？

李　哲：我还得上三门课。我想拿双学位，再选一门物理课，另外再选两门电脑系的课，学分就够了。

张天明：你毕业以后打算做什么呢？

李　哲：我想念研究所*，要么是工学院，要么是管理学院。你想选什么专业？

张天明：我想学文学。可是我妈妈说，学文科将来不容易找工作，而且赚钱也少，她让我念医学院。但是，我最不愿意当医生，整天跟病人打交道，多没意思。

李　哲：唉，我的父母跟你的父母差不多。其实，我最喜欢的是哲学，因为我喜欢想问题。西方人一般不太管孩子选什么专业，比我们自由。

张天明：你想申请哪些学校？

李　哲：我想申请离家比较近的学校，这样我就可以搬回家去住，把房租跟饭钱省下来。

张天明：不过在家里住太不自由了。

李　哲：是吗？那我再考虑考虑。

张天明：也许你可以先找个地方实习一下，有点工作经验，这样对你写履历有好处，将来申请学校、找工作都可以提一提。

李　哲：我明天去找指导教授的时候，再听听他的意见。

张天明：明天我也要去找指导教授。希望他们能给咱们一些好的建议。

二·生詞表

選	选	v	xuǎn	choose
專業	专业	n	zhuānyè	major; specialization
選課	选课	vo	xuǎn kè	choose courses

這個學期我選了三門課。

門	门	m	mén	measure word for (academic) courses
東亞史	东亚史	n	dōngyà shǐ	East Asian history
統計學	统计学	n	tǒngjìxué	statistics
文學	文学	n	wénxué	literature
其他*		pr	qítā	other
準備	准备	v	zhǔnbèi	prepare
學到	学到	vc	xuédào	learn
受不了		vc	shòu bu liǎo	can't take it

今天太熱，我真的受不了。

很久沒吃中國飯了，小張有點兒
受不了了。

對...來說	对...来说		duì...lái shuō	to so and so; so far as so and so is concerned
反復	反复	adv	fǎnfù	repeatedly
記住	记住	vc	jì zhù	remember
大半			dàbàn	more than half; most
為	为	prep	wèi	for
後天	后天	t	hòutian	the day after tomorrow
指導教授	指导教授	n	zhǐdǎo jiàoshòu	advisory professor
討論	讨论	v	tǎolùn	discuss

我們正在討論選專業的事。

這件事很重要，你們討論討論吧。

聊*		v	liáo	chat
選好	选好	vc	xuǎn hǎo	finish choosing
想法		n	xiǎngfǎ	idea; opinion
肯定		adv	kěndìng	definitely
至於	至于	conj	zhìyú	as for; as to
畢業	毕业	v	bìyè	graduate
雙學位	双学位	n	shuāng xuéwèi	double major
物理		n	wùlǐ	physics
電腦*	电脑	col	diànnǎo	computer; lit. electric brain
系		n	xì	(university) department
學分	学分	n	xuéfēn	academic credit
打算		v	dǎsuàn	plan
研究所		n	yánjiūsuǒ	graduate school
要麼...	要么...	conj	yàome...	if it's not A, it's B; either...or...
要麼...	要么...		yàome...	
工學院	工学院	n	gōngxuéyuàn	school of engineering
管理學院	管理学院	n	guǎnlǐ xuéyuàn	school of management
文科		n	wénkē	humanities
賺錢	赚钱	vo	zhuàn qián	make money
醫學院	医学院	n	yīxuéyuàn	school of medicine
願意	愿意	av	yuànyi	be willing to

我不願意去圖書館看書，喜歡在家看書。

你願意跟我去城裏跳舞嗎？

| 當* | 当 | v | dāng | be; work as |

整天			zhěngtiān	all day long

他姐姐很忙，整天不在家。

你整天打球，累不累？

病人*		n	bìngrén	patient
(跟)…打交道		vo	dǎ jiāodào	deal with
唉		exc	āi	an exclamation indicating resignation
哲學	哲学	n	zhéxué	philosophy
西方		n	xīfāng	the West
孩子		n	háizi	child
管		col	guǎn	mind; meddle
申請	申请	v	shēnqǐng	apply
這樣*	这样	pr	zhèyàng	in this way
房租*		n	fángzū	rent
飯錢	饭钱	n	fàn qián	money for food
省下來	省下来	vc	shěng xialai	save (money, time)
不過	不过	conj	búguò	but; however
考慮*	考虑	v	kǎolǜ	consider
實習	实习	v	shíxí	practice; have an internship
經驗	经验	n	jīngyàn	experience

申請研究所，我沒有經驗。

有工作經驗對找工作很有幫助。

履歷	履历	n	lǚlî	curriculum vitae; resume
提		v	tí	mention

哥哥來信時，工作的事一點兒
也沒提。

昨天老師上課提到下個星期考試
的事了。

意見	意见	n	yìjiàn	opinion
咱們	咱们	pr	zánmen	we (including the listener;我們 does not necessarily include the listener)
建議	建议	v/n	jiànyì	suggest; suggestion

我建議你學電腦。

我不知道選什麼專業，你能不能給我提一點兒建議？

專名 Proper Noun

| 李哲 | | | Lǐ Zhé | a masculine name |

難寫的字：

選　專　導　畢　腦　醫　慮　履

Note:

*In mainland China, the word "研究所" refers to research institutes, which may or may not be affiliated with universities; the word for "graduate school" on the mainland is "研究生院." In Taiwan, however, "研究所" or "研究院" can mean either "graduate school" or "research institute."

三・語法註釋　Grammar Notes

1. "只是 / 就是" (it's just that)：

"只是" signifies a turn in thought. It is similar to "不過" in usage. It is more moderate in tone than "但是,可是."

(1) 你要跟他結婚，我不是不同意，只是我覺得太早了一點。

你要跟他结婚，我不是不同意，只是我觉得太早了一点。

It's not that I object to your wanting to marry him. It's just that it's too soon.

(2) 他這個人好是好，就是身體差一些。

他这个人好是好，就是身体差一些。

He *is* a good person, but he is a bit too frail.

(3) 那兒冬天的天氣暖和是暖和，只是常常颱風。

那儿冬天的天气暖和是暖和，只是常常刮风。

It's true that it's warm there in the winter, but it is very windy.

It should be noted that "只是/就是" usually appears in the second clause. The first clause is often positive in meaning whereas the second clause modifies the first clause, pointing out a flaw in something that might otherwise be perfect. In this respect "只是" is different from "但是,可是,不過."

2. "對他來說" (to him)：

"對他來說" means "from his point of view." For example,

(1) 對妹妹來說，今年最重要的事情是選一個好大學。

对妹妹来说，今年最重要的事情是选一个好大学。

As far as my sister is concerned, the most important thing this year is to pick a good college.

Note: "對他來說" is different from "他認為." "對他來說" actually conveys the speaker's impression of somebody else's point of view.

(2) (我認為)對他來說，有工作總比沒工作好，可是他認為工作不好還不如沒有工作。

(我认为)对他来说，有工作总比没工作好，可是他认为工作不好还不如没有工作。

[I thought,] for him, having *a* job is better than having no job. However, in his view, having a bad job is worse than having no job.

(3) 對她媽媽來說，她是最重要的。

对她妈妈来说，她是最重要的。

To her mother, she is the most important person.
(Her mother might agree or might disagree with the speaker's statement.)

(4) 對我來說，找一個好工作是第一位的事情。

对我来说，找一个好工作是第一位的事情。

For me, landing a good job is the number one [priority].
= Landing a good job is my number one [priority].
(I =the speaker)

3. " 至於 " :

"至於" is used to introduce a new subject which is somehow related to the one mentioned in the preceding discourse. For instance,

(1) A：我們明天去旅行還是後天去？

我们明天去旅行还是后天去？

When are we going to take the trip, tomorrow or the day after tomorrow?

B：我們先討論去不去，至於明天去還是後天去，我想都可以。

我们先讨论去不去，至於明天去还是后天去，我想都可以。

Let's first decide [discuss] if we're going or not. As for when, [whether it's tomorrow or the day after tomorrow], we can decide [discuss that] later.

(2) A ：你認識那兩個人嗎？

你认识那两个人吗？

Do you know those two people?

B：我認識那個男的，至於那個女的，我從來沒見過。

我认识那个男的，至于那个女的，我从来没见过。

I know the man. As for the woman, I've never seen her before.

86

(3) A：你跟你太太喜歡吃中國飯還是日本飯？

你跟你太太喜欢吃中国饭还是日本饭？

Do you and your wife like to eat Chinese or Japanese food?

B：我喜歡吃中國飯，至於我太太，她喜歡吃日本飯。

我喜欢吃中国饭，至于我太太，她喜欢吃日本饭。

I like Chinese food. As for my wife, she likes Japanese food.

(4) A：我想買衣服，這個商店怎麼樣？

我想买衣服，这个商店怎麼样？

I would like to buy some clothes. How about this store?

B：買日用品，這個商店不錯，比較便宜，至於買衣服，還是去大一點的購物中心吧。

买日用品，这个商店不错，比较便宜，至于买衣服，还是去大一点的购物中心吧。

This store is good for [buying] daily necessities. [The prices are cheap[er][there]. As for clothes, you'd better go to a bigger shopping center.

4. "要麼...，要麼..." (either...or)：

"要麼..., 要麼" is a selective conjunction. It is used to mean "choosing between several (often two) possibilities," or two "desires." For instance,

(1) 你要麼學醫，要麼學工程，反正不能學文科。

你要么学医，要么学工程，反正不能学文科。

You have to study either medicine or engineering. It can't be the humanities [no matter what you say.]

(2) A：你說明天做什麼？

你说明天做什么？

What do you say we should do tomorrow?

B： 要麼聽音樂，要麼看電影。

要么听音乐，要么看电影。

Either go to a concert or a movie.

A： 去公園看紅葉怎麼樣？

去公园看红叶怎么样？

How about enjoying the foliage in the park?

B： 不行。

不行。

No way.

(3) **A：** 明天誰去送你爸爸去飛機場？

明天谁去送你爸爸去飞机场？

Who's going to give your father a ride to the airport tomorrow?

B： 要麼你去，要麼我哥哥去。

要么你去，要么我哥哥去。

Either you or my older brother.

5. "另外" (another; other) :

There are two usages of "另外." One of them is before a noun:

(1) 另外兩門課選什麼，還不知道。

另外两门课选什么，还不知道。

As for the other two courses [to be taken], I haven't decided yet.

(2) 這裏有兩個大學，一個男校，另外一個是女校，都很不錯。

这里有两个大学，一个男校，另外一个是女校，都很不错。

There are two colleges here. One is a men's college. The other one is a women's college. Both are quite good.

(3) 他有三個妹妹，一個上大學，另外兩個已經工作了。

他有三个妹妹，一个上大学，另外两个已经工作了。

He has three younger sisters. One is at college. The other two are already working.

(4) 我有四個中文老師，三個是從中國大陸來的，另外一個是從台灣來的。

我有四个中文老师，三个是从中国大陆来的，另外一个是从台湾来的。

Of my four Chinese teachers, three are from mainland China. The other one is from Taiwan.

"另外" can also be used before a verb or at the beginning of a sentence. We have already studied this usage. Here are some more examples:

(5) 再選一門物理課，另外再選兩門電腦系的課，學分就夠了。

再选一门物理课，另外再选两门电脑系的课，学分就够了。

One more course in physics, and two more in computer science, and I'll have enough credits.

(6) 我明年想去日本旅行，另外還想去中國看看。

我明年想去日本旅行，另外还想去中国看看。

I'd like to take a trip to Japan next year. I'd also like to go to China as well.

(7) 上個週末我看了一個電影，另外還聽了一個音樂會。

上个周末我看了一个电影，另外还听了一个音乐会。

Last weekend I saw a movie. I also went to a concert.

6. Resultative Complements (I) :

In Chinese a verb can be followed by an adjective or another verb to indicate the result of the action. We call the second verb or adjective a resultative complement. Resultative complements fall into several categories:

A: Resultative complement elucidating the verb:

(1) 我做完了功課再看電視。（完）

我做完了功课再看电视。（完）

I'll watch TV after I've finished doing my homework. (完=the action will have been completed by the time I watch TV.)

(2) 一個字得反復練習才能記住。（住）（第五課）

一个字得反复练习才能记住。（住）（第五课）

One has to repeat a word several times before one can remember it. (住: fixed; here "lodged in memory")

(3) 下學期的課你選好了嗎？（好）（第五課）

下学期的课你选好了吗？（好）（第五课）

Have you finished choosing the classes for next semester? (done choosing)

B: Resultative complement, indicating a new state or a change on the part of the agent of the action:

(4) 老師講的我聽懂了。（懂）

老师讲的我听懂了。（懂）

I understood the teacher. (Now the material is clear to me.)

(5) 你吃飽了嗎？（飽）

你吃饱了吗？（饱）

Are you full? (sated)

C: Complement of result, indicating a new state or change on the part of the recipient of the action or the object:

(6) 你怎麼把妹妹打哭了？（哭）

你怎么把妹妹打哭了？（哭）

Why did you hit your sister and make her cry? (She is crying now.)

(7) 他把椅子搬走了。（走）

他把椅子搬走了。（走）

He took away the chair. (The chair is gone.)

(8) 我洗乾淨了衣服就睡覺。（乾淨）

我洗干净了衣服就睡觉。（干净）

I'll go to bed after I do the laundry. (The clothes will be clean.)

It should be noted that any one verb can only take certain other verbs or adjectives as its resultative complements. Therefore, it is best to remember each verb together with its resultative complements as if they were one word.

7. "再"、"又"、"還" Compared :

Both "又"and "再" indicate the repetition of an action. "又" is usually used with actions which have already taken place. "再," on the other hand, indicates future recurrences:

(1) 我上星期看了一個中國電影，昨天又看了一個。

我上星期看了一个中国电影，昨天又看了一个。

I saw a Chinese movie last week. I saw another one yesterday.

(2) 您剛才說的我沒聽清楚，請您再說一次。

您刚才说的我没听清楚，请您再说一次。

I didn't hear what you just said very clearly. Please say it again.

However, when the main verb is "想", "能", "可以", "要", or "是," one can only use "又:"

(3) 她今天下午又要去見指導教授了。

她今天下午又要去见指导教授了。

She is going to see her advisor again this afternoon.

(4) 明天又是星期天了。

明天又是星期天了。

Tomorrow is Sunday again.

"還" indicates increase in quantity or amount:

(5) 這本書我買了一本了，還得買一本。

这本书我买了一本了，还得买一本。

I've already bought a copy of this book. I have to get one more.

(6) 這個電影我看了一次了，還想再看一次。

这个电影我看了一次了，还想再看一次。

I've seen this movie once. I'd like to see it one more time.

四‧詞語練習

1. "反復" (repeatedly)："反復" often follows verbs such as "說、念、寫、記、思考、討論、練習".

Example: 一個字得反復練習才能記住。

　　　　一个字得反复练习才能记住。

(1) 課文要反復_____，才能念好。

课文要反复_____，才能念好。

(2) 這個字你反復_____，就能記住了。

这个字你反复_____，就能记住了。

(3) 老師反復解釋那個詞的_____，我還是不懂。

老师反复解释那个词的_____，我还是不懂。

2. "肯定" (definitely)：

Example: 我肯定要選電腦和中文。

　　　　我肯定要选电脑和中文。

(1) 這麼晚了，他肯定不會_____了。

这么晚了，他肯定不会_____了。

(2) 點了那麼多的菜，肯定_____。

　　点了那么多的菜，肯定_____。

(3) 你讓她做那麼多的事，她肯定_____。

　　你让她做那么多的事，她肯定_____。

3. "跟...打交道" (deal with) :

The phrase is used to mean to come in contact with certain people or objects because of the nature and the need of one's work.

Example: 整天跟病人打交道，多沒意思。

　　　　整天跟病人打交道，多没意思。

(1) 數學家整天跟_____打交道。

　　数学家整天跟_____打交道。

(2) 我媽媽在學校工作，天天跟_____打交道。

　　我妈妈在学校工作，天天跟_____打交道。

(3) 張天明的叔叔是翻譯，常常和_____人打交道。

　　张天明的叔叔是翻译，常常和_____人打交道。

4. "這樣" (in this way) :

Example: 我想申請離家比較近的學校，這樣我就可以搬回家去住。

　　　　我想申请离家比较近的学校，这样我就可以搬回家去住。

(1) 課文多念幾次，這樣就可以_____了。

　　课文多念几次，这样就可以_____了。

(2) 你開車去，這樣_____。

　　你开车去，这样_____。

(3) 你去他家前，給他打個電話，這樣他_____。

　　你去他家前，给他打个电话，这样他_____。

93

5. " 不過 " (but)：

    Example: 不過在家裏住太不自由了。

              不过在家里住太不自由了。

    (1) 張天明的房間不錯，不過有一點兒_____。

         張天明的房间不错，不过有一点儿_____。

    (2) 住在宿舍很方便，不過_____。

         住在宿舍很方便，不过_____。

    (3) 那本書很有意思，不過_____。

         那本书很有意思，不过_____。

五·看圖說話

第六課　租房子

一 · 課文

　　開學已經兩個多月了，張天明一直住在學生宿舍裏。小張的房間在二樓，離樓梯很近。每天早上不到六點，就開始有人上下樓梯。晚上，常常到十一、二點，還有人在走廊裏大聲地打招呼或開玩笑，吵得張天明早晚都睡不好覺。住在他隔壁的是安德森。自從上個星期大學籃球比賽開始以後，安德森差不多每天晚上都看球，常常激動得大喊大叫。大學籃球比賽到明年三月才結束，張天明想，這樣下去學習非受影響不可，最好趕緊搬出學校，找個安靜的地方住。

　　他找來一張報紙，翻到廣告欄，看了幾個出租房子的廣告，就打起電話來。

第六課　租房子

一・課文

　　开学已经两个多月了，张天明一直住在学生宿舍里。小张的房间在二楼，离楼梯很近。每天早上不到六点，就开始有人上下楼梯。晚上，常常到十一、二点，还有人在走廊里大声地打招呼或开玩笑，吵得张天明早晚都睡不好觉。住在他隔壁的是安德森。自从上个星期大学篮球比赛开始以後，安德森差不多每天晚上都看球，常常激动得大喊大叫。大学篮球比赛到明年三月才结束，张天明想，这样下去学习非受影响不可，最好赶紧搬出学校，找个安静的地方住。

　　他找来一张报纸，翻到广告栏，看了几个出租房子的广告，就打起电话来。

（一）

張天明： 喂，你們有一套房子出租，是嗎？

房　東： 對，有兩間臥室，帶家俱，有地毯，而且有空調。

張天明： 每個月租金是多少？

房　東： 要是租一年的話，每個月四百六十塊。

張天明： 我想你們的房子一定很不錯，不過對我來說，稍微貴了點兒。

房　東： 沒關係，你先找別的地方試試，要是找不到合適的，再來找我。

張天明： 那太好了！多謝！

（二）

張天明： 喂，你好！可以告訴我你們要出租的是什麼樣的房子嗎？

房　東： 不是房子，只是一個房間，帶家俱，可是沒有空調。

張天明： 在什麼地方？

房　東： 十七街四百二十五號，離體育場很近。如果你是個球迷的話，住在這兒最理想不過了。

張天明： 不瞞您說，如果我是個球迷的話，就不用搬家了。

（一）

张天明： 喂，你们有一套房子出租，是吗？

房　东： 对，有两间卧室，带家具，有地毯，而且有空调。

张天明： 每个月租金是多少？

房　东： 要是租一年的话，每月四百六十块。

张天明： 我想你们的房子一定很不错，不过对我来说，稍微贵了点儿。

房　东： 没关系，你先找别的地方试试，要是找不到合适的，再来找我。

张天明： 太好了！多谢！

（二）

张天明： 喂，你好！可以告诉我你们要出租的是什么样的房子吗？

房　东： 不是房子，只是一个房间，带家具，可是没有空调。

张天明： 在什么地方？

房　东： 十七街四百二十五号，离体育场很近。如果你是个球迷的话，住在这儿最理想不过了。

张天明： 不瞒您说，如果我是个球迷的话，就不用搬家了。

（三）

張天明：　你好！你們的房子租出去了嗎？

房　東：　還沒有，不過已經有好幾個人打過電話了。

張天明：　請問，是什麼樣的房子？

房　東：　是一室一廳的，廚房很大。如果你每天自己做飯的話，住在這兒最合適不過了。

張天明：　租金是多少？

房　東：　每個月三百塊，包水電。

張天明：　是嗎？不算很貴。你們附近有球場嗎？

房　東：　這兒離球場很遠，環境不錯。後面是一片樹林，前面是一條小河，可能對你來說太安靜了吧？

張天明：　我就是要找一個安靜的地方，嗯，就是離學校遠了一點兒。

房　東：　不過這兒交通很方便。

張天明：　好極了。我可以去看看房子嗎？

房　東：　可以，可以。

（三）

张天明：　你好！你们的房子租出去了吗？

房　东：　还没有，不过已经有好几个人打过电话了。

张天明：　请问，是什么样的房子？

房　东：　是一室一厅的，厨房很大。如果你每天自己做饭的话，住在这儿最合适不过了。

张天明：　租金是多少？

房　东：　每个月三百块，包水电。

张天明：　是吗？不算很贵。你们附近有球场吗？

房　东：　这儿离球场很远，环境不错。后面是一片树林，前面是一条小河，可能对你来说太安静了吧？

张天明：　我就是要找一个安静的地方。嗯，就是离学校远了一点儿。

房　东：　不过这儿交通很方便。

张天明：　好极了。我可以去看看房子吗？

房　东：　可以，可以。

二・生詞表

租房子*		vo	zū fángzi	rent a house/room
一直*		adv	yìzhí	always; continuously
樓梯	楼梯	n	lóutī	staircase
走廊		n	zǒuláng	hallway
大聲	大声	adv	dàshēng	loudly

弟弟睡覺了，別大聲說話！
大聲點兒，我聽不見。

打招呼		vo	dǎ zhāohu	greet
或		conj	huò	or
開玩笑	开玩笑	vo	kāi wánxiào	joke around
吵		vc	chǎo	disturb; make a noise
睡不好覺	睡不好觉	vc	shuì bu hǎo jiào	not able to sleep well
隔壁		n	gébì	next door
自從	自从		zìcóng	ever since; since
籃球*	篮球	n	lánqiú	basketball
比賽	比赛	v	bǐsài	competition season
激動	激动	v	jīdòng	excited

聽了這個歌，我很激動。
她激動地對我說...

大喊大叫			dà hǎn dà jiào	yell and scream
受影響	受影响	vo	shòu yǐngxiǎng	be affected
趕緊	赶紧	adv	gǎnjǐn	in a hurried fashion; right away
翻到		vc	fān dào	turn to

廣告欄	广告栏	n	guǎnggào lán	ad columns
出租*		v	chūzū	rent out; let
喂*			wèi	(on the phone) hello
套		m	tào	a suite of
間	间	m	jiān	measure word for rooms
臥室*	卧室*	n	wòshì	bedroom
帶	带	v	dài	be equipped with
地毯		n	dìtǎn	carpet
租金		n	zūjīn	rent
稍微		adv	shāowēi	a little bit; somewhat
試*	试	v	shì	try
找不到		vc	zhǎo bu dào	not able to find
什麼樣	什麼样		shénmeyàng	what kind
街		n	jiē	street
體育場	体育场	n	tǐyùchǎng	stadium
球迷		n	qiúmí	fans (of ball games: basketball, football,etc.)
理想		n/adj	lǐxiǎng	ideal

我的理想是在一個好大學當
教授。

這個工作不太理想，我想再
找一個新工作。

| 瞞 | 瞞 | v | mán | hide the truth from |

有什麼事情應該告訴我，不
要瞞我。

你什麼都瞞著媽媽，這很不
好。

| 室 | | n | shì | room |

廳	厅	n	tīng	room; living-room
廚房*	厨房	n	chúfáng	kitchen
包		v	bāo	include
水電	水电	n	shuǐ diàn	water and electricity
算		v	suàn	count; to be counted as
球場	球场	n	qiúchǎng	basketball court
環境	环境	n	huánjìng	environment; surroundings
後面	后面		hòumian	in the back; back
樹林	树林	n	shùlín	woods
河*		n	hé	river
嗯*		exc	ng	interjection indicating minor regret over an otherwise satisfactory situation
交通		N	jiāotōng	transportation; communications

難寫的字：

樓 聲 籃 賽 響 欄 微 廚 環 境 樹

三・語法註釋 Grammar Notes

1. Descriptive complements with "得"：

The descriptive complements can be divided into three categories, depending on their structure and function:

A: The complement comments on the preceding verb. For example,

(1) 我每天起得很早。

我每天起得很早。

Everyday I get up very early.

(2) 他跑得很快。

他跑得很快。

He runs very fast.

(3) 妹妹寫字寫得很好。

妹妹写字写得很好。

[My] younger sister writes beautifully (has very beautiful penmanship.)

If there is an object after the verb as in (3), one must repeat the verb.

B: The complement describes the mood of the subject or object, which results from the action or state signified by the verb or adjective before the complement. For instance,

(1) 他聽到老師說明天不考試了，高興得跳了起來。

他听到老师说明天不考试了，高兴得跳了起来。

When he heard the teacher say there was no test tomorrow, he lept with joy.

("跳了起來" is the result of "高興;" it also describes "他.")

(2) 同學開他玩笑，説得他很不高興。

同学开他玩笑，说得他很不高兴。

His classmates teased him, which made him very angry.

("很不高興" is the result of "說;" but it also describes "他.")

(3) 她把房子打掃得乾乾淨淨的。

她把房子打扫得干干净净的。

She tidied up the house.

("乾乾淨淨" is the result of "打掃." It also describes "房子.")

This kind of complement is descriptive. It is used to describe what has already happened. It cannot be used in the negative.

C: The complement indicates degree. For instance,

快過年了，飛機場裏人多得很。

快过年了，飞机场里人多得很。

New Year is almost here. There are lots of people at the airport.

This kind of complement of degree also describes what has already happened. It cannot be used in the negative.

2. "...以後" compared with "...的時候":

"...以後" is different from "...的時候". The former means "after (something happened)"; the latter "when (something happens or happened)". Compare:

(1) a. 我看見他的時候，他正在打電話。

我看见他的时候，他正在打电话。

When I saw him, he was making a phone call.

b. 我看見他以後，跟他打了聲招呼。

我看见他以后，跟他打了声招呼。

After I saw him, I said 'hi.'

(2) a. 他出去的時候忘了帶錢。

他出去的时候忘了带钱。

When he went out, he forgot to take some money with him.

b. 他出去以後想起來沒有帶錢。

他出去以后想起来没有带钱。

After he had gone out, he remembered that he hadn't brought any money.

(3) a. 沒有事情的時候，他常常打電話。

没有事情的时候，他常常打电话。

When he doesn't have anything to do, he often makes phone calls.

b. 下了課以後，他給小王打了一個電話。

下了课以后，他给小王打了一个电话。

After the class, he gave Xiao Wang a call.

3. "...的話" :

"...的話" is a particle. It is used in a hypothetical clause. It must be followed by another clause. For example,

(1) 你要是去的話，一定給我打電話。

你要是去的话，一定给我打电话。

If you are going, make sure that you give me a call.

(2) 媽媽要是非讓我學醫不可的話，我就不上大學了。

妈妈要是非让我学医不可的话，我就不上大学了。

If Mother insists on my studying medicine, then I'm not going to college.

(3) 電影，有意思的話，我就看完，沒有意思的話，我看一點就不看了。

电影，有意思的话，我就看完，没有意思的话，我看一点就不看了。

If the movie is interesting, I'll watch the whole thing. If not, I'll just watch a bit of it.

4. "最...不過了" :

"最...不過了" means "沒有比...更...的了 ." It is a rather forceful expression. For instance,

(1) 她過生日，買花送她最好不過了。

她过生日，买花送她最好不过了。

Nothing would be a better gift for her birthday than flowers.

(2) 這本書對東亞史的介紹最清楚不過了。

這本书对东亚史的介绍最清楚不过了。

This book contains the best introduction to the history of East Asia.

(3) 小王的妹妹最聰明不過了。

小王的妹妹最聪明不过了。

No one is smarter than Wang's younger sister.

5. Directional complements (I):

Verbs of direction can be used as direcitonal complements after other verbs. Verbs of direction include "來," "去," "上," "下," "進," "出," "回," "過," "起," "開," "到." "來" and "去" can be combined with other verbs of direction: "上來," "上去," "下來," "下去," "進來," "進去," "出來," "出去," "回來," "回去," "過來," "過去," "起來," "開來," "開去," "到...來," "到...去," etc. We call all of these directional complements. Directional complements fall into three categories: **A.** directional complements indicating direction; **B.** directional complements indicating result; **C.** directional complements indicating state. In this lesson, we are concerned with the first category. Take a look at the following examples:

(1) 你回家去吧。（去）

你回家去吧。（去）

You'd better go home.

(2) 張天明想最好趕緊搬出學校。（出）（第六課）

张天明想最好赶紧搬出学校。（出）（第六课）

Zhang Tianming thought it was best to move off campus. (**Lesson Six**)

(3) 我明天搬進宿舍來。（進...來）

我明天搬进宿舍来。（进...来）

I'll move into the dorm tomorrow.

(4) 請你們拿出一張紙來。（出...來）

请你们拿出一张纸来。（出...来）

Please take out a sheet of paper.

(5) 我帶回來了一個客人。（回來）

　　我带回来了一个客人。（回来）

I brought back a guest.

When using a directional complement, one should pay attention to the position of the object. If "來," and "去"are used as complements, the object denoting a person or object can be placed either before or after "來" or "去:"

(6) 他搬來了一把椅子。

　　他搬来了一把椅子。

He brought a chair.
(When the object appears after the complement, the action is more often than not completed.)

(7) 請搬一把椅子來。

　　请搬一把椅子来。

Please bring a chair. (future action)

(8) 他從家裏搬了一把椅子來。

　　他从家里搬了一把椅子来。

He brought a chair from home. (completed action)

It should be noted that if the object signifies a place, it can only be placed before "來" and "去:"

(9) 我九月回北京去。

　　我九月回北京去。

I'm going back to Beijing in September.

(10) 你快一點進房間來。

　　你快一点进房间来。

Get into the room quickly.

When 上，下，進，出，etc., are used as complements, they have to be placed in between the verb and the object, as in (2).

When "上來" and "下去" are involved, if the object signifies a place, it should be inserted between the verbs of direction. See (3). If the object is a normal noun, it can be inserted into "上來" and "下去", and can also go before or after the complements. See (5).

"上" and "上來," "上去" indicate the same direction. However, "上來" signifies a movement toward the speaker, whereas "上去" denotes a movement away from the speaker. For instance,

他把椅子搬上樓來了。

他把椅子搬上楼来了。

He brought the chair upstairs.
(The speaker is upstairs. The chair is now also upstairs.)

他把椅子搬下樓去了。

他把椅子搬下楼去了。

He took the chair downstairs.
(The speaker is upstairs. The chair is now downstairs.)

The distinction between "下" and "下來," "下去;" between "進," and "進來," "進去" is the same.

6. Chinese numerical series:

In Chinese, large numbers go before small ones. That is to say general information goes before specific information. A date, address, list, etc. begins with the most general information and ends with the most specific. For instance:

1997年10月25日

October 25, 1996

中國北京中山路25號1樓2門3號

#3 Gate 2 1st flr., 25 Zhongshan Rd., Beijing, China

四 · 詞語練習

1. " 一直 " (all along; continuously):

Example: 開學已經兩個多月了，張天明一直住在學生宿舍裏。

開学已经两个多月了，张天明一直住在学生宿舍里。

(1) 我們問她爲什麼不高興，可她一直＿＿＿＿＿＿＿＿。

我们问她为什么不高兴，可她一直＿＿＿＿＿＿＿。

(2) 大學畢業以後，他一直＿＿＿＿＿＿＿，不教日文。

大学毕业以后，他一直＿＿＿＿＿＿＿，不教日文。

(3) 小張上研究所以後，一直＿＿＿＿＿＿＿＿＿＿。

小张上研究所以后，一直＿＿＿＿＿＿＿＿＿＿。

2. " 或（者）" (or: only in declarative sentences):

(1) A: 你喜歡看哪國電影？

你喜欢看哪国电影？

B: 美國電影或（者）中國電影我都喜歡看。

美国电影或（者）中国电影我都喜欢看。

(2) A: 你想喝點兒什麼？

你想喝点儿什么？

B: 可樂或（者）咖啡都可以。

可乐或（者）咖啡都可以。

" 還是 " (or: in interrogative sentences):

(3) 今天晚上你在家吃飯還是去飯館吃飯？

今天晚上你在家吃饭还是去饭馆吃饭？

(4) 你喜歡看中國電影還是美國電影？

你喜欢看中国电影还是美国电影？

3. "**差不多**" (almost):

Example: 安德森差不多每天晚上都看球。

安德森差不多每天晚上都看球。

(1) 他差不多＿＿＿＿＿打球。

他差不多＿＿＿＿＿打球。

(2) 他功課差不多＿＿＿＿＿＿了。

他功课差不多＿＿＿＿＿＿了。

(3) 開學差不多已經有＿＿＿＿＿＿＿了。

开学差不多已经有＿＿＿＿＿＿＿了。

4. "**最好**" (had better; it's best that...):

Example: 張天明想，這樣下去學習非受影響不可，最好趕緊
搬出學校。

张天明想，这样下去学习非受影响不可，最好赶紧
搬出学校。

(1) 我晚上有事，你最好＿＿＿＿＿來。

我晚上有事，你最好＿＿＿＿＿来。

(2) 他現在很忙，最好不要＿＿＿＿＿。

他现在很忙，最好不要＿＿＿＿＿。

(3) 這件事我不太清楚，你最好＿＿＿＿＿，她知道。

这件事我不太清楚，你最好＿＿＿＿＿，她知道。

5. **" 稍微...點兒 "** (slightly):

It is often used to indicate a bit off from the ideal situation or standard set by the speaker.

Example: 我想你們的房子一定很不錯，不過對我來說，稍微貴了點兒。

我想你们的房子一定很不错，不过对我来说，稍微贵了点儿。

(1) 今天天氣還不錯，就是_____了點兒。

今天天气还不错，就是_____了点儿。

(2) 現在給他打電話稍微___了一點，都晚上十二點了。

现在给他打电话稍微___了一点，都晚上十二点了。

(3) 請你說話稍微____點兒，別人都睡了。

请你说话稍微____点儿，别人都睡了。

五‧看圖說話

第七課　男朋友

一‧課文

　　前幾天張天明給他妹妹天華打電話，在電話裏，天華聽起來好像有什麼心事。張天明問了她 好幾次，天華才說，她跟男朋友鬧翻了。她還說等心情好 一些以後，再把詳細情況告訴天明。

　　天華的男朋友湯姆是張天明的高中同學，湯姆經常到天明家去玩兒，天華就是這樣認識湯姆的。湯姆人很好，性格十分開朗，學習也不錯，就是脾氣有點兒急躁。在興趣上，他跟天華不太一樣。湯姆是個球迷，電視裏一有體育節目，他就非看

第七课 男朋友

一·课文

前几天张天明给他妹妹天华打电话，在电话里，天华听起来好像有什么心事。张天明问了她好几次，天华才说，她跟男朋友闹翻了。她还说等心情好一些以后，再把详细情况告诉天明。

天华的男朋友汤姆是张天明的高中同学，汤姆经常到天明家去玩儿，天华就是这样认识汤姆的。汤姆人很好，性格十分开朗，学习也不错，就是脾气有点儿急躁。在兴趣上，他跟天华不太一样。汤姆是个球迷，电视里一有体育节目，他就非看不可；天華是個戲迷，一有新戲就去看。她喜歡古典音樂，湯姆喜歡搖滾樂。雖然兩個人興趣不同，可是交往了一年多以後，他們相處得越來越好。張天明想來想去想不出他們為什麼鬧翻了。是因為文化背景不同嗎？還是湯姆有了新的女朋友？正好今天晚上有空，張天明就給妹妹打了一個電話。

張天明：　喂？

妹　　妹：　噢，哥哥，是你啊。

張天明：　你怎麼樣？

妹　　妹：　好多了。

張天明：　你跟湯姆怎麼了？

妹　　妹：　他最近老喝醉酒。

張天明：　醉得很厲害嗎？

妹　　妹：　嗯。兩個星期以來，這已經是第四次了。有一次，他醉得把屋裏的鏡子都打破了，還對我說了很多難聽的話。我真想跟他吹了。

張天明：　難怪你心情不好，原來是湯姆喝酒的事。我知道湯姆喜歡喝酒，可是從來沒見到他喝醉過。要不要我給他打個電話，跟他說說？

妹　　妹：　我想你最好別管。我們吵架以後，他好像挺後悔的。你跟麗莎怎麼樣？

張天明：　挺好的。對了，這個週末我們放三天假，想去你那兒看看你們。這兒真把我們憋死了。

妹　　妹：　那太好了。我們學校校園很美，附近有很多餐館、酒吧，還有不少電影院。有一家正在演幾部中國電影。

張天明：　你看了嗎？

不可；天华是个戏迷，一有新戏就去看。她喜欢古典音乐，汤姆喜欢摇滚乐。虽然两个人兴趣不同，可是交往了一年多以后，他们相处得越来越好。张天明想来想去想不出他们为什么闹翻了。是因为文化背景不同吗？还是汤姆有了新的女朋友？正好今天晚上有空，张天明就给妹妹打了一个电话。

张天明：　喂？

妹　　妹：　噢，哥哥，是你啊。

张天明：　你怎么样？

妹　　妹：　好多了。

张天明：　你跟汤姆怎么了？

妹　　妹：　他最近老喝醉酒。

张天明：　醉得很厉害吗？

妹　　妹：　嗯。两个星期以来，这已经是第四次了。有一次，他醉得把屋里的镜子都打破了。还对我说了很多难听的话。我真想跟他吹了。

张天明：　难怪你心情不好，原来是汤姆喝酒的事。我知道汤姆喜欢喝酒，可是从来没见到他喝醉过。要不要我给他打个电话，跟他说说？

妹　　妹：　我想你最好别管。我们吵架以后，他好象挺后悔的。你跟丽莎怎么样？

张天明：　挺好的。对了，这个周末我们放三天假，想去你那儿看看你们。这儿真把我们憋死了。

妹　　妹：　那太好了。我们学校校园很美，附近有很多餐馆、酒吧，还有不少电影院。有一家正在演几部中国电影。

张天明：　你看了吗？

妹　　妹：　我看了一部，很不錯，另外兩部還沒看。等你們來了
　　　　　　一起去看。

張天明：　好，等我們見面以後，再好好談談。

妹　　妹：　好吧，來以前打個電話。

張天明：　好，再見。

妹　　妹：　我看了一部，很不错，另外两部还没看。等你们来了
　　　　　　一起去看。

张天明：　好，等我们见面以后，再好好谈谈。

妹　　妹：　好吧，来以前打个电话。

张天明：　好，再见。

二·生詞表

心事		n	xīnshì	something weighing on one's mind
鬧翻	闹翻	vc	nào fān	fall out with somebody
心情		n	xīnqíng	mood
詳細	详细	adj	xiángxì	in detail
情況	情况	n	qíngkuàng	situation

他最近的健康情況怎麼樣？
你把學生情況說給我聽聽。

高中		n	gāozhōng	senior high school
經常	经常	adv	jīngcháng	frequently
性格		n	xìnggé	personality; disposition
十分		adv	shífēn	very
開朗	开朗	adj	kāilǎng	outgoing
脾氣	脾气	n	píqi	temper; temperament
急躁		adj	jízào	impetuous; impatient
體育	体育	n	tǐyù	physical education; sport
節目	节目	n	jiémù	(TV, radio) program; performance
戲迷	戏迷	n	xìmí	theater buff
戲	戏	n	xì	play
古典音樂	古典音乐	n	gǔdiǎn yīnyuè	classical music
搖滾樂	摇滚乐	n	yáogǔnyuè	rock 'n' roll music
不同		adj/n	bùtóng	different; difference

中文和日文的語法很不同。
"天"和"夫"有什麼不同？

交往		v	jiāowǎng	socialize

他們兩個人交往很久了。

這個人不好，你別跟他交往。

相處	相处	v	xiāngchǔ	get along

他很好相處，跟大家的關係不錯。

我跟她相處一年多了，從來沒跟她吵過架。

文化*		n	wénhuà	culture
背景		n	bèijǐng	background
有空		vo	yǒu kòngr	have free time
噢			ò	oh
喝醉酒		vo	hē zuì jiǔ	get drunk
醉		adj	zuì	drunk
厲害	厉害	adj	lìhai	terrible; terribly
...以來	...以来		yǐlái	since
屋裏	屋里		wūli	inside the room
鏡子	镜子	n	jìngzi	mirror
打破		vc	dǎ pò	break into pieces
難聽	难听	adj	nántīng	(of words) ugly
吹		col	chuī	break up
難怪	难怪	adv	nánguài	no wonder
從來	从来	adv	cónglái	ever

我上課從來沒晚過。

他從來不喜歡抽煙喝酒。

吵架		v	chǎo jià	quarrel
挺		col	tǐng	quite; rather

後悔	后悔	v	hòuhuǐ	regret

我很後悔昨天沒去上課。
跟他分手是好事，不必後悔。

放假*		vo	fàng jià	have a holiday; have a day off
憋死		vc	biē sǐ	suffocate; feel oppressed
校園	校园	n	xiàoyuán	campus
酒吧		n	jiǔbā	bar
電影院	电影院	n	diànyǐngyuàn	cinema
演*		v	yǎn	(of plays or movies) to show
部		m	bù	measure word (for movies, books, etc.)
等*		v	děng	wait
見面	见面	vo	jiàn miàn	meet

你們在哪兒見面？
我從來沒跟他見過面，不認識他。
（incorrect: 我昨天見面他了。）

談*	谈	v	tán	talk; discuss

專名 Proper Nouns

天華	天华		Tiānhuá	a unisex name
湯姆	汤姆		Tāngmǔ	Tom
麗莎	丽莎		Lìshā	Lisa

難寫的字：

脾 戲 噢 屬 裏 鏡 憋

三・語法註釋　Grammar Notes

1. "...，才"：

In the sentence, "張天明問了好幾次，妹妹才告訴他...，" "張天明問了好幾次" is the condition for "妹妹告訴他." In other words, "才" can be used to indicate the conditions under which someone will do something. For instance,

(1) 你先給我錢，我才能給你東西。

你先给我钱，我才能给你东西。

Give me the money first. Then I'll give you the stuff.

(2) 你得把你的看法告訴我，我才把我的看法告訴你。

你得把你的看法告诉我，我才把我的看法告诉你。

You have to tell me your point of view. Then I'll tell you mine.

(3) 爸爸對我說："你今年能畢業，我才給你錢去中國旅行。"

爸爸对我说："你今年能毕业，我才给你钱去中国旅行。"

My dad said to me, "Unless you graduate this year, I won't give you money to travel to China.

2. "（先...）再..."：

"（先）...，再..." is used to mean "someone does not want to (not cannot) do something now, but will do it later." For instance,

(1) 老師，我今天不想考試，準備好了以後再考，可以嗎？

老师，我今天不想考试，准备好了以后再考，可以吗？

Laoshi, I don't feel like taking the exam today. Can I take it when I'm ready?

(2) A：咱們今年夏天去台灣旅行好嗎？

咱们今年夏天去台湾旅行好吗？

Can we travel to Taiwan this summer?

B：我今年不想去，畢業以後再去。

我今年不想去，毕业以后再去。

I don't feel like going this year. [I want to wait] until after I graduate.

(3) 你先吃飯吧，我寫完這封信再吃。

你先吃饭吧，我写完这封信再吃。

You go ahead and eat first. I'll eat after I finish writing this letter.

比較：

Compare:

(1) 你寫完功課才能吃飯。

你写完功课才能吃饭。

You have to finish writing your homework. Then you can eat.
= You can't eat now.

(2) 我寫完功課再吃飯。

我写完功课再吃饭。

I want to finish my homework first, and then eat.
= I don't want to eat now.

Note that modal verbs like "能" cannot be used after "再."

3. "...上"：

"...上" can be used after abstract nouns. It means "in terms of." For instance, in terms of "character, interest, study, work, etc."

(1) 在興趣上，湯姆跟天華不太一樣。（第七課）

在兴趣上，汤姆跟天华不太一样。（第七课）

In terms of interests, Tom and Tianhua are very different.

(2) 小林學習上，工作上都很不錯。

小林学习上，工作上都很不错。

Xiao Lin excels both in her studies and her work.

(3) 在性格上，她以前的男朋友比現在的男朋友好多了。

在性格上，她以前的男朋友比现在的男朋友好多了。

Her old boyfriend is much better than her current boyfriend in terms of personality.

4. " V 來 V 去 " :

"V來V去" signifies a repetitive action. For instance, "走來走去 (walk back and forth), 飛來飛去 (fly here and there), 想來想去 (think again and again), 說來說去 (say again and again), 討論來討論去 (discuss again and again), 研究來研究去 (consider (research) again and again)."

5. Directional complement (II): indicating result

Directional complements that indicate result are similar to resultative complements, although not all directional complements indicate result. Here are some examples from the previous lessons:

(1) 先生，加上稅一共是三百八十六塊四。（加上，第四課）

先生，加上税一共是三百八十六块四。（加上，第四课）

Sir, with tax, it's three hundred eighty-six and forty cents. (***Lesson Four***)

(2) 其他的課......也學到了不少東西。（學到，第五課）

其他的课......也学到了不少东西。（学到，第五课）

From the other classes, (he) also learned a lot. (***Lesson Five***)

(3) 把房租跟飯錢省下來。（省下來，第五課）

把房租跟饭钱省下来。（省下来，第五课）

Save the money for room and board. (***Lesson Five***)

Every directional complement indicating result is different. Some can have several different meanings. Although we can explain the meaning of each directional complement, it is better to treat the complement and its preceding verb as one word. We will list them as such in the vocabulary sections.

6. "V + 出 (來)": indicating result

"V + 出來" signifies a change in status, from non-being to being, from obscurity to clarity, etc. When there is an object, one can often leave out the word "來." When the construction occurs at the end of a sentence, however, one must use the full construction. For instance,

(1) 我想出來一個好辦法。

我想出来一个好办法。

I came up with a good idea.

(2) 這兩本書有什麼不同，我沒看出來。

这两本书有什么不同，我没看出来。

I didn't see any difference between these two books.

(3) 從電話裏我聽出來是姐姐的聲音。

从电话里我听出来是姐姐的声音。

I recognized my sister's voice on the phone.

7. "...以後" and "...以來" compared:

"...以後" means "after a certain point in time." For instance,

(1) 上大學以後，我們一直沒有見過她。

上大學以后，我們一直沒有見過她。

After college, we haven't seen her.

(2) 她跟我吵架以後，我就不喜歡她了。

她跟我吵架以后，我就不喜欢她了。

After she quarreled with me, I began to dislike her.

(3) 95年我們住在一個宿舍，96年以後我搬走了。

95年我们住在一个宿舍，96年以后我搬走了。

In 1995, we lived in the same dormotory. In '96, I moved out.

"...以來" means "from a certaint point in time up to now." For example,

(1) 上大學以來，我一直沒有見過她。

上大学以来，我一直没有见过她。

Since college, I haven't seen her.

(2) 1995年以來，我沒有搬過家。

1995年以来，我没有搬过家。

Since 1995, I haven't moved.

(3) 自從我認識她以來，沒有看見她哭過。

自从我认识她以来，没有看见她哭过。

Ever since I became acquainted with her, I've never seen her cry.

(4) 他們結婚以來，一直相處得很好。

他们结婚以来，一直相处得很好。

Since they got married, they have been getting along very well.

(5) 三天以來，他一直在考試。

三天以来，他一直在考试。

He's been taking exams for three days.

　　If we want to say from/after a certain point, we can use "以來" or "以後," although they mean different things. See (1) and (4). "... 以來" means "from a certain point up to now." "...以後" means "after a certain point in time," and has nothing to do with the present. If the phrase before "以後/ 以來" is one of time duration, "...以後" cannot be replaced by "以來." See (5).

四・詞語練習

1. "**聽起來好像**" (sound as if) :

　　Example: 天華聽起來好像有什麼心事。

　　　　　　 天华听起来好像有什么心事。

　　(1) 你說話的聲音跟平常不一樣，聽起來好像＿＿＿＿了。

　　　　 你说话的声音跟平常不一样，听起来好像＿＿＿了。

　　(2) 這本書她給我介紹了，聽起來好像＿＿＿＿＿。

　　　　 这本书她给我介绍了，听起来好像＿＿＿＿＿。

　　(3) 她聽起來好像是＿＿＿人。

　　　　 她听起来好像是＿＿＿人。

2. "**電視裏**" (on television):

　　Example: 電視裏一有體育節目，他就非看不可。

　　　　　　 电视里一有体育节目，他就非看不可。

　　(1) 週末電視裏的節目，都＿＿＿＿＿。

　　　　 周末电视里的节目，都＿＿＿＿＿。

　　(2) 今天電視裏＿＿＿＿＿＿＿？

　　　　 今天电视裏＿＿＿＿＿＿＿？

3. "**跟...一樣**" (the same as...) :

　　(1) 我跟我哥哥一樣，都＿＿＿＿＿＿。

　　　　 我跟我哥哥一样，都＿＿＿＿＿＿。

　　(2) 她跟她媽媽＿＿＿＿＿。

　　　　 她跟她妈妈＿＿＿＿＿。

　　(3) 我的＿＿＿跟你不一樣。

　　　　 我的＿＿＿跟你不一样。

4. " **越來越** " (more and more) :

(1) 上二年級以來，功課_____。

上二年级以来，功课_____。

(2) 不知道爲什麼，我越來越不喜歡_____。

不知道为什麽，我越来越不喜欢_____。

(3) 自從工作以後，她越來越想_____。

自从工作以後，她越来越想_____。

5. " **難怪** " (no wonder) :

Example: 難怪你心情不好！

难怪你心情不好！

(1) 難怪他_____，原來他從來不看報紙！

难怪他_____，原来他从来不看报纸！

(2) 難怪他沒來上課，原來_____了。

难怪他没来上课，原来_____了。

(3) 難怪這兩天他這兩天心情不好，原來_____。

难怪这两天他这两天心情不好，原来_____。

6. " **見面** " (meet) :

Example: 等我們見面以後，再好好談談。

等我们见面以后，再好好谈谈。

(1) A: 你跟小張見過面嗎？

你跟小张见过面吗？

B: _____，我們認識。

_____，我们认识。

(2) A: 明天你跟他_____？

明天你跟他＿＿＿＿＿＿＿？

B: 我們在購物中心門口見面。

我们在购物中心门口见面。

(3)A: 你跟老師約好＿＿＿＿＿＿＿？

你跟老师约好＿＿＿＿＿＿＿？

B: 我跟老師下午兩點鐘見面。

我跟老师下午两点钟见面。

五‧看圖說話

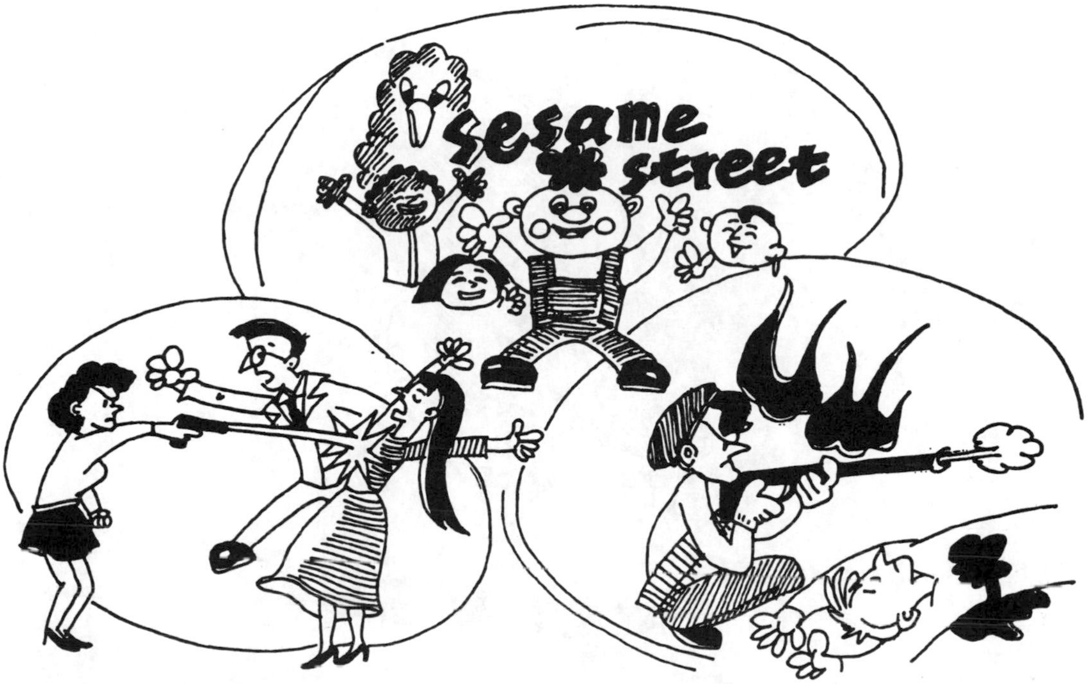
sesame street

第八課 電視和電影的影響

一‧課文

　　張天明的女朋友麗莎很喜歡看電影，新電影一上演，她就去看。這個學期她選了一門電影課，得看很多電影，張天明有空也陪她一起看。

　　學校附近有兩、三家電影院，演的都是商業片。學校禮堂幾乎每天晚上都演電影，演的多半是藝術片，偶爾也有紀錄片。今天上午麗莎來電話說，晚上想去看一部外國電影。張天明閑著沒事，坐在沙發上一邊看電視，一邊等他的女朋友。八頻道* 正在播一條新聞說，MTV 的卡通片對兒童的影響很不

第八课 电视和电影的影响

一·课文

　　张天明的女朋友丽莎很喜欢看电影，新电影一上演，她就去看。这个学期她选了一门电影课，得看很多电影，张天明有空也陪她一起看。

　　学校附近有两、三家电影院，演的都是商业片。学校礼堂几乎每天晚上都演电影，演的多半是艺术片，偶尔也有纪录片。今天上午丽莎来电话说，晚上想去看一部外国电影。张天明闲着没事，坐在沙发上一边看电视，一边等他的女朋友。八频道*正在播一条新闻说，MTV的卡通片对儿童的影响很不好，引起了很多家長的反對。據說加州有一個小男孩看了MTV的卡通片以後，模仿片裏的人物玩火柴，引起了一場火災，把他的妹妹燒死了。張天明看到這兒，他的女朋友走了進來。

張天明：　你聽說了嗎？加州的一個小男孩看了MTV以後玩火，結果不小心把他的妹妹燒死了。

麗　莎：　真的？唉，電視裏老播些亂七八糟的東西，小孩兒能學好嗎？

張天明：　這也不見得是電視的影響。大人不好好教育孩子，反而怪電視！電視裏也有不少好的節目啊，像《芝蔴街》什麼的，爲什麼不學？

麗　莎：　像那樣的節目有幾個？小孩學壞容易，學好難哪！就是大人也難免會受電視電影的影響。你沒聽說有個女的向她男朋友的女兒開槍，她說她以爲她男朋友的女兒是他的另一個女朋友，還說她開槍是因爲受了一部電影的影響！

張天明：　她完全是找藉口。她是個大人，不是孩子，難道可以對自己的行爲不負責任嗎？

麗　莎：　你剛才不是說小孩不見得會受電視的影響嗎？你這不是自相矛盾嗎？

張天明：　我並沒有自相矛盾。好了，好了，我不跟你爭論了，我們還是去看電影吧。

麗　莎：　電影不演了，有人威脅要炸禮堂。我敢說，這肯定是什麼人從哪個電影裏學來的。

張天明：　你是在開玩笑吧？

* "頻道"也可以說"台"，"第五頻道"也可以說"第五台"。
Another word for "頻道" is "台." One can also say "第五台" for "第五頻道."

好，引起了很多家长的反对。据说加州有一个小男孩看了MTV
的卡通片以后，模仿片里的人物玩火柴，引起了一场火灾，把
他的妹妹烧死了。张天明看到这儿，他的女朋友走了进来。

张天明：　你听说了吗？加州的一个小男孩看了MTV以后玩火，
　　　　　结果不小心把他的妹妹烧死了。

丽　莎：　真的？唉，电视里老播些乱七八糟的东西，小孩儿能
　　　　　学好吗？

张天明：　这也不见得是电视的影响。大人不好好教育孩子，反
　　　　　而怪电视！电视里也有不少好的节目啊，像《芝麻
　　　　　街》什么的，为什么不学？

丽　莎：　像那样的节目有几个？小孩学坏容易，学好难哪！就
　　　　　是大人也难免会受电视电影的影响。你没听说有个女
　　　　　的向她男朋友的女儿开枪。她说她以为她男朋友的女
　　　　　儿是他的另一个女朋友，还说她开枪是因为受了一部
　　　　　电影的影响！

张天明：　她完全是找藉口。她是个大人，不是孩子，难道可以
　　　　　对自己的行为不负责任吗？

丽　莎：　你刚才不是说小孩不见得会受电视影响吗？你这不是
　　　　　自相矛盾吗？

张天明：　我并没有自相矛盾。好了，好了，我不跟你争论了，
　　　　　我们还是去看电影吧。

丽　莎：　电影不演了，有人威胁要炸礼堂。我敢说，这肯定是
　　　　　什么人从哪个电影里学来的。

张天明：　你是在开玩笑吧？

＊“频道”也可以说“台”，“第五频道”也可以说“第五台”。
Another word for "频道" is "台." One can also say "第五台" for "第五频道."

二·生詞表

影響*	影响	n	yǐngxiǎng	influence

每天花很多時間看電視，
會影響孩子的學習。
這件事對我有很大的影響。

上演		v	shàngyǎn	(of plays or movies) to show
商業片	商业片	n	shāngyè piàn	commercial film
禮堂	礼堂	n	lǐtáng	auditorium
幾乎	几乎	adv	jīhū	almost
多半		adv	duōbàn	mostly
藝術片	艺术片	n	yìshù piàn	art film
偶爾	偶尔片	adv	ǒu'ěr	occasionally
紀錄片	纪录	n	jìlù piàn	documentary film
閑著沒事	闲着没事		xián zhe méi shì	idle with nothing to do
沙發*	沙发	n	shāfā	sofa
頻道	频道	n	píndào	TV channel
播		v	bō	broadcast
新聞	新闻	n	xīnwén	news
卡通		n	kǎtōng	cartoon
兒童	儿童	n	értóng	children

兒童節；兒童用品
他有兩個孩子。
那兒有幾個小孩在玩。

引起		v	yǐnqǐ	give rise to

135

家長	家长	n	jiāzhǎng	parent

冬冬的媽媽到學校去參加家長會了。

學校請學生家長來學校和老師見面。

小張的父母反對他學醫。

反對	反对	v	fǎnduì	oppose

我爸爸反對我搬到校外去住。

據說	据说	vp	jùshuō	it is said; allegedly
小男孩		n	xiǎo nánhái	a little boy
模仿		v	mófǎng	imitate

他很喜歡模仿別人說話。

人物		n	rénwù	character in a play, story, etc.
火柴		n	huǒchái	match
火災	火灾	n	huǒzāi	fire (disaster)
燒死	烧死	vc	shāo sǐ	burn to death
火		n	huǒ	fire
結果	结果	conj/n	jiéguǒ	as a result; result

他申請學校還沒有結果。

那個孩子常常看不好的電視，結果學壞了。

亂七八糟*	乱七八糟		luàn qī bā zāo	at sixes and sevens; junk; messy
大人		n	dàrén	adult
教育		v	jiàoyù	educate
反而		conj	fǎn'ér	on the contrary

怪		v	guài	blame

你們別怪他，他沒有錯。

這個人做錯了事常常喜歡怪別人。

那樣	那样	pn	nàyàng	that manner; that kind
小孩		n	xiǎoháir	small kid
難免	难免	adv	nánmiǎn	hard to avoid; inevitably
向		prep	xiàng	toward
開槍	开枪	vo	kāi qiāng	fire a gun shot
以為*	以为	v	yǐwéi	think erroneously
另			lìng	the other; another
完全		adv	wánquán	completely

老師說的話我完全聽不懂。

這件事不能完全怪他。

(找)藉口	(找)借口	n	(zhǎo) jièkǒu	(look for) excuse
行為	行为	n	xíngwéi	behavior
負責任	负责任	vo	fù zérèn	take responsibility

他這個人做事很負責任。

父母應該對自己的孩子負責任。

自相矛盾			zìxiāng máodùn	contradict oneself; self-contradictory
威脅	威胁	v	wēixié	threaten

那個人用槍威脅他，可是他不怕。

炸		v	zhà	bomb
敢		v	gǎn	dare

外面太黑，我不敢出去。

這件事我不敢告訴爸爸。

專名 Proper Nouns

加州*	Jiā Zhōu	(abbr.) the state of California
芝蔴街　　芝麻街	Zhīmájiē	Sesame Street

難寫的字：

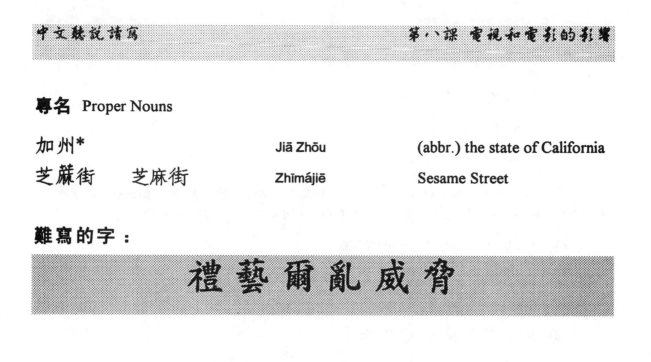

禮 藝 爾 亂 威 脅

三・語法註釋 Grammar Notes

1. Distinguishing among "的, 地, 得:"

A: "的" is used after attributives. "的" is generally followed by nouns, sometimes by verbs or adjectives; "的" can be preceded by pronouns, nouns, adjectives, verbs, etc, but not adverbs. For instance,

(1) 我的專業是統計學，妹妹的專業是文學。

我的专业是统计学，妹妹的专业是文学。

I major in statistics. My sister majors in literature.

(2) 小張買的衣服不太好看。

小张买的衣服不太好看。

The clothes that Xiao Zhang buys do not look very good.

(3) 我喜歡跟性格開朗的人交朋友。

我喜欢跟性格开朗的人交朋友。

I prefer to make friends with people who are outgoing.

(4) 你的建議不錯。

你的建议不错。

Your suggestion isn't bad.

B: "地" is an adverbial marker. It is used before verbs; "地" is often preceded by adjectives, adverbs or set phrases, but not nouns or pronouns. For instance,

(1) 老師慢慢地走進教室來。

老师慢慢地走进教室来。

The teacher slowly walked into the classroom.

(2) 孩子們很快地跑了出去。

孩子们很快地跑了出去。

The kids quickly ran out.

(3) 學生們正在努力地學習中文。

学生们正在努力地学习中文。

The students are studying Chinese hard.

"得" signals complements. It is used after verbs or adjectives. "得" is generally followed by adjectives, verbal phrases, or adverbs. For instance,

(1) 妹妹跑得很快。

妹妹跑得很快。

(My) sister runs very quickly.

(2) 李明聽說不考試了，高興得跳了起來。

李明听说不考试了，高兴得跳了起来。

When Li Ming heard that there would be no exam, he lept with joy.

(3) 今天熱得很。

今天热得很。

It's really hot today.

2. "一邊...，一邊..." :

"一邊...，一邊..." is used to describe two simultaneous actions. Often the second verb denotes the main action whereas the first verb denotes the accompanying action. For example,

(1) 我喜歡一邊吃飯一邊看電視。

我喜欢一边吃饭一边看电视。

I like to watch TV while I'm eating.

(2) 他一邊聽古典音樂一邊給他家人寫信。

他一边听古典音乐一边给他家人写信。

He wrote to his family while listening to classical music.

(3) 你不要一邊走路一邊看書。

你不要一边走路一边看书。

Don't read while you're walking.

3. "就是...，也..." (even if... still...) :

The conjunction "就是 ...,也 ..." expresses supposition. There are two usages:

A: The two clauses or phrases refer to two related things. The first clause or phrase signifies a hypothesis; the second clause or phrase indicates that that hypothesis will not in anyway change the result. For instance,

(1) 南加州的天氣很好，就是冬天也很暖和。

南加州的天气很好，就是冬天也很暖和。

The weather in southern California is very nice. It is pretty warm even in the winter.

(2) A：外邊很黑，他要是不來，你就不要去看電影了。

外边很黑，他要是不来，你就不要去看电影了。

It's dark out. If he doesn't come, then don't go to see the movie.

B：我不怕，他就是不來，我一個人也要去。

我不怕，他就是不来，我一个人也要去。

I'm not afraid. Even if he doesn't come, I'll go by myself.

(3) **A：**明天要是天氣不好，我們還去波士頓嗎？

明天要是天气不好，我们还去波士顿吗？

If the weather is bad tomorrow, are we still going to Boston?

B：這件事已經説定了，就是天氣不好，也要去。

这件事已经说定了，就是天气不好，也要去。

It's already been settled. Even if the weather is bad, we still have to go.

The hypothese described in the first clause is often extreme:

(4) 你就是給我一百萬塊錢，我也不跟你結婚。

你就是给我一百万块钱，我也不跟你结婚。

Even if you gave me a million dollars, I still wouldn't marry you.

(5) 他眼睛很好，就是芝麻大的字，他都看得清楚。

他眼睛很好，就是芝麻大的字，他都看得清楚。

His eyesight is very good. Even a word as small as a sesame seed, he can still read it.

"就是…," can be followed by a noun. What appears after "也…" is the predicate of the noun. For instance,

(6) 我餓得很，誰有吃的，就是一小塊糖也可以。

我饿得很，谁有吃的，就是一小块糖也可以。

I'm starved to death. Who [can give me] something to eat, even if it's just a piece of candy？

(7) 別説是你，就是指導教授我也不怕。

别说是你，就是指导教授我也不怕。

Even my advisor wouldn't be able to intimidate me. Let alone you.

(8) 這兒很暖和，就是冬天也不用穿毛衣。

这儿很暖和，就是冬天也不用穿毛衣。

It's very warm here. You don't need to wear a sweater even in the winter.

B: The two clauses or phrases refer to the same thing. The second clause or phrase signifies a concessionary guess:

(1) A：這個音樂會聽說很不錯，現在還有票嗎？

这个音乐会听说很不错，现在还有票吗？

I hear this is going to be a good concert. Are there still tickets available?

B：我想，就是有也不多了。

我想，就是有也不多了。

I don't think there are many left, if any.

(2) 明天的晚會我可能去不了，就是去也得很晚。

明天的晚会我可能去不了，就是去也得很晚。

I probably won't make it to tomorrow's party. Even if I can make it, I'll be very late.

4. "反而"：

"反而" expresses a turn or twist. The second clause signifies something that is contrary to one's expectation. For example,

(1) 難的字他都會寫，容易的字他反而不會寫。

难的字他都会写，容易的字他反而不会写。

He can write difficult characters, but not simple ones!

(2) 他很奇怪，這次考試考得很好，好像反而不高興了。

他很奇怪，这次考试考得很好，好像反而不高兴了。

He's weird. He did really well on this exam, but he seemed unhappy [for some strange reason].

(3) 他每天都是第一個來，今天有這麼重要的事，反而來
晚了。

他每天都是第一个来，今天有这么重要的事，反而来
晚了。

He is the first one to get here every day, but he was late today when we had
such an important thing [to attend to.]

Note that "反而" is an adverb. If there is a subject in the second clause, "反而" should
appear after the subject. Because "反而" signifies a shift in thought, there must be some
context; in other words, one cannot use "反而" out of the blue.

5. "難免":

"難免" means "difficult to avoid." For example,

(1) 兒童難免會受電視的影響。

儿童难免会受电视的影响。

It's inevitable that children will be affected by TV.

(2) 第一次教課，緊張總是難免的。

第一次教课，紧张总是难免的。

It's inevitable that [you will] get nervous when [you] teach for the first time.

(3) 你在女同學面前說難聽話，難免讓人不高興。

你在女同学面前说难听话，难免让人不高兴。

You use [such] foul language in front of female classmates. No wonder [they]
find you unpleasant.

(4) 就是兩個好朋友，有時也難免意見不同。

就是两个好朋友，有时也难免意见不同。

Even between two good friends, disagreements are inevitable.

143

6. 反問句 (Rhetorical Questions)：

Some sentences are in the form of questions, but they do not require answers. They are used to emphasize a point. For instance,

(1) 這麼簡單的道理，難道你都不懂嗎？

這么简单的道理，难道你都不懂吗？

Such a simple idea. Can't you understand it?
[You should be able to understand it.]

(2) A：小明，你剛才拿我的東西了吧？

小明，你刚才拿我的东西了吧？

Xiaoming, did you just take my stuff?

B：誰拿你的東西了？你別亂說。

谁拿你的东西了？你别乱说。

Who would take your stuff?　Don't talk nonsense.
[I didn't take your stuff.]

(3) 這麼貴的衣服，我怎麼買得起呢？

这么贵的衣服，我怎么买得起呢？

These clothes are so expensive.　How could I afford them?
[I can't afford them.]

(4) 電視里老播些亂七八糟的東西，小孩能學好嗎？

电视里老播些乱七八糟的东西，小孩能学好吗？

Would kids be able to learn to be good by example?　[They wouldn't.]

 (*Lesson Eight*)

(5) 我每天去工作得換三次車，你說麻煩不麻煩？

我每天去工作得换三次车，你说麻烦不麻烦？

I have to change buses three times when I go to work every day.
Isn't that a drag?
[It's a drag.]

(6) 你說我應該給你錢，我是你的媽媽還是你的爸爸？

你说我应该给你钱，我是你的妈妈还是你的爸爸？

You said I should give you money. Am I your mother or your father?
[I'm neither your mother nor your father.]

From these examples, it is clear that rhetorical questions in the form of affirmative sentences are used to negate; rhetorical questions in the form of negative sentences are used to affirm. Rhetorical questions are much more emphatic than non-rhetorical questions.

四·詞語練習

1. " 幾乎 " (almost [more formal than 差不多]):

Example: 學校禮堂幾乎每天晚上都演電影。

學校礼堂几乎每天晚上都演电影。

(1) 他是個球迷，幾乎每個週末＿＿＿＿＿＿＿＿。

他是个球迷，几乎每个周末＿＿＿＿＿＿＿＿。

(2) 這個星期天氣不好，幾乎天天＿＿＿＿＿＿＿ 。

这个星期天气不好，几乎天天＿＿＿＿＿＿＿ 。

(3) 他＿＿＿＿＿＿＿，幾乎天天去酒吧喝酒。

他＿＿＿＿＿＿＿，几乎天天去酒吧喝酒。

2. " 偶爾 " (occasionally) :

Example: 學校禮堂...演的多半是藝術片，偶爾也有紀錄片。

學校礼堂...演的多半是艺术片，偶尔也有纪录片。

(1) 我一般自己做飯，偶爾也去＿＿＿＿＿＿＿。

我一般自己做饭，偶尔也去＿＿＿＿＿＿＿。

(2) 他喜歡聽搖滾樂，不過偶爾也＿＿＿＿＿＿＿＿＿＿＿。

他喜欢听摇滚乐，不过偶尔也＿＿＿＿＿＿＿＿＿＿＿。

(3) 她一般都在自己的房間看書，偶爾＿＿＿＿＿＿＿＿＿。

她一般都在自己的房间看书，偶尔＿＿＿＿＿＿＿＿＿。

3. "多半" (lit. more than half) (used before verbs)：

Example: 學校禮堂...演的多半是藝術片，偶爾也有紀錄片。

學校礼堂...演的多半是艺术片，偶尔也有纪录片。

(1) 這些電影我多半都看過。

这些电影我多半都看过。

(2) 下午他多半都在家，你去找他吧。

下午他多半都在家，你去找他吧。

(3) 今天來的客人你多半不認識，他們不太有名。

今天来的客人你多半不认识，他们不太有名。

4. "引起...反對/火災/興趣/爭論"

(provoke/ignite...opposition/fire/interest/dispute)：

Example: 加州的一個小男孩玩火柴引起了一場火災。

加州的一个小男孩玩火柴引起了一场火灾。

(1) 報上的文章引起很多人的＿＿＿＿＿。

报上的文章引起很多人的＿＿＿＿＿。

(2) 這本書引起孩子們很大的＿＿＿＿＿。

这本书引起孩子们很大的＿＿＿＿＿。

(3) 他的看法引起很多人的＿＿＿＿＿。

他的看法引起很多人的＿＿＿＿＿。

5. Adverb " 老 " (colloq. always) :

　　Example: 電視裏老播些亂七八糟的東西。
　　　　　　 电视里老播些乱七八糟的东西。

　　(1) 他老買些＿＿＿＿＿＿＿東西。
　　　　 他老买些＿＿＿＿＿＿＿东西。

　　(2) 別老喝酒，＿＿＿＿＿＿＿＿＿ ！
　　　　 别老喝酒，＿＿＿＿＿＿＿＿＿ ！

　　(3) 你怎麼老穿＿＿＿＿＿＿衣服？
　　　　 你怎么老穿＿＿＿＿＿＿衣服？

6. " 還是 " (had better) :

　　Example: 我們還是去看電影吧。
　　　　　　 我们还是去看电影吧。

　　(1) 你還是＿＿＿＿＿＿＿＿＿，他不會幫你忙的。
　　　　 你还是＿＿＿＿＿＿＿＿＿，他不会帮你忙的。

　　(2) 你還是明天問老師吧，＿＿＿＿＿＿。
　　　　 你还是明天问老师吧，＿＿＿＿＿＿。

　　(3) 我們還是＿＿＿＿＿，不然她會生氣的。
　　　　 我们还是＿＿＿＿＿，不然她会生气的。

五·看圖說話

第九課　旅　行

一・課　文

　　快放假了，這幾天張天明一直在考慮假期的旅行計劃。張天明的父母是五十年代從中國南京移民來美國的。張天明自己是在美國出生，在美國長大的，從來沒去過中國。他的父母曾經多次讓他去中國大陸看看，特別是去南京看看。張天明自己也確實想去看看爸爸媽媽出生的地方。可是他覺得除非麗莎跟他一起去，否則，一個人旅行有什麼意思？這天晚飯後，張天明和麗莎一邊散步，一邊談起了旅行的事。

第九課　旅 行

一·课 文

　　快放假了，这几天张天明一直在考虑假期的旅行计划。张天明的父母是五十年代从中国南京移民来美国的。张天明自己是在美国出生，在美国长大的，从来没去过中国。他的父母曾经多次让他去中国大陆看看，特别是去看看南京。张天明自己也确实想去看看爸爸妈妈出生的地方。可是他觉得除非丽莎跟他一起去，否则，一个人旅行有什么意思？这天晚饭后，张天明和丽莎一边散步，一边谈起了旅行的事。

張天明：　就要放假了，你說我們該去哪兒玩兒？

麗　莎：　哪兒好玩兒就去哪兒。

張天明：　以前咱們不是去東岸就是去西岸，都快玩兒膩了。
　　　　　這次咱們去遠一點的地方怎麼樣？出國旅行！

麗　莎：　出國？好啊。去墨西哥！

張天明：　墨西哥太近，還有，聽說一打開電視，節目有一半
　　　　　都是在美國演過的。

麗　莎：　你說的這些都是藉口。要是不去墨西哥，那你說咱們
　　　　　去哪兒？

張天明：　去中國好嗎？我真的很想去南京看看，當然還有北
　　　　　京、上海。

麗　莎：　難怪這幾天你老看中國地圖！可是我聽說夏天南京
　　　　　熱得很，像個大火爐一樣。

張天明：　其實沒那麼可怕，我父母的老家就在南京。我有一
　　　　　個姑媽住在那兒，我應該去看看她。我要是今年不
　　　　　去南京，就得等到畢業以後了。

麗　莎：　好吧，既然你這麼想去，我就陪你去一趟吧。你現
　　　　　在就給旅行社打電話訂機票吧。

　　　　　＊　　　　　　　　　＊　　　　　　　　　＊

張天明：　我已經打過電話了，沒有從紐約直飛南京的飛機。
　　　　　一條路線是從芝加哥到上海，再從上海坐火車到南
　　　　　京，是東方航空公司；另一條是先到香港，然後從
　　　　　香港飛南京，是韓國航空公司。我們得商量商量走
　　　　　哪條路線好。

麗　莎：　走香港！我們可以順便去看看斯蒂夫。他在香港做
　　　　　生意，可以讓他開車到機場接我們，當我們的導
　　　　　遊。

张天明：　就要放假了，你说我们该去哪儿玩儿？

丽　莎：　哪儿好玩儿就去哪儿。

张天明：　以前咱们不是去东岸就是去西岸，都快玩儿腻了。
这次咱们去远一点的地方怎么样？出国旅行！

丽　莎：　出国？好啊。去墨西哥！

张天明：　墨西哥太近，还有，听说一打开电视，节目有一半
都是在美国演过的。

丽　莎：　你说的这些都是借口。要是不去墨西哥，那你说咱们
去哪儿？

张天明：　去中国好吗？我真的很想去南京看看，当然还有北
京、上海。

丽　莎：　难怪这几天你老看中国地图！可是我听说夏天南京
热得很，象个大火炉一样。

张天明：　其实没那么可怕，我父母的老家就在南京。我有一
个姑妈住在那儿，我应该去看看她。我要是今年不
去南京，就得等到毕业以后了。

丽　莎：　好吧，既然你这么想去，我就陪你去一趟吧。你现
在就给旅行社打电话订机票吧。

*　　　　　　　*　　　　　　　*

张天明：　我已经打过电话了，没有从纽约直飞南京的飞机。
一条路线是从芝加哥到上海，再从上海坐火车到南
京，是东方航空公司；另一条是先到香港，然后从
香港飞南京，是韩国航空公司。我们得商量商量走
哪条路线好。

丽　莎：　走香港！我们可以顺便去看看斯蒂夫。他在香港做
生意，可以让他开车到机场接我们，当我们的导
游。

張天明：　你總是忘不了你那個斯蒂夫！

麗　莎：　別吃醋，我跟他只不過是一般的朋友。

張天明：　我知道。我只是怕時間來不及。

麗　莎：　我們可以在南京少待兩天，那麼熱的地方。對了，
　　　　　我還得去郵局辦護照呢，聽說一般要等兩個禮拜。

張天明：　咱們還得辦簽證。這麼多事情，得趕快辦。

麗　莎：　我馬上去照相。

張天明：　好，我也去打聽打聽中國領事館的電話和地址。

张天明： 你总是忘不了你那个斯蒂夫！

丽　　莎： 别吃醋，我跟他只不过是一般的朋友。

张天明： 我知道。我只是怕时间来不及。

丽　　莎： 我们可以在南京少待两天，那么热的地方。对了，
我还得去邮局办护照呢，听说一般要等两个礼拜。

张天明： 咱们还得办签证。这么多事情，得赶快办。

丽　　莎： 我马上去照相。

张天明： 好，我也去打听打听中国领事馆的电话和地址。

二・生詞表

假期	假期	n	jiàqī	vacation
年代		n	niándài	decade
移民		v	yímín	emigrate
曾經	曾经	adv	céngjīng	indicating past action
大陸	大陆	n	dàlù	mainland; continent
確實	确实	adv	quèshí	indeed; in truth
除非		conj	chúfēi	unless
否則	否则	conj	fǒuzé	otherwise
散步		v	sàn bù	take a walk

我們去公園散散步吧。

他每天吃了晚飯就去散步。

該	该	av	gāi	應該
東岸	东岸	n	dōng'àn	east coast
西岸		n	xǐ'àn	west coast
(玩)膩(了)	(玩)膩(了)	col	(wár) nì (le)	bored; tired; sick of

這道菜我天天吃，都吃膩了。

這種電影太多了，我看膩了。

出國	出国	v	chū guó	go abroad
火爐	火炉	n	huǒlú	furnace
可怕		adj	kěpà	terrible

那個地方壞人很多，很可怕。

剛才他講了一個可怕的故事。

姑媽	姑妈	n	gūmā	father's sister

既然*		conj	jìrán	since; now that
趟		m	tàng	once; a round trip
旅行社*		n	lǚxíngshè	travel agency
訂*	订	v	dìng	reserve; book
				打電話給飯館訂位子。
機票*	机票	n	jīpiào	plane ticket
直飛*	直飞		zhí fēi	fly directly
路線	路线	n	lùxiàn	route
火車	火车	n	huǒchē	train
東方	东方	n	dōngfāng	east; the orient
航空公司			hángkōng gōngsī	airline
公司		n	gōngsī	company
然後*	然后		ránhòu	then; after that
商量		v	shāngliang	discuss
				你們商量一下明天旅行的路線。
				你提出來的事我們正在商量。
順便	顺便	adv	shùnbiàn	in passing
做生意		vo	zuò shēngyì	do business
機場*	机场	n	jīchǎng	airport
導遊*	导游	n	dǎoyóu	tour guide
忘不了		vc	wàng bu liǎo	cannot forget; unable to forget
吃醋		col	chī cù	jealous (because of rivalry in love); lit. eat vinegar
不過*	不过	adv	búguò	no more than; just; only
怕*		v	pà	be afraid of; perhaps
來不及		vc	lái bu jí	there's not enough time for
待		v	dāi	stay

郵局*	邮局	n	yóujú	post office
護照	护照	n	hùzhào	passport
禮拜*	礼拜	col	lǐbài	week
簽證*	签证	n	qiānzhèng	visa
趕快*	赶快	adv	gǎnkuài	quickly

趕快走，快上課了。

他病了，趕快帶他去醫院吧。

| 照相 | | vo | zhào xiàng | have a picture taken; take a picture |
| 打聽 | 打听 | v | dǎtīng | ask about; inquire about |

你去打聽一下，這附近有沒有中國飯館。

剛才我去打聽了，明天放假，圖書館不開。

| 領事館 | 领事馆 | n | lǐngshìguǎn | consulate |
| 地址 | | n | dìzhǐ | address |

專名 Proper Nouns

南京		Nánjīng	Nanjing
墨西哥	墨西哥	Mòxīgē	Mexico
芝加哥		Zhījiāgē	Chicago
香港		Xiānggǎng	Hong Kong
韓國	韩国	Hánguó	(South) Korea
斯蒂夫		Sīdìfū	Steve

難寫的字：

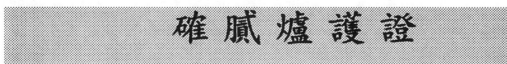

確　膩　爐　護　證

157

三 · 語法註釋 Grammar Notes

1. " 過 " (indicating experience)

To indicate that someone has had the experience of doing something, we use the dynamic particle "過." It differs from "了" in two ways.

A: "了" is descriptive in nature, and is used to describe the realization of an action. For instance,

(1) 八點鐘了，上課了，同學們都進了教室。

八点钟了，上课了，同学们都进了教室。

> It was eight o'clock. The class began. The students all walked into the classroom.

(2) 第二天早晨，我很早就起來了，起床後就去體育場跑步。

第二天早晨，我很早就起来了，起床后就去体育场跑步。

> The following morning I got up really early. After I got up, I went jogging on the track field.

(3) 客人們進來以後，找到了自己的位子，坐了下來。

客人们进来以后，找到了自己的位子，坐了下来。

> The guests walked in, found their seats, and sat down.

There isn't an explicit time phrase in (3). The implied time is a relative one. "過" is explanatory in nature. It is used to explain the rationale behind the action mentioned in a separate clause. For instance,

(1) (以前)我們在一起學過英文，我知道他英文很好。

(以前)我们在一起学过英文，我知道他英文很好。

(因為我們在一起學過英文，所以我知道他英文很好。)

(因为我们在一起学过英文，所以我知道他英文很好。)

> We used to study English together. I know his English is very good.

> (i.e., because we studied English together, I know his English is very good.)

(2) A：你去過中國，請給我們一個建議，去哪兒旅行最好。

你去过中国，请给我们一个建议，去哪儿旅行最好。

（因為你去過中國，所以請給我們一個建議，去哪兒
旅行最好。）

（因为你去过中国，所以请给我们一个建议，去哪儿
旅行最好。）

You've been to China. Give us some tips on where are some of the best
places to go.

(i.e., because you've been to China, you can give us some tips on where
are some of the best places to go.)

B： 誰說我去過中國？對不起，我不能給你們什麼建議。

　　谁说我去过中国？对不起，我不能给你们什麽建议。

Who says I've been to China? I'm sorry. I can't offer you any
suggestions.

(3) 他學過好幾年中文，都能看中文電影了。

他学过好几年中文，都能看中文电影了。

（因為他學過好幾年中文，所以都能看中文電影了。）

（因为他学过好几年中文，所以都能看中文电影了。）

He's been studying Chinese for several years now. He can now read
Chinese movies
(i.e., because he's been studying Chinese for several years, he can now read
Chinese novels.)

In the above sentences the clauses containing "過" all explain the reason for the action
in the following clauses.

B: When one uses "了," there is often a specific time phrase, which is often absent from
sentences with "過." When we use "過," the time implied is often rather vague: "before,"
and "in the past." Only when one wants to be more precise does one use a time phrase.
Note that when "過" is used in the experiential sense, it usually cannot be followed by
"了."

2. " 過 " (indicating completion) ：

"過" can also indicate completion as in "我已經打過電話了 (I've called.)" More
examples:

(1) 你叫我看的那本書我看過了，很不錯。

你叫我看的那本书我看过了，很不错。

I've read the book that you asked me to read. It's not bad.

(2) A：今天我們去看這個電影好嗎？

今天我们去看这个电影好吗？

Let's go and see this movie today, all right?

B：這個電影我看過了。

这个电影我看过了。

I've seen this movie already.

(3) A：你在我們這兒吃飯吧。

你在我们这儿吃饭吧。

Why don't you eat with us?

B：不，我吃過了。

不，我吃过了。

Oh no, I've already eaten.

Verbs that can be used with "過" in this way have to do with actions that are known or familiar to the speaker. "過" in this usage is interchangeable with "了." One could also put "了" after "過."

3. "除非"：

"除非" is a conjunction. It introduces a precondition. There is usually a second clause containing a "才."

(1) 明天除非你來接我，我才去。

明天除非你来接我，我才去。

I'm not going unless you come and pick me up tomorrow.

(2) A：今天的討論會你去嗎？

今天的讨论会你去吗？

Are you going to the lecture today?

　　B：除非做完了功課，我才會去。

　　　　除非做完了功课，我才会去。

　　　　Only if I can finish my homework; otherwise, I'm not going.

(3) A：今天去看電影好不好？

　　　　今天去看电影好不好？

　　　　Shall we go to a movie today?

　　B：除非看外國電影我才去。

　　　　除非看外国电影我才去。

　　　　Only if we're going to see a foreign movie.

After "除非…, 才…", one can also add "(要)不然/否則…"

(1) A：今天去看電影好不好？

　　　　今天去看电影好不好？

　　　　Shall we go to a movie today?

　　B：除非看外國電影，我才去，否則我就不去。

　　　　除非看外国电影，我才去，否则我就不去。

　　　　I'll go only if it's a foreign one. Otherwise I'm not going.

Often the middle clause with "才" can be omitted.

(2) A：明天我的生日晚會她會來嗎？

　　　　明天我的生日晚会她会来吗？

　　　　Do you think she'll come to my birthday party tomorrow evening?

　　B：除非你自己去請她，否則她不會來。

　　　　除非你自己去请她，否则她不会来。

　　　　She won't come unless you ask her in person,

(3) 除非天氣特別好，否則我是不會出去散步的。

　　除非天气特别好，否则我是不会出去散步的。

　　I won't go out for a walk unless the weather is exceptionally good.

　　In the construction "…, 除非…", the conclusion can also be introduced before the precondition. For example,

(1) 這本書這個星期我一定要看完，除非我女朋友來看我。

這本书这个星期我一定要看完，除非我女朋友来看我。

I'll definitely finish reading this book this week unless my girlfriend comes to visit me.

(2) 明天我們一定去打籃球，除非下大雨。

明天我们一定去打篮球，除非下大雨。

We'll definitely play basketball tomorrow unless it rains.

(3) 他一般十點鐘就睡了，除非第二天有考試。

他一般十点钟就睡了，除非第二天有考试。

Usually he's asleep by ten, unless there's an exam the next day.

4. "哪兒...，哪兒..." :

Some interrogative pronouns can be used for non-interrogative purposes. In this lesson, the same interrogative pronoun "哪兒...哪兒" appears in both clauses, and refers to the same indefinite person, thing, time or place.

(1) A：咱們點菜吧。你想吃什麼？

咱们点菜吧。你想吃什么？

Let's order. What would you like to eat?

B：什麼都可以，你喜歡吃什麼，我就吃什麼。

什么都可以，你喜欢吃什么，我就吃什么。

Anything would do. I'll eat whatever you like to eat.

(2) 每天姐姐去哪兒，她去哪兒。

每天姐姐去哪儿，她去哪儿。

Everyday, wherever the elder sister goes, she goes.

(3) 你什麼時候有時間，什麼時候來。

你什么时候有时间，什么时候来。

Come whenever you have time.

(4) 這個問題，誰會請誰回答。

这个问题，谁会请谁回答。

Whoever knows the answer to this question can answer.

(5) A：咱們怎麼走？

咱们怎么走？

Which way shall we go?

B：怎麼近怎麼走。

怎么近怎么走。

Whichever way is the nearest.

Note that when interrogative pronouns are used in this way, their positions remain unchanged. For instance, in (1) "你喜歡吃什麼，我就吃什麼," "什麼" is the object. Therefore it stays in the position of the object. In (3), "你什麼時候有時間，什麼時候來," "什麼時候" is the adverbial. Therefore it stays in the position of the adverbial.

5. "既然，...就..."：

"既然" introduces a fact or circumstance which is the cause of the condition indicated in the second clause. Conversely, the second clause expresses a conclusion that is derived from the fact or circumstance mentioned in the first clause. For instance,

(1) A：老師，這本書我看過了。

老师，这本书我看过了。

Laoshi, I've read this book.

B：既然你看過了，那麼就不必再看了。

既然你看过了，那么就不必再看了。

In that case, you don't have to read it again.

(2) A：我很不喜歡這兒的天氣。

我很不喜欢这儿的天气。

I really don't like the weather here.

B：既然你不喜歡這兒的天氣，就應該搬家。

既然你不喜欢这儿的天气，就应该搬家。

Well, if you don't like the weather here, you should move.

(3) 既然你同意了，咱們就決定了吧。

既然你同意了，咱们就决定了吧。

Since you've agreed to it, let's make a decision.

Note: "既然" introduces a fact or circumstance which is already known. In this respect, it differs from "因爲." Please compare:

(4) A：爲什麼中國人一家只能生一個孩子？

為什麼中國人一家只能生一个孩子？

Why each Chinese family can only have one child?

B：因爲中國的人口太多了，所以不得不這麼做。

因为中国的人口太多了，所以不得不这么做。

Because there are too many people in China. There is no other way.

B：*既然中國的人口太多了，所以不得不這麼做。(incorrect)

*既然中国的人口太多了，所以不得不这么做。

(5) A：老師，我有一點不舒服。

老师，我有一点不舒服。

Laoshi, I don't feel well.

B：既然你不舒服，就回去休息吧。

既然你不舒服，就回去休息吧。

In that case [since you're not feeling well], go home and take a rest.

B：*因爲你不舒服，就回去休息吧。(incorrect)

*因为你不舒服，就回去休息吧。

6. "然後"：

"然後" is used to describe two consecutive actions. They are usually future actions, but can also be past actions. For example,

(1) 你們先復習這一課的語法，然後預習下一課的生詞。

你们先复习这一课的语法，然後预习下一课的生词。

Review the grammar for this lesson first. Then study the vocabulary for the following lesson.

(2) 在這個學校，你得先念碩士，然後才能念博士。

在这个学校，你得先念硕士，然后才能念博士。

At this school, you have to get a master's degree before you can go on to the Ph.D. [program].

(3) 昨天他們先去看了一場電影，然後又去一家中國餐館
吃了一頓飯，很晚才回家。

昨天他们先去看了一场电影，然后又去一家中国餐馆
吃了一顿饭，很晚才回家。

Yesterday they first saw a movie, and then went to a Chinese restaurant. They
got home very late.

Note: "然後" is different from "後來":

A: "後來" can only be used to refer to past actions.

B: When "然後" is used to speak of the past, it connects two concrete actions or events.
Furthermore, they must be consecutive actions or events. This restriction does not apply
to "後來." Compare:

(4) 他們認識了一年多，後來就結婚了。

他们认识了一年多，后来就结婚了。

About one year after they met each other, they got married.

*他們認識了一年多，然後就結婚了。(incorrect)

*他们认识了一年多，然后就结婚了。

(5) 我們學了兩年日文，後來就不學了。

我们学了两年日文，后来就不学了。

We studied Japanese for two years. Then we quit.

*我們學了兩年日文，然後就不學了。(incorrect)

*我们学了两年日文，然后就不学了。

7. Word Order in Chinese (II)

Chinese word order follows the chronological principle. For instance,

(1) 我還得去郵局辦護照呢。（先去郵局，才能辦護照）

我还得去邮局办护照呢。（先去邮局，才能办护照）

I have to go to the post office to get my passport.
(One has to get to the office first before one can get one's passport.)

(2) 一條路線是從芝加哥到上海，再從上海坐火車到南京。

一条路线是从芝加哥到上海，再从上海坐火车到南京。

（先在芝加哥，然后在上海；在上海先坐上火車才能到南京）

One route is from Chicago to Shanghai, and then from Shanghai to Nanjing. (You have to be in Chicago first before you can go on to the next destination, Shanghai; you have to be in Shanghai first before you can board the train to Nanjing.)

(3) 他在香港做生意，可以讓他開車到機場接我們。

他在香港做生意，可以让他开车到机场接我们。

（先開車才能到機場，才能接我們）

（先开车才能到机场，才能接我们）

He does business in Hong Kong. We could let him drive to the airport to pick us up.
(He would have to drive to the airport first before he can pick up us.)

Please remember this important principle.

四 · 詞語練習

1. " 從來不/沒 " (never)：

Example: 張天明自己是在美國出生，在美國長大的，從來沒去過中國。

張天明自己是在美国出生，在美国长大的，从来没去过中国。

(1) 他上大學以後，從來沒＿＿＿＿＿＿過。

他上大学以后，从来没＿＿＿＿＿＿过。

(2) 我弟弟性格開朗，很容易相處，從來＿＿＿＿＿＿。

我弟弟性格开朗，很容易相处，从来＿＿＿＿＿＿。

(3) 小林很喜歡吃墨西哥飯，可是＿＿＿＿＿＿ 。

小林很喜欢吃墨西哥饭，可是＿＿＿＿＿＿ 。

2. " 曾（經）" (indicating past action)：

Example: 他的父母曾經多次讓他去中國大陸看看。

他的父母曾经多次让他去中国大陆看看。

(1) 我小時候_____，可是我都忘了。（學日文）

我小时候_____，可是我都忘了。（学日文）

(2) 我們可以叫柯林介紹一下的華盛頓，他_____。

我们可以叫柯林介绍一下的华盛顿，他_____。

(3) 張天明有一點工作經驗，他_____。

（在波士頓的一家旅行社實習）

張天明有一点工作经验，他_____。

（在波士顿的一家旅行社实习）

3. " 就要...了" (almost) (indicating an imminent action or state)：

Example: 就要放假了，你說我們該去哪兒玩兒？

就要放假了，你说我们该去哪儿玩儿？

(1) 就要_____了，你想上哪兒去？

就要_____了，你想上哪儿去？

(2) 就要_____了，你怎麼還不準備一下？

就要_____了，你怎么还不准备一下？

(3) 就要_____了，我們進屋吧。

就要_____了，我们进屋吧。

4. " 不是..., 就是..." (if it's not A, it's B; either A or B)：

Example: 以前咱們不是去東岸就是去西岸。

以前咱们不是去东岸就是去西岸。

(1) 這個學期我很忙，不是在圖書館_____，就是在電腦房
_____。

这个学期我很忙，不是在图书馆_____，就是在电脑房
_____。

(2) 她每年夏天不是去_____就是去_____。

她每年夏天不是去_____就是去_____。

(3) 張天明只買_____的運動鞋，不是阿迪達斯的就是耐
克(Nàikè: Nike)的。

张天明只买_____的运动鞋，不是阿迪达斯的就是耐
克(Nàikè: Nike)的。

5. "像...一樣"(like a...; resemling):

Example: 夏天南京熱得很，像個大火爐一樣。

夏天南京热得很，像个大火炉一样。

(1) 我的事他都管，像_____一樣。

我的事他都管，像_____一样。

(2) 他們的校園，又大又漂亮，像_____一樣。

他们的校园，又大又漂亮，像_____一样。

(3) 那個人很喜歡看卡通，像_____一樣。

那个人很喜欢看卡通，像_____一样。

6. "順便"(in passing):

Example: 我們可以順便去看看斯蒂夫。

我们可以顺便去看看斯蒂夫。

(1) 你去商店的時候，順便替我_____好嗎？

你去商店的时候，顺便替我_____好吗？

(2) 你要還書嗎？我現在去圖書館，可以順便_____。

你要还书吗？我现在去图书馆，可以顺便_____。

(3) 我弟弟住在波士頓,你_____的時候,順便替我看
看他好嗎?

我弟弟住在波士顿,你_____的时候,顺便替我看
看他好吗?

7. " 趕快 " (hurry up):

Example: 這麼多事情,得趕快去辦。

這么多事情,得赶快去办。

(1) 這本書今天得還,圖書館就要關門了,你_____吧。

这本书今天得还,图书馆就要关门了,你_____吧。

(2) 他病得這麼厲害,你_____吧。

他病得这么厉害,你_____吧。

(3) 電影快開始了,_____吧。

电影快开始了,_____吧。

五·看圖說話

第十課 在郵局

一・課文

在南京

　　星期六下午張天明和麗莎去逛街，他們走著走著來到了中山路。 他們看見馬路對面的一棟大樓上寫著 " 郵電局 " 三個大字。很多人進進出出，張天明和麗莎很好奇，就走了過去。

張天明： 奇怪，星期六下午郵局還辦公？
麗　莎： 這跟美國的郵局不一樣。

第十课　在邮局

一·课文

在南京

　　星期六下午张天明和丽莎去逛街，他们走着走着来到了中山路。他们看见马路对面的一栋大楼上写着"邮电局"三个大字。很多人进进出出，张天明和丽莎很好奇，就走了过去。

张天明：　奇怪，星期六下午邮局还办公？
丽　莎：　这跟美国的邮局不一样。

張天明： 麗莎，我正好可以買一些明信片跟郵票，給美國的朋友寫信。

麗　莎： 對。那邊好像可以打長途電話，我去給你母親和我母親打電話，告訴她們我們一路上都很順利，請她們放心。

（二十分鐘以後）

張天明： 我把東西都買好了，你呢？電話打通了嗎？

麗　莎： 對，都打通了。排隊打電話的人真多，等了半天才輪到我。

張天明： 趁你打電話的時候，我寫了三張明信片，寄給李哲、柯林和我妹妹。信筒在門口。我現在就把明信片寄了。你等我一下。

*　　　　　　*　　　　　　*

麗　莎： 咱們還應該買些郵簡，在去西安的路上，我可以寫幾張寄給我的大學同學和斯蒂夫。

張天明： 又是斯蒂夫。為了他，我們特地去了香港，沒想到他卻跑到台北去了。對了，我們還應該給西安拍個電報，把我們的日程告訴那邊的旅行社。

麗　莎： 今天真的來對了，一下子辦了這麼多事。你趕快去拍電報，我去買郵簡。

张天明：　丽莎，我正好可以买一些明信片跟邮票，给美国的朋
　　　　　友写信。

丽　莎：　对。那边好像可以打长途电话，我去给你母亲和我母
　　　　　亲打电话，告诉她们我们一路上都很顺利，请她们放
　　　　　心。

（二十分钟以后）

张天明：　我把东西都买好了，你呢？电话打通了吗？

丽　莎：　对，都打通了。排队打电话的人真多，等了半天才轮
　　　　　到我。

张天明：　趁你打电话的时候，我写了三张明信片，寄给李哲、
　　　　　柯林和我妹妹。信筒在门口。我现在就把明信片寄
　　　　　了。你等我一下。

＊　　　　　　　　＊　　　　　　　　＊

丽　莎：　咱们还应该买些邮简，在去西安的路上，我可以写几
　　　　　张寄给我的大学同学和斯蒂夫。

张天明：　又是斯蒂夫。为了他，我们特地去了香港，没想到他
　　　　　却跑到台北去了。对了，我们还应该给西安拍个电
　　　　　报，把我们的日程告诉那边的旅行社。

丽　莎：　今天真的来对了，一下子办了这么多事。你赶快去拍
　　　　　电报，我去买邮简。

在台北

　　斯蒂夫從香港到台北出差，買了些台灣特產，想寄給麗莎。

斯蒂夫：　小姐，我要把這個包裹寄到美國。

櫃　台：　好的，你要寄空運，海運，還是陸空聯運？

斯蒂夫：　哪個快，哪個便宜，就寄哪個。

櫃　台：　那就寄航空掛號吧，又快又安全，就是貴一點。**裏邊是什麼東西？**

斯蒂夫：　台灣特產和糖果、餅乾什麼的。

櫃　台：　我幫你稱稱。不太重，四百二十塊台幣。

斯蒂夫：　好。萬一東西寄丟了，怎麼辦？

櫃　台：　航空掛號一向安全可靠，不會有什麼問題的。給你這張收據，有問題可以打電話來問。

在台北

　　斯蒂夫从香港到台北出差，买了些台湾特产，想寄给丽莎。

斯蒂夫： 小姐，我要把这个包裹寄到美国。

柜　台： 好的，你要寄空运，海运，还是陆空联运？

斯蒂夫： 哪个快，哪个便宜，就寄哪个。

柜　台： 那就寄航空挂号吧，又快又安全，就是贵一点。里边是什么东西？

斯蒂夫： 台湾特产和糖果、饼干什么的。

柜　台： 我帮你称称。不太重，四百二十块台币。

斯蒂夫： 好。万一东西寄丢了，怎么办？

柜　台： 航空挂号一向安全可靠，不会有什么问题的。给你这张收据，有问题可以打电话来问。

二 · 生 詞 表

郵局	邮局	n	yóujú	post office
對面	对面	n	duìmiàn	opposite; the other side

郵局在商店的對面。
對面的大樓是一個醫院。

大樓	大楼	n	dàlóu	tall building
郵電局	邮电局	n	yóudiànjú	post and telecommunications office
好奇		v	hàoqí	curious

他對什麼什麼事情都很好奇。
孩子差不多都有好奇心。

| -過去 | -过去 | | -guoqu | ... toward |
| 奇怪 | | v | qíguài | strange; unfamiliar |

他今天怎麼沒來上課？
我覺得很奇怪。
學校最近常常有些奇怪的事。

辦公	办公	vo	bàn gōng	work (in an office); in this lesson: open for business
明信片		n	míngxìnpiàn	postcard
郵票	邮票	n	yóupiào	stamp
長途	长途	n	chángtú	long distance
母親	母亲	adj	mǔqin	mother
路上			lùshang	on the way

在回宿舍的路上，他碰到了一個老朋友。
這次去日本，一路上都很順利。

順利	順利	adj	shùnlì	without a hitch
放心		v	fàngxīn	relax; rest assured

你放心吧，他的病很快
就會好。

媽媽給他打了電話，他
好幾天不回電話，媽媽
很不放心。

打通		vc	dǎ tōng	(of calls) go through
排隊	排队	vo	pái duì	queue up; line up
輪到	轮到	vc	lún dào	be somebody's turn
趁		prep	chèn	take the opportunity
寄*		v	jì	send; mail
郵簡	邮简	n	yóujiǎn	aerogram
信筒	信筒	n	xìntǒng	postbox
特地		adv	tèdì	specially
卻	却	conj	què	however
一下子			yí xiàzi	at one go; at once

弟弟的書丟了，我幫他
找，一下子就找到了。

老師說的話，他下了課，
一下子就忘了。

拍		v	pāi	pat; send (a telegram)
電報	电报	n	diànbào	telegram
日程		n	rìchéng	itinerary
來對了	来对了	vc	lái duì le	(it's a) right (decision) to come
出差		v	chū chāi	go on a business trip
特產	特产	n	tèchǎn	unique local product
包裹		n	bāoguǒ	parcel

空運	空运		kōngyùn	transport by air
海運	海运		hǎiyùn	transport by sea
陸空聯運	陆空联运		lù kōng liányùn	land-air linked transport
掛號	挂号	v	guàhào	registered
糖果		n	tángguǒ	candies
餅乾	饼干	n	bǐnggān	cookies; crackers
稱*	称	v	chēng	weigh
台幣	台币	n	Táibì	Taiwan dollar
萬一	万一	adv	wànyī	in case
寄丟了		vc	jì diū	get lost in the mail
一向		adv	yíxiàng	consistently; always
可靠		adj	kěkào	reliable

專名 Proper Nouns

中山路	Zhōngshān lù	Zhongshan Road
西安	Xǐān	Xi'an, famous tourist city in western China

難寫的字：

輪　簡　裹　聯　幣

三 · 語法註釋 Grammar Notes

1. "V著V著..." :

"V著 V著..." must be followed by a verbal phrase. It signifies that while the first action denoted in the "V著 V著..." phrase is going on, a second action happens without one's realizing it.

(1) 那個孩子哭著哭著睡著了。

那个孩子哭着哭着睡着了。

The child cried and cried and fell asleep.

(2) 老人走著走著迷路了。

老人走着走着迷路了。

The old man was walking. [Before he knew it,] he was lost.

(3) 弟弟想著想著笑起來了。

弟弟想着想着笑起来了。

[My] brother was thinking when he burst out laughing.

2. Resultative Complements II :

A verb or adjective can be followed by another adjective or verb. When the second verb or adjective signifies the result of the first verb or adjective, it is called a resultative complement. We have learned several kinds of resultative complements. For instance,

A: The complement clarifies the action or state:

睡著了

睡着了

fall asleep

B: The complement clarifies the subject:

> 他喝醉了
>
> 他喝醉了
>
> He got himself drunk. (He was drunk.)
>
> 我聽懂了
>
> 我听懂了
>
> I listened and understood. (I was clear.)
>
> 書放在桌子上
>
> 书放在桌子上
>
> The book was put on the desk. (The book was lying on the desk.)
>
> 信寄給哥哥
>
> 信寄给哥哥
>
> The letter was sent to [my] elder brother. (He now has the letter.)
>
> 我走到學校
>
> 我走到学校
>
> I walked to school. (I'm now at school.)

C: The complement clarifies the object:

> 打破了鏡子
>
> 打破了镜子
>
> broke the mirror (The mirror is now broken.)
>
> 寄丟了明信片
>
> 寄丢了明信片
>
> lost the postcard in the mail (the postcard was lost.)

寫錯了一個字

写错了一个字

wrote a character incorrectly (The character was wrong.)

做完了功課

做完了功课

finished doing the homework (The homework is now done.)

洗乾淨衣服

洗干净衣服

washed the clothes until they're clean (The clothes are now clean.)

D: Some complements that appear after adjectives or verbs that denote psychological activities indicate an extreme degree:

好極了 (extremely good)

好极了

高興極了 (extremely happy)

高兴极了

急死了 (extremely worried)

急死了

Note: Although the resultative complement is closely related to the preceding verb or adjective, they are mutually selective. In other words, their combination is not unrestricted. One must remember which complement can be used after which verb or adjective, or which verb or adjective can take which complement. One must learn resultative complements the way one learns new words.

3. " 把 " structure :

If one wants to say that someone causes something or some other person to undergo some change, or somehow affects that thing or person through an action, one needs to use the "把" structure. For instance,

(1) 請把那個杯子給我。

　　请把那个杯子给我。

　　Please hand me that glass.

(2) 他一出門，就把媽媽剛才說的話忘了。

　　他一出门，就把妈妈刚才说的话忘了。

　　The minute he stepped out he forgot what his mother had said to him.

(3) 考試的時候，我把＂人＂字寫成了＂入＂字。

　　考试的时候，我把＂人＂字写成了＂入＂字。

　　I wrote＂人＂incorrectly as＂入＂during the exam.

When using the 把 structure, one should note the following:

A: The noun after 把 is prominent information and can be treated as a topic. Therefore, it is generally specific and known information. The agent of the action can often be omitted.

B: There have to be some other words or phrases after the verbs. Usually, it is a complement as in (3), or an indirect object as in (1). Or it can be a ＂了.＂ When there is only a ＂了,＂ it often implies disappearance, as in (2). However, when the topic involved is known by both the speaker and the listener, ＂了＂ is probably used to indicate realization.

4. Attributives and ＂的＂:

Some simple rules governing the use of ＂的＂ between attributives and nouns:

A: Nouns modifying nouns:

If the relationship between the nouns is one of possession, then ＂的＂ must be used:

> 媽媽的衣服 (mother's clothes)
>
> 妈妈的衣服
>
> 老師的筆 (the teacher's pen)
>
> 老师的笔
>
> 學校的名字 (the name of the school)
>
> 学校的名字

商店的東西 (the store's goods)

商店的东西

If the relationship between the nouns is not possessive, however, but modifies the following noun, then "的" is not needed.

中文老師 (teacher of Chinese)

中文老师

體育節目 (sportscast)

体育节目

兒童用品 (daily necessities for children)

儿童用品

電影藝術 (cinematic art)

电影艺术

汽車廣告 (auto ads.)

汽车广告

Modification indicates profession, quality and material, etc. It is different from possession. Please compare:

中國的城市一定在中國。

中国的城市一定在中国。

Chinese cities must be China. (possession)

中國城不在中國。

中国城不在中国。

Chinatowns are not in China. (modification)

B: Adjectives modifying nouns:

Generally, "的" is not needed after monosyllabic adjectives:

紅花 (a red flower)

红花

小桌子 (a small table)

小桌子

白紙 (a piece of white paper)

白纸

新書 (a new book)

新书

舊報紙 (an old newspaper)

旧报纸

"的" is usually required after disyllabic adjectives:

漂亮的衣服 (beautiful clothes)

漂亮的衣服

可愛的孩子 (a cute kid)

可爱的孩子

重要的事情 (an important event)

重要的事情

聰明的學生 (a bright student)

聪明的学生

"的" is not used in familiar adjectival nominal phrases:

客氣話 (polite and modest language)

客气话

重要人物 (an important person)

重要人物

新鮮水果 (fresh fruit)

新鲜水果

"的" is required after adjectival phrases:

> 很小的桌子(a very small table)
>
> 很小的桌子
>
> 非常新的房子(a brand new house)
>
> 非常新的房子
>
> 大大的眼睛 (big eyes)
>
> 大大的眼睛
>
> 深藍色的襯衫(a dark blue shirt)
>
> 深蓝色的衬衫

C: Pronouns modifying nouns. "的" is required to indicate possession:

> 我的書(my book)
>
> 我的书
>
> 他們的問題(their problem)
>
> 他们的问题
>
> 你的事情(your matter)
>
> 你的事情
>
> 我們的朋友(our friend)
>
> 我们的朋友
>
> 你們的時間 (your time)
>
> 你们的时间

D: "的" is generally required if the modifier is a verb, verbal phrase, or a subject-predicate phrase.

> 吃的東西 (edible things)
>
> 吃的东西
>
> 買的書 (purchased book)
>
> 买的书

寫信用的紙 (paper for writing letters)

写信用的纸

剛照的照片 (a recently taken photograph)

刚照的照片

打破的杯子 (a broken cup)

打破的杯子

我看的書 (the book I'm reading)

我看的书

你說的事情 (the thing you're saying)

你说的事情

妹妹穿的衣服 (the clothes my sister wears)

妹妹穿的衣服

老師給的功課 (the homework assigned by the teacher)

老师给的功课

E: "的" is unnecessary if a numeral modifies a noun:

一本書 (a book)

一本书

兩雙鞋 (two pairs of shoes)

两双鞋

三件衣服 (three pieces of clothing)

三件衣服

四棟大樓 (four buildings)

四栋大楼

五張照片 (five photos)

五张照片

Set phrases that have become part of familiar vocabulary do not require "的."

拿手菜 (specialty [cuisine])

拿手菜

知識份子 (intellectual)

知识分子

清蒸魚 (steamed fish)

清蒸鱼

指導教授 (advisor)

指导教授

5. "一向" and "一直":

"一向" often indicates an incessant action or a consistent state persisting "from the past up to the present." It is usually followed by a word that denotes habit or predilection. For instance,

(1) 我姐姐一向不喜歡看電影。

我姐姐一向不喜欢看电影。

My sister has never liked going to the movies.

(2) 我一向早睡早起，從來不睡懶覺。

我一向早睡早起，从来不睡懒觉。

I always go to bed early and get up early. I never sleep in.

(3) 她的男朋友一向不吸煙、不喝酒。

她的男朋友一向不吸烟、不喝酒。

Her boyfriend never smokes or drinks.

(4) 他跟朋友一向相處得很好，很少有矛盾。

他跟朋友一向相处得很好，很少有矛盾。

He is always getting along with his friends fine. There is seldom any conflict.

"一直" is used to suggest an incessant action or a consistent state within a specific time frame. The implied time period is usually shorter than "一向."

(1) 昨天一直下雨，我沒有出去跑步。

昨天一直下雨，我没有出去跑步。

Yesterday it rained all day. I didn't go out and run.

(2) 上個星期她一直生病，沒來上課。

上个星期她一直生病，没来上课。

Last week she was sick all week. She didn't go to school.

(3) 這件事過去我一直不知道，今天老師才告訴我。

这件事过去我一直不知道，今天老师才告诉我。

I didn't know about this for some time. The teacher didn't tell me till today.

四 · 詞語練習

1. " 輪到 " (it's someone's turn) :

Example: 排隊打電話的人真多，我等了半天才輪到我。

排队打电话的人真多，我等了半天才轮到我。

(1) 上個禮拜你請我吃飯，這個禮拜＿＿＿＿＿＿＿＿。

上个礼拜你请我吃饭，这个礼拜＿＿＿＿＿＿＿＿。

(2) 買票的人太多，票太少，等輪到我的時候，票都＿＿＿＿＿
了。

买票的人太多，票太少，等轮到我的时候，票都＿＿＿＿＿
了。

(3) 老師對學生說：這兩天要來找我的人很多，下星期三
才能＿＿＿＿＿你。

老师对学生说：这两天要来找我的人很多，下星期三
才能＿＿＿＿＿你。

2. " 趁 " (take advantage of the fact that...) :

Example: 趁你打電話的時候，我寫了三張明信片。

趁你打电话的时候，我写了三张明信片。

(1) 趁_____ 都在，我說一下明天的工作。

趁_____ 都在，我说一下明天的工作。

(2) 趁我現在有錢，我們_____好好吃一頓。

趁我现在有钱，我们_____好好吃一顿。

(3) _____，我想問你幾個問題。

_____，我想问你几个问题。

3. " 特地 " (specially; for a special purpose) :

Example: 爲了他，我們特地去了香港，沒想到他卻跑到
台北去了。

为了他，我们特地去了香港，没想到他却跑到
台北去了。

(1) 小王聽說老師病了，_____。

小王听说老师病了，_____。

(2) 我們知道你喜歡吃清蒸魚_____。

我们知道你喜欢吃清蒸鱼_____。

(3) 她的男朋友特地從加州坐飛機來看她，她卻

_____。

她的男朋友特地从加州坐飞机来看她，她却

_____。

4. " 卻 " (however)：

Example: 爲了他，我們特地去了香港，沒想到他卻跑到
台北去了。

為了他，我们特地去了香港，没想到他却跑到
台北去了。

(1) 她讓我在這兒等她，自己卻先_____了。

她让我在这儿等她，自己却先_____了。

(2) 他讓別人工作，自己卻去_____了。

他让别人工作，自己却去_____了。

(3) 我要去南京，他卻要去_____。

我要去南京，他却要去_____。

5. " 萬一 " (in case)：

Example: 萬一東西寄丟了，怎麼辦？

万一东西寄丢了，怎麼办？

(1) 你把護照給我吧。_____，怎麼辦？

你把护照给我吧。_____，怎麼办？

(2) 買東西應該拿收據，_____還可以換。

买东西应该拿收据，_____还可以换。

(3) 你把我的電話寫下來，_____，你可以給我打
電話。

你把我的电话写下来，_____，你可以给我打
电话。

五·看圖說話

第十一課　一封信

一・課文

爸爸、媽媽：

　　你們好！我們到南京已經快一個星期了。幾天來，我們遊覽了南京的許多名勝古蹟，南京比我想像的好得多。我小的時候就從你們那兒聽到不少南京的故事，可是到現在才真的看到了南京！

　　我們到南京的第二天，表弟就陪我們去了夫子廟，我們是坐公共汽車去的。那天是星期天，汽車上的人真多。到了夫子廟，我們好不容易才從車上擠下來。夫子廟那兒真是人山人海。我以前老聽說中國人口多，可是想像不出多到什麼程度，到了夫子廟才體會到什麼叫"擠"。不過我們很喜歡那裏的建築，夫子廟的遊客所以那麼多，可能正是因為那裏的建築別具風格吧。夫子廟旁邊就是秦淮河，聽說秦淮河以前很漂亮，可是現在我看不出那條窄窄的小河有什麼吸引人的地方。也許它當年是妙齡少女，現在已經人老珠黃了吧。我跟麗莎這麼說以後，她狠狠地瞪了我一眼。

　　前幾天我們去了玄武湖公園，在湖上划了船，還去了古城牆。不過給我們印象最深的還是中山陵。我不說你們也知道，中山陵就是孫中山先生的陵墓。陵墓在山上，從中山陵向下看，是一片樹海，非常壯觀。麗莎特別喜歡這個地方，在山上待了很長時間，我再三催她下山，她都不肯走。最後她總算戀戀不捨地跟我下了山。我們等公共汽車的時候，她突然對我說："天明，咱們死後也葬到這兒吧。"我聽了，忍不住哈哈

193

第十一课　一封信

一·课文

爸爸、妈妈：

　　你们好！我们到南京已经快一个星期了。几天来，我们游览了南京的许多名胜古迹，南京比我想象的好得多。我小的时候就从你们那儿听到不少南京的故事，可是到现在才真的看到了南京！

　　我们到南京的第二天，表弟就陪我们去了夫子庙，我们是坐公共汽车去的。那天是星期天，汽车上的人真多。到了夫子庙，我们好不容易才从车上挤下来。夫子庙那儿真是人山人海。我以前老听说中国人口多，可是想象不出多到什么程度，到了夫子庙才体会到什么叫“挤”。不过我们很喜欢那里的建筑，夫子庙的游客所以那么多，可能正是因为那里的建筑别具风格吧。夫子庙旁边就是秦淮河，听说秦淮河以前很漂亮，可是现在我看不出那条窄窄的小河有什么吸引人的地方。也许它当年是妙龄少女，现在已经人老珠黄了吧。我跟丽莎这么说以后，她狠狠地瞪了我一眼。

　　前几天我们去了玄武湖公园，在湖上划了船，还去了古城墙。不过给我们印象最深的还是中山陵。我不说你们也知道，中山陵就是孙中山先生的陵墓。陵墓在山上，从中山陵向下看，是一片树海，非常壮观。丽莎特别喜欢这个地方，在山上待了很长时间，我再三催她下山，她都不肯走。最后她总算恋恋不舍地跟我下了山。我们等公共汽车的时候，她突然对我说：“天明，咱们死后也葬到这儿吧。”我听了，忍不住哈哈大笑起來。我說："你以爲誰死後都可以葬到這兒嗎？你知道孫中山是一位偉大的 大人物啊！"没想到麗莎一本正經地問我："你怎麼知道我們幾十年以後不會成爲大人物呢？"我一想，她的話也有點道理，就說："好，我們就這麼說定了：我們倆以後就葬在中山陵旁邊的山上，我的墓碑上寫‘南京的兒子張天明’，你的墓碑上寫‘南京的媳婦麗莎’。"媽媽，別生氣，我們在開玩笑。明天我們就要去西安了，告訴你們一個小秘密。麗莎說，她今天不洗澡了，明天要到楊貴妃洗澡的華清池裏好好洗一洗。不過，我們回美國以後你們千萬別跟她提洗澡的事，要不然她又要跟我瞪眼睛了！

　　姑媽在叫我們吃飯呢。好吧，到了西安再給你們寫信。

　　　敬祝

安好！

　　　　　　　　　　　　兒

　　　　　　　　　　　　天明

　　　　　　　　　　　　六月五日

大笑起来。我说："你以为谁死后都可以葬到这儿吗？你知道孙中山是一位伟大的大人物啊！"没想到丽莎一本正经地问我："你怎么知道我们几十年以后不会成为大人物呢？"我一想，她的话也有点道理，就说："好，我们就这么说定了：我们俩以后就葬在中山陵旁边的山上，我的墓碑上写'南京的儿子张天明'，你的墓碑上写'南京的媳妇丽莎'。"妈妈，别生气，我们在开玩笑。明天我们就要去西安了，告诉你们一个小秘密。丽莎说，她今天不洗澡了，明天要到杨贵妃洗澡的华清池里好好洗一洗。不过，我们回美国以后你们千万别跟她提洗澡的事，要不然她又要跟我瞪眼睛了！

　　姑妈在叫我们吃饭呢。好吧，到了西安再给你们写信。

　　　敬祝

安好！

　　　　　　　　　　　儿

　　　　　　　　　　天明

　　　　　　　　　　　六月五日

二. 生詞表

遊覽	游览	v	yóulǎn	go sight-seeing
許多	许多		xǔduō	many; a lot
名勝古蹟	名胜古迹		míngshèng gǔjī	scenic spots and historical sites
想像	想象	v	xiǎngxiàng	imagine; visualize

波士頓的冬天比我想像的更冷。

你一定想像不出來這兒的風景多麼美。

故事		n	gùshì	story
表弟*		n	biǎodì	(younger male) cousin
擠下來	挤下来	vc	jǐ xialai	push one's way off
人山人海			rén shān rén hǎi	huge crowds of people
人口		n	rénkǒu	population
程度		n	chéngdù	degree; extent
體會到	体会到	vc	tǐhuì	learn from experience; realize

離開了家才體會爸爸媽媽對我們有多重要。

你上大學快一個月了，有什麼體會？

擠	挤	v/adj	jǐ	crowded; push against
建築	建筑	n/v	jiànzhù	architecture; to build
遊客	游客	n	yóukè	tourist
別具風格	别具风格		bié jù fēnggé	have a distinctive style
窄		adj	zhǎi	narrow

吸引		v	xīyǐn	attract
				中山陵每年都吸引很多的遊客。
				這本書很吸引人。
當年	当年		dāngnián	in those years
妙齡	妙龄	adj	miàolíng	(of young girls) wonderful or best age
少女		n	shàonǚ	young girl
人老珠黃			rén lǎo zhū huáng	(metaphor) people grow old and pearls turn yellow; (usually of women) not as beautiful as before
狠狠地		adv	hěnhěn de	vigorously; with a great deal of intensity
瞪		v	dèng	glare
湖		n	hú	lake
划船		vo	huá chuán	row a boat; paddle
古城牆	古城墙	n	gǔ chéngqiáng	ancient city wall
印象*		n	yìnxiàng	impression
				我對那個女孩的印象很好。
				我在那兒只待了一天，印象已經不深了。
深		adj	shēn	deep
陵墓		n	língmù	mausoleum; tomb
海洋		n	hǎiyáng	ocean
壯觀	壮观	adj	zhuàngguān	(of buildings, monuments, scenery etc.) grand
再三		adv	zàisān	over and over again
催		v	cuī	hurry; urge

肯		av	kěn	be willing to
總算	总算	adv	zǒngsuàn	finally
戀戀不捨	恋恋不舍		liànliàn bù shě	be reluctant to part with
突然		adv	tūrán	suddenly

突然門開了，一個人跑了進來。

死		v	sǐ	die
葬		v	zàng	bury (a person)
忍不住		vc	rěn bú zhù	unable to bear
哈哈大笑			hāhā dà xiào	laugh heartily; guffaw
偉大	伟大	adj	wěidà	great; mighty

什麼人最偉大？

大人物		n	dà rénwù	important person
一本正經	一本正经		yì běn zhèngjīng	in all seriousness
說定	说定	vc	shuō dìng	agree on; settle
墓碑		n	mùbēi	tombstone
媳婦	媳妇	n	xífù	daughter-in-law
生氣	生气	v	shēng qì	angry

學生沒復習課文，老師很生氣。

他一生氣就又喊又叫。

秘密		n/adj	mìmì	secret

他們倆秘密地談了很長時間。

洗澡		v	xǐ zǎo	take a bath (shower)
千萬	千万	adv	qiānwàn	be sure to
敬祝			jìngzhù	respectfully wish
安好			ānhǎo	safe and sound

199

專名 Proper Nouns

夫子廟	夫子庙	Fūzǐ Miào	The Temple of Confucius
秦淮河		Qínhuái Hé	The Qinhuai River
玄武湖		Xuánwǔ Hú	Lake Xuanwu
中山陵		Zhōngshān Líng	Sun Yat-sen Mausoleum
孫中山	孙中山	Sūn Zhōngshān	Sun Yat-sen
楊貴妃	杨贵妃	Yáng Guìfēi	Imperial Concubine Yang
華清池	华清池	Huáqīng Chí	Huaqing Springs

難寫的字：

覽　齡　牆　陵　墓　觀　戀　葬　萬

三 · 語法註釋 Grammar Notes

1. "幾天來" :

The word "來" in "幾天來" means the same thing as "以來." It also denotes continuation from a certain point in time in the past to the present, but it is used after phrases that suggest durations of time: 三年來(from three years ago up to the present), 一年來 (from one year ago to the present), 五個月來(from five months ago to the present). It cannot be preceded by "自" or "自從;" neither can it be used after phrases other than those that suggest durations of time. (Cf. "以來" in *Lesson Seven's* 詞語練習)

2. "才" and "就" Compared:

The adverb "才" is used to suggest that an action occurred later or more slowly than expected. "就" is the opposite. It suggests that an action occurred sooner or more quickly than expected.

(1) 八點上課，她八點一刻才來。

八点上课，她八点一刻才来。

The class began at eight o'clock. She didn't come till eight fifteen.

八點上課，她七點半就來了。

八点上课，她七点半就来了。

The class began at eight. She came (as early as) seven thirty.

(2) 我過一個鐘頭才能去。

我过一个钟头才能去。

I won't be able to go till an hour later.

我馬上就去。

我马上就去。

I'll go right away.

(3) 她念了六年才大學畢業。

她念了六年才大学毕业。

She didn't graduate till after six years at college.

他念了三年半就大學畢業了。

他念了三年半就大学毕业了。

He graduated after just three years.

Note that when using "就," if the action already took place, there should be a "了" at the end of the sentence.

3. " 好不容易 " ：

Both "好不容易" and "好容易" mean "很不容易" (with a lot of difficulty):

(1) 這本書很難買，我好容易(好不容易)才在香港買到一本。

这本书很难买，我好容易(好不容易)才在香港买到一本。

This book was really hard to get. It took me a lot of trouble to get it in Hong Kong.

(2) 今天的功課真多，我好不容易(好容易)才做完。

今天的功课真多，我好不容易(好容易)才做完。

There's so much homework today. It took me forever to get it done.

(3) 這個生詞昨天我好容易記住了，可是今天又忘了。

这个生词昨天我好容易记住了，可是今天又忘了。

I finally managed to remember this new word yesterday, but I forgot it again today.

4. "再三"：

"再三" means to do something "again and again." The actions involved usually have to do with speaking and thinking. For instance,

(1) 我再三向他説明我給他打電話只是想聊聊天，沒有別的事，可是他不相信。

我再三向他说明我给他打电话只是想聊聊天，没有别的事，可是他不相信。

I told him again and again that I called just to chat with him; there was no other reason, but he wouldn't believe me.

(2) 那個導遊幫了我很多忙，我再三向他表示感謝。

那个导游帮了我很多忙，我再三向他表示感谢。

That tour guide helped me a great deal. I thanked him repeatedly.

(3) 我離開家的時候，媽媽再三告訴我要注意身體，要常常打電話。

我离开家的时候，妈妈再三告诉我要注意身体，要常常打电话。

When I left home, my mother told me again and again to take care of myself and call home often.

"再三" can also be used after "考慮(to consider)," and "斟酌(to deliberate)."

(4) 爸爸讓我考醫學院，我考慮再三，選了統計學。

爸爸让我考医学院，我考虑再三，选了统计学。

Dad wanted me to go to medical school. After a lot of thinking, I chose statistics.

5. The Prepositions "跟/向/對" Compared:

"跟", "向" and "對" all have several meanings, which overlap but also differ from one another. For example,

(1) 我在走廊裏看見他的時候，他跟我笑了笑。

我在走廊里看见他的时候，他跟我笑了笑。

("我" 是 "(他)笑" 的對象)

("我" 是 "(他)笑" 的对象)

When I saw him in the hallway, he gave me a smile.
["I" is the object of "his smile."]

(2) 在中國，在路上遇到一個認識的人，跟他點點頭就可以了，不必説什麼。

在中国，在路上遇到一个认识的人，跟他点点头就可以了，不必说什么。

In China, when one runs into an acquaintance, one only has to give him a nod. One doesn't have to say anything.

(3) 我把我的想法跟他説了説，他沒説什麼。

我把我的想法跟他说了说，他没说什么。

I told him my idea. He didn't say anything.

(1a) 我在走廊裏看見他的時候，他對我笑了笑。

我在走廊里看见他的时候，他对我笑了笑。

(2a) 在中國，在路上遇到一個認識的人，<u>對</u>他點點頭就可以了，不必說什麼。

在中国，在路上遇到一个认识的人，<u>对</u>他点点头就可以了，不必说什么。

(3a) 我把我的想法<u>對</u>他說了說，他沒說什麼。

我把我的想法<u>对</u>他说了说，他没说什么。

(1c) 我在走廊裏看見他的時候，他<u>向</u>我笑了笑。

我在走廊里看见他的時候，他<u>向</u>我笑了笑。

(2c) 在中國，在路上遇到一個認識的人，<u>向</u>他點點頭就可以了，不必說什麼。

在中国，在路上遇到一个认识的人，<u>向</u>他点点头就可以了，不必说什么。

(3c) 我把我的想法<u>向</u>他說了說，他沒說什麼。

我把我的想法<u>向</u>他说了说，他没说什么。

Both "跟" and "向" suggest "from someone or some place..." although they also introduce the object of an action, but they do not have the connotation of "facing someone or some place". For instance,

(4) 剛才我<u>跟/向</u>一個同學借了一本書，那本書很有意思。

刚才我<u>跟/向</u>一个同学借了一本书，那本书很有意思。

I just borrowed a book from a classmate. It's really an interesting book.

(5) 我<u>跟/向</u>你打聽一件事，不知道你知道不知道。

我<u>跟/向</u>你打听一件事，不知道你知道不知道。

I'd like to ask you something [get some information from you]. I don't know if you would know.

"對" cannot be used in this way.

When these prepositions are used to mean something else, they cannot be used interchangeably.

6. "了" after a verb and "了" at the end of a sentence:

"了" at the end of a sentence signals the completion of a sentence. There is a significant pause after it. For instance,

(1) A：昨天上午你去哪兒了？

昨天上午你去哪儿了？

Where did you go yesterday morning?

B：昨天上午我進城了。

昨天上午我进城了。

Yesterday morning I went to the city.

(2) 做完功課以後我就睡覺了。

做完功课以后我就睡觉了。

I went to sleep after I finished my homework.

"了" after a verb is rather different. Compare,

(3) 昨天我先在一個飯館吃了飯，然後又去買了一些東西，後來就回家了。

昨天我先在一个饭馆吃了饭，然后又去买了一些东西，后来就回家了。

Yesterday I first had dinner at a restaurant, and then did some shopping. After that I went home.

If a sentence is not yet complete, or if it is immediately followed by another clause, "了" generally goes after the verb. If the sentence is complete, "了" should go to the end of the sentence.

四・詞語練習

1. " 快 . . . 了 " (soon; before long) :

　　Example: 我們到南京已經快一個星期了。

　　　　　　我们到南京已经快一个星期了。

　　(1) 現在是十一月了，快_____ 了。

　　　　現在是十一月了，快_____ 了。

　　(2) 咱們_____吧，快上課了。

　　　　咱们_____吧，快上课了。

　　(3) 我快要畢業了，學習_____。

　　　　我快要毕业了，学习_____。

2. " 催 " (urge) :

　　Example: 我再三催她下山，她都不肯走。

　　　　　　我再三催她下山，她都不肯走。

　　(1) 上山的時候，我_____，常常有人催我快走。

　　　　上山的时候，我_____，常常有人催我快走。

　　(2) 電影七點鐘開演，現在已經六點三刻了，我催大家
　　　　_____。

　　　　电影七点钟开演，现在已经六点三刻了，我催大家
　　　　_____。

　　(3) 別催我，我_____來。

　　　　别催我，我_____来。

3. " 忍不住 " (cannot help doing sth.) :

　　Example: 我聽了，忍不住哈哈大笑起來。

　　　　　　我听了，忍不住哈哈大笑起来。

(1) 妹妹看見電影裏的小狗被打死了，忍不住＿＿＿＿＿起來。

妹妹看见电影里的小狗被打死了，忍不住＿＿＿＿＿起来。

(2) 妹妹想讓弟弟著急，不叫我告訴弟弟他的女朋友來電話的事，可是我看見弟弟著急的樣子，就＿＿＿＿＿＿＿了他。

妹妹想让弟弟着急，不叫我告诉弟弟他的女朋友来电话的事，可是我看见弟弟着急的样子，就＿＿＿＿＿＿＿了他。

(3) 在郵局，有一個人對櫃台的服務員很不客氣，我＿＿＿＿＿＿
＿＿＿＿＿＿＿＿＿＿＿＿＿＿＿＿＿＿＿＿＿＿了起來。

在邮局，有一个人对柜台的服务员很不客气，我＿＿＿＿＿＿
＿＿＿＿＿＿＿＿＿＿＿＿＿＿＿＿＿＿＿＿＿了起来。

4. " 千萬 " (be sure) :

Example: 你千萬別跟她提洗澡的事。

你千万别跟她提洗澡的事。

(1) 我聽説他跟他的女朋友鬧翻了，你＿＿＿＿＿＿＿＿＿＿。

我听说他跟他的女朋友闹翻了，你＿＿＿＿＿＿＿＿＿＿。

(2) 千萬別讓小孩玩火柴，很容易＿＿＿＿＿＿＿＿＿＿。

千万别让小孩玩火柴，很容易＿＿＿＿＿＿＿＿＿＿。

(3) 明天是你姑媽的生日，＿＿＿＿＿＿＿＿＿＿＿。

明天是你姑妈的生日，＿＿＿＿＿＿＿＿＿＿＿。

五 · 看圖說話

第十二課　中國的節日

一・課文

（一）對　話

　　今天是端午節。早晨起床後，姑媽給張天明和麗莎每人一個很漂亮的小東西。姑媽說那是荷包，戴在身上就不會生病了。不過姑媽笑著說，這只是過去的一種風俗習慣，戴著玩，不一定有什麼特別的用處。

　　中午，他們和姑媽一家人吃飯，因爲是過節，所以菜特別豐盛。除了雞鴨魚肉以外，還有幾盤在美國根本吃不到的青菜。最後姑媽又端上一大盤粽子。

第十二课　中国的节日

一·课文

（一）

　　今天是端午节。早晨起床后，姑妈给张天明和丽莎每人一个很漂亮的小东西。姑妈说那是荷包，戴在身上就不会生病了。不过姑妈笑着说，这只是过去的一种风俗习惯，戴着玩，不一定有什么特别的用处。

　　中午，他们和姑妈一家人吃饭，因为是过节，所以菜特别丰盛。除了鸡鸭鱼肉以外，还有几盘在美国根本吃不到的青菜。最后姑妈又端上一大盘粽子。

麗　莎：　這是什麼？

表　哥：　這是粽子，是端午節特別要吃的東西。

張天明：　表哥，為什麼粽子是端午節特別要吃的東西？

表　哥：　這裏邊有一個故事。兩千多年前，楚國有一個大官叫屈原。他看出來秦國雖然表面上對楚國不錯，可是實際上早晚要來打楚國，所以就建議楚國國王要早一點做準備。可是楚國國王不但不聽屈原的話，反而把他趕到南方去了。屈原因為憂國憂民，最後投江自殺了。

張天明：　屈原還是一位大詩人吧？我上中文學校的時候，好像聽我們的老師說過。

表　哥：　對，他是中國最偉大的詩人之一。他寫的詩表現了他的愛國精神。

麗　莎：　那粽子跟屈原有什麼關係呢？

表　哥：　為了祭祀屈原，老百姓把米放在竹筒裏，然後投到江裏。這就是後來的粽子。

麗　莎：　我聽說端午節還常常賽龍舟，跟屈原有關係嗎？

姑　媽：　有啊。那象徵當時人們爭先恐後地去救屈原呀。

麗　莎：　真是個動人的故事！

（二）閱　讀

　　中國傳統的節日很多，除了端午節以外，最重要的節日還有春節（中國新年）、中秋節、和元宵節。

　　春節是中國最大的節日。過春節的時候，人們要放鞭炮，到親朋好友家拜年，大人要給小孩壓歲錢。

丽　莎： 这是什么？

表　哥： 这是粽子，是端午节特别要吃的东西。

张天明： 表哥，为什么粽子是端午节特别要吃的东西？

表　哥： 这里边有一个故事。两千多年前，楚国有一个大官叫屈原。他看出来秦国虽然表面上对楚国不错，可是实际上早晚要来打楚国，所以就建议楚国国王要早一点做准备。可是楚国国王不但不听屈原的话，反而把他赶到南方去了。屈原因为忧国忧民，最后投江自杀了。

张天明： 屈原还是一位大诗人吧？我上中文学校的时候，好像听我们的老师说过。

表　哥： 对，他是中国最伟大的诗人之一。他写的诗表现了他的爱国精神。

丽　莎： 那粽子跟屈原有什么关系呢？

表　哥： 为了祭祀屈原，老百姓把米放在竹筒里，然后投到江里。这就是后来的粽子。

丽　莎： 我听说端午节还常常赛龙舟，跟屈原有关系吗？

姑　妈： 有啊。那象征当时人们争先恐后地去救屈原呀。

丽　莎： 真是个动人的故事！

（二）阅 读

　　中国传统的节日很多，除了端午节以外，最重要的节日还有春节（中国新年）、中秋节、和元宵节。

　　春节是中国最大的节日。过春节的时候，人们要放鞭炮，到亲朋好友家拜年，大人要给小孩压岁钱。

　　元宵節也叫燈節，是農曆的正月（一月）十五，那一天家家吃元宵，有的地方人們會做各種各樣好看的燈掛在門口，晚上人們都上街看燈。

　　中秋節是農曆的八月十五，那一天月亮最圓、最亮。中秋節是一家人團圓的日子，在外面工作的人，儘可能回家過節。晚上，一家人常常坐在院子裏，一邊吃著象徵著團圓的月餅，一邊賞月。

　　元宵节也叫灯节，是农历的正月（一月）十五，那一天家家吃元宵，有的地方人们会做各种各样好看的灯挂在门口，晚上人们都上街看灯。

　　中秋节是农历的八月十五，那一天月亮最圆、最亮。中秋节是一家人团圆的日子，在外面工作的人，尽可能回家过节。晚上，一家人常常坐在院子里，一边吃着象征着团圆的月饼，一边赏月。

二・生詞表

節日	节日	n	jiérì	festival; holiday
早晨			zǎochén	morning
荷包		n	hébāo	pouch
戴		v	dài	wear

戴手錶，戴首飾，戴帽子

身上			shēnshang	on the body
風俗	风俗	n	fēngsú	custom
習慣*	习惯	n	xíguàn	usual practice; custom
用處	用处	n	yòngchu	use
過節	过节	vo	guòjié	celebrate a festival or holiday
豐盛	丰盛	adj	fēngshèng	sumptuous (to describe feast)
雞	鸡	n	jī	chicken
鴨	鸭	n	yā	duck
盤*	盘	n	pán	plate
根本		adv	gēnběn	fundamentally; (often used in the negative form) not at all

那個女孩我根本不認識，可是媽媽讓她做我女朋友。

這筆生意根本沒希望，不要再談了。

端		v	duān	hold something level with both hands
粽子		n	zòngzi	a kind of dumpling eaten during the Dragon Boat Festival
大官		n	dà guān	high-ranking official

表面上			biǎomiàn shang	on the surface
實際上	实际上		shíjì shang	actually
早晚		adv	zǎowǎn	sooner or later
				你不好好學習，早晚會後悔。
				別著急，他早晚會來。
國王	国王	n	guówáng	king
趕	赶	v	gǎn	drive away
南方		n	nánfāng	the south
憂國憂民	忧国忧民		yōu guó yōu mín	concerned about one's country and one's people
投江		vo	tóu jiāng	jump into the river
自殺	自杀	v	zìshā	commit suicide
詩人	诗人	n	shīrén	poet
之一			zhīyī	one of
詩	诗	n	shī	poem; poetry
表現	表现	v	biǎoxiàn	display; manifest
愛國	爱国	vo	àiguó	patriotic
精神		n	jīngshen	spirit
祭祀		v	jìsì	offer sacrifices to
老百姓		n	lǎobǎixìng	"old hundred names;" ordinary folks
米		n	mǐ	(uncooked) rice
竹筒		n	zhútǒng	bamboo tube
投		v	tóu	throw
江		n	jiāng	river
賽	赛	v	sài	race; compete

龍舟	龙舟	n	lóngzhōu	dragon boat
象徵	象征	v	xiàngzhēng	symbolize
當時	当时		dāngshí	at that time; of that time
人們	人们	n	rénmen	people
爭先恐後	争先恐后		zhēng xiān kǒng hòu	strive to be the first and fear to lag behind; vie with each other in doing sth.
救		v	jiù	save
動人	动人	adj	dòngrén	moving; touching
傳統	传统	n/adj	chuántǒng	tradition; traditional

我很喜歡中國的傳統文化。
過中秋節吃月餅是一種
傳統。

鞭炮		n	biānpào	firecracker
親朋好友	亲朋好友		qīn péng hǎo yǒu	good friends and dear relatives
拜年		v	bài nián	pay a New Year call; wish someone a happy New Year
壓歲錢	压岁钱	n	yāsuìqián	money given to children as a lunar New Year gift
農曆	农历	n	nónglì	lunar calendar
正月		n	zhēngyuè	the first month of the lunar calendar
元宵		n	yuánxiāo	sweet dumplings made of glutinous rice
各種各樣	各种各样		gè zhǒng gè yàng	of various kinds
燈	灯	n	dēng	lamp; light
上街		vo	shàng jiē	go to the street
月亮		n	yuèliang	the moon

圓	圓	adj	yuán	round
亮		adj	liàng	bright
團圓	团圆	v	tuányuán	reunion
日子		n	rìzi	days; time; life
外面			wàimian	outside
儘可能	尽可能		jǐn kěnéng	try one's best
院子		n	yuànzi	courtyard
月餅	月饼	n	yuèbǐng	moon cake
賞月	赏月	vo	shǎng yuè	admire the full moon

專名 Proper Nouns

端午節	端午节	Duānwǔ Jié	the Dragon Boat Festival
戰國	战国	Zhànguó	the Warring States (475-221 B.C.)
楚國	楚国	Chǔguó	the State of Chu (740-330 B.C.)
屈原		Qū Yuán	Qu Yuan (343-290 B.C.)
秦國	秦国	Qínguó	the State of Qin (879-221 B.C.)
春節	春节	Chūn Jié	the Spring Festival (Chinese New Year)
中秋節	中秋节	Zhōngqiū Jié	the Mid-autumn Festival
元宵節	元宵节	Yuánxiāo Jié	the Lantern Festival
燈節	灯节	Dēng Jié	the Lantern Festival

難寫的字：

戴豐雞鴨憂龍徵鞭壓歲團圓

三 · 語法註釋 Grammar Notes

1. Potential Complements:

One can insert 得/不 between a verb and its resultative or directional complement to indicate if one has the ability to carry out an action, or if circumstances permit the realization of an objective. For instance,

(1) 今天的功課太多了，我做不完。

今天的功课太多了，我做不完。

There is too much homework today. I can't finish it.
(I don't have the ability.)

(2) 這是誰的聲音？我怎麼聽不出來？

这是谁的声音？我怎么听不出来？

Whose voice is this? How come I can't tell?
(I don't have the ability to tell.)

(3) 這個房間太小，擺不下三張床。

这个房间太小，摆不下三张床。

This room is too small. There isn't room for three beds.
(The room doesn't have the capacity.)

(4) A：他說的話你聽得懂聽不懂？

他说的话你听得懂听不懂？

Can you understand what he says?

B：我聽得懂。

我听得懂。

Yes, I can.

It should be noted that directional complements very often appear in their negative form to indicate that one doesn't have the ability to realize a certain action or that circumstances do not permit the realization of such an action. Besides, very often there must be a potential complement to convey this meaning. One can't use this pattern: "能/不能＋ Verb ＋ resultative complement / potential complement." The following sentences are all incorrect:

(1)*今天的功課太多了，我不能做完。

今天的功课太多了，我不能做完。

(2)*這是誰的聲音？我怎麼不能聽出來？

这是谁的声音？我怎么不能听出来？

(3)*這個房間太小，不能擺下三張床。

这个房间太小，不能摆下三张床。

When asking questions, one can use either the affirmative or the negative form. When answering a question containing a positive potential complement, one can answer the question by using the positive form of the potential complement. See (4).

Sometimes the pattern "不能 +動詞 + resultative complement/directional complement" differs from its corresponding potential complement in meaning. For instance,

(5) 你給我的飯太多了，我吃不完。

你给我的饭太多了，我吃不完。

You gave me too much food. I can't eat it all.
(I don't have the ability to finish all the food.)

(6) 飯你不能吃完，給你哥哥留一點。

饭你不能吃完，给你哥哥留一点。

You may not eat all the food. You have to leave some for your brother.
(You are not allowed to all the food.)

Potential complements are an important means of expression in Chinese. Try to use them whenever it is appropriate.

2. "戴著玩"：

Phrases like "戴著玩" are made up of two parts. The first part consists of a verb plus "著." The second part is a verb or an adjectival phrase. The second part indicates the purpose of the action. For instance, in "戴著玩" from this lesson, "玩" is the purpose of "戴著(荷包)" More examples,

(1) 你別生氣，他是跟你説著玩呢。

你別生气，他是跟你说着玩呢。

Don't get mad. He's saying this to tease you.

(2) 媽媽：　你怎麼剛吃完飯，又在吃？

妈妈：　你怎么刚吃完饭，又在吃？

Mother:　You just ate. How come you're eating again?

女兒：　您看，這是餅乾，我吃著玩。

女儿：　您看，这是饼乾，我吃着玩。

Daughter: Look, Mom, this is just a cookie. I'm eating it for fun.

(3) A：你看什麼書呢，是電腦書嗎？

你看什么书呢，是电脑书吗？

What book are you reading? Is it a book on computer?

B：不是，我在看閒書，看著玩。

不是，我在看闲书，看着玩。

No. It's just light reading. I'm reading it for fun.

(4) A：你怎麼買那麼多明信片？要寄給誰？

你怎么买那么多明信片？要寄给谁？

Why did you buy so many postcards? Whom do you want to send them to?

B：不寄給誰，買著玩兒。

不寄给谁，买着玩儿。

Nobody. I got them for fun.

3.　The Indefinite Use of the Interrogative Pronoun "什麼":

The interrogative pronoun "什麼" can refer to an indefinite person or thing. For instance,

(1) A： 你爲什麼問我這個問題？

你为什么问我这个问题？

Why did you ask me this question?

B： 我只是問問，並沒有什麼特別的目的。

我只是问问，并没有什么特别的目的。

I was simply asking. No particular reason.

(2) 別念了，這本書沒什麼意思。

别念了，这本书没什么意思。

Don't read anymore. The book is not that interesting.

(3) A： 你馬上就要畢業了，有什麼打算？

你马上就要毕业了，有什么打算？

You're graduating soon. Do you have any particular plans?

B： 我還沒有什麼打算。

我还没有什么打算。

No, I don't have any particular plans yet.

In the above sentences "什麼" is followed by a noun. The meaning of the sentence would not be affected if one left out "什麼," but with it the tone of voice is moderate.

There is also an indefinite use of the interrogative pronoun. This kind of usage is not limited to "什麼." Note that there is no noun after it.

(4) 我餓了，想吃點什麼。

我饿了，想吃点什么。

I'm hungry. I'd like to eat something.

(5) 今天下午沒事，我想找誰聊聊。

今天下午没事，我想找谁聊聊。

I've nothing to do this afternoon. I'd like to find someone to chat with.

(6) 今年夏天我想去哪兒旅行幾天。

今年夏天我想去哪儿旅行几天。

This summer I'd like to take a trip somewhere.

4. Cohesion:

When we speak or write at any length, we need to string together discrete clauses which would otherwise seem independent of each other. There are several ways to do this in Chinese.

First, we can use the following cohesive devices:

    a. time expressions, e.g., "今天," "1998年," "星期五," "後來," "然後," "這時後," "以後," "突然," "立刻," etc.

    b. place expressions, e.g., "在那兒," "房間裏," "前面," "街上," etc.

    c. connectives, e.g., "因爲…所以," "不但…而且," "就," "也," etc.

All cohesive devices are missing from the following story. The story will read much smoother with the appropriate cohesive devices. See if you can fill in the blanks with the correct phrases from below.

1) 古時候，…時候，…以後，先（古时候，...时候，...以后，先）
2) 在集市上   （在集市上）
3) 可是，於是，就，就，才   （可是，于是，就，就，才）

鄭人買履 (lǚ: shoe)

    _____，鄭國有個人想買一雙鞋。他_____在家裏拿一根繩子比著自己的腳量好了尺寸，他_____高高興興地到集市上去了。

    _____他找到了賣鞋的地方，他挑選了一雙，他想比比合適不合適。他往身上一摸，____發現忘了把量好的尺寸帶來了。他很著急，他心想：“自己真是太粗心了，白跑了一趟。”_____他急急忙忙跑回家去拿。_____等他回到集市來的_____，天已經很晚，賣鞋的早就走了。他的鞋沒有買成。

    別人知道了這件事_____，_____問他：“你給你自己買鞋，你在腳上試試不就可以了嗎？你怎麼還要跑回去拿尺寸呢？”他回答說：“我只相信量好的尺寸，我不相信自己的腳。”

郑人买履 (lǚ: shoe)

    _____，郑国有个人想买一双鞋。他_____在家里拿一根绳子比著自己的脚量好了尺寸，他_____高高兴兴地到集市上去了。

    _____他找到了卖鞋的地方，他挑选了一双，他想比比合适不合适。他往身上一摸，____发现忘了把量好的尺寸带来了。他很着急，他心想：“自己真是太粗心了，白跑了一趟。”_____他急急忙忙跑回家去拿。＿＿＿＿＿等他回到集市来的＿＿＿＿＿，天已经很晚，卖鞋的早就走了。他的鞋没有买成。

　　别人知道了这件事＿＿＿＿＿，＿＿＿＿＿问他："你给你自己买鞋，你在脚上试试不就可以了吗？你怎么还要跑回去拿尺寸呢？"他回答说："我只相信量好的尺寸，我不相信自己的脚。"

Second, we can delete any superfluous nouns or pronouns. In a complex sentence with multiple clauses, there is no need to repeat the subject if it has already appeared in the first clause. This is something that we must particular attention to.

Third, we can readjust the word order. For instance, we can put known information at the front, in other words, treat it as a topic, and put new information in the position of the object. In the above story, when the word "尺寸" first appears, it is new information. Therefore it appears as the object of the clause: "量好了尺寸". When it makes its second appearance, instead of "忘了帶量好的尺寸", it is far more idiomatic to use the "把" structure and say, "忘了把量好的尺寸帶來了." Likewise when the word "鞋" appears for the first time, it is new information. Therefore it appears as the object of the clause: "想買一雙鞋." When it reappears, it becomes the topic of the clause, "他的鞋沒買成," since it is now known information. You may wonder, "這件事" is also known information, why does it appear as the object, "別人都知道了這件事"? That is because like "這件事," "別人", which is the agent of the action is also known information. Therefore it can be used as the subject of the clause. Notice that we are also looking at the beginning of a new paragraph, and a change in point of view. The narrative focus shifts from storytelling, i.e., what happens to the character, to others' reaction. If we do not want to shift the point of view, we can change this sentence to "這件事別人知道了."

Here is another version of the story with all the appropriate devices:

鄭人買履

　　古時侯，鄭國有個人想買一雙鞋。他先在家裏拿一根繩子比著自己的腳量好了尺寸，就高高興興地到集市上去了。

　　在集市上他找到了賣鞋的地方，他挑選了一雙，想比比合適不合適。往身上一摸，才發現忘了把量好的尺寸帶來了。他很著急，心想："自己真是太粗心了，白跑了一趟。"

　　於是他急急忙忙跑回家去拿。可是等回到集市來的時候，天已經很晚，賣鞋的早就走了。他的鞋沒有買成。

　　別人知道了這件事以後，就問他："你給你自己買鞋，在腳上試試不就可以了嗎？怎麼還要跑回去拿尺寸呢？"他回答說："我只相信量好的尺寸，不相信自己的腳。"

郑人买履

古时侯，郑国有个人想买一双鞋。他先在家里拿一根绳子比着自己的脚量好了尺寸，就高高兴兴地到集市上去了。

在集市上他找到了卖鞋的地方，他挑选了一双，想比比合适不合适。往身上一摸，才发现忘了量好的尺寸带来了。他很着急，心想："自己真是太粗心了，白跑了一趟。"

于是他急急忙忙跑回家去拿。可是等回到集市来的时候，天已经很晚，卖鞋的早就走了。他的鞋没有买成。

别人知道了这件事以後，就问他："你给你自己买鞋，在脚上试试不就可以了吗？怎么还要跑回去拿尺寸呢？"他回答说："我只相信量好的尺寸，不相信自己的脚。"

四 · 詞語練習

1. "**表面上**"（on the surface）：

Example: 他看出來秦國雖然表面上對楚國不錯，可是實際上早晚要來打楚國。

他看出来秦国虽然表面上对楚国不错，可是实际上早晚要来打楚国。

(1) 他表面上＿＿＿＿＿＿＿＿，可是實際上＿＿＿＿＿＿＿＿。

（ 同意你的意見　他的想法跟你完全不同 ）

他表面上＿＿＿＿＿＿＿＿，可是实际上＿＿＿＿＿＿＿＿。

（ 同意你的意见　他的想法跟你完全不同 ）

(2) 這個人＿＿＿＿＿＿看起來很厲害，＿＿＿＿＿＿人很好。

（ 表面上　實際上 ）

这个人＿＿＿＿＿＿看起来很厉害，＿＿＿＿＿＿人很好。

（ 表面上　实际上 ）

2. " 好像 " (seem like; seem as if) :

Example: 我上中文學校的時候，好像聽我們的老師說過。

我上中文学校的时候，好像听我们的老师说过。

(1) 他是我的老同學，怎麼見面＿＿＿＿＿＿＿＿＿似的？

（ 不認識我 ）

他是我的老同学，怎么见面＿＿＿＿＿＿＿＿＿似的？

（ 不认识我 ）

(2) 我今天很不舒服，＿＿＿＿＿＿＿＿。（ 病了 ）

我今天很不舒服，＿＿＿＿＿＿＿＿。（ 病了 ）

(3) 王先生：我來介紹一下，這是張先生，這是李小姐。

王先生：我来介绍一下，这是张先生，这是李小姐。

張先生：你好，李小姐！哎，我們＿＿＿＿＿＿＿＿。

（ 在哪兒見過 ）

张先生：你好，李小姐！哎，我们＿＿＿＿＿＿＿＿。

（ 在哪儿见过 ）

李小姐：你好，對不起，我不記得我們見過面。

李小姐：你好，对不起，我不记得我们见过面。

注意，"女兒長得很像爸爸"，不能說 " 女兒長得好像爸爸 "。

3. " 跟...有關係 " (have to do with) :

Example: 我聽說端午節還常常賽龍舟，跟屈原有關係嗎？

我听说端午节还常常赛龙舟，跟屈原有关系吗？

(1) 這件事情＿＿＿＿＿＿＿＿，你不必管。（ 你 ）

这件事情＿＿＿＿＿＿＿＿，你不必管。（ 你 ）

(2) 他考試考得不好，跟＿＿＿＿＿＿＿＿＿。

（ 他平常不夠努力 ）

他考试考得不好，跟＿＿＿＿＿＿＿＿＿。

（ 他平常不够努力 ）

(3) A：你身體為什麼這麼好？

你身体为什么这么好？

B：我身體很好，＿＿＿＿＿＿＿＿＿＿＿＿＿＿。（經常運動）

我身体很好，＿＿＿＿＿＿＿＿＿＿＿＿。（经常运动）

4. "各種各樣" (of various kinds)：

Example: 有的地方人們會做各種各樣好看的燈掛在門口。

有的地方人们会做各种各样好看的灯挂在门口。

(1) 上課的時候，學生提出＿＿＿＿＿＿＿＿＿，老師都回答得很清楚。（問題）

上课的时候，学生提出＿＿＿＿＿＿＿＿，老师都回答得很清楚。（问题）

(2) 購物中心裏有＿＿＿＿＿＿＿＿＿＿，你想買什麼，就買什麼。（東西）

购物中心里有＿＿＿＿＿＿＿＿＿＿，你想买什么，就买什么。（东西）

(3) 公園裏種著＿＿＿＿＿＿＿＿＿，好看極了。（花）

公园里种着＿＿＿＿＿＿＿＿＿，好看极了。（花）

5. "...之一" (one of the...)：

Example: 屈原是中國最偉大的詩人之一。

屈原是中国最伟大的诗人之一。

(1) 中山陵是南京＿＿＿＿＿＿＿＿＿。

中山陵是南京＿＿＿＿＿＿＿＿＿。

(2) 那家飯館的清蒸魚是他們＿＿＿＿＿＿＿＿＿。

那家饭馆的清蒸鱼是他们＿＿＿＿＿＿＿＿＿。

(3) 《芝麻街》是小孩＿＿＿＿＿＿＿＿＿＿＿＿。

《芝麻街》是小孩＿＿＿＿＿＿＿＿＿＿＿＿。

6. "**儘可能**" (try one's best):

　　Example: **中秋節是一家人團圓的日子，在外面工作的人，儘可能回
　　　　　　家過節。**

　　　　　　中秋节是一家人团圆的日子，在外面工作的人，尽可能回
　　　　　　家过节。

　(1)明天考試，我＿＿＿＿＿＿＿＿＿＿＿。

　　　明天考试，我＿＿＿＿＿＿＿＿＿＿。

　(2)醫生說你吃得太油，希望你＿＿＿＿＿＿＿＿＿。

　　　医生说你吃得太油，希望你＿＿＿＿＿＿＿＿。

　(3)出去旅行的時候，＿＿＿＿＿＿＿＿＿＿。

　　　出去旅行的时候，＿＿＿＿＿＿＿＿＿＿。

五 · 看 圖 說 話

第十三課　談體育

一・課文

（一）對　話

　　張天明搬出學生宿舍已經好幾個月了。他一個人住在校外比住在校內安靜多了，有很多時間做功課。可是有的時候一個人也會覺得寂寞。這天晚上張天明做完了功課，閑著沒事，就給安德森打了一個電話。

張天明：　喂，安德森嗎？

安德森：　對，我是安德森。請問您是⋯⋯

張天明：　怎麼，你連我的聲音都聽不出來了？

安德森：　啊，天明，是你！看今天晚上的球賽了嗎？

張天明：　球賽？今天晚上我根本沒看電視。

安德森：　怎麼，連這麼重要的籃球比賽你都不看。

張天明：　誰跟誰比賽？

安德森：　咱們學校跟密西根。

張天明：　結果怎麼樣？

安德森：　唉，咱們輸了。

張天明：　又輸了？太讓人失望了。

安德森：　可不是，密西根隊個個身強體壯，特別是他們的五號，速度快極了⋯⋯

張天明：　我聽說咱們隊的速度也不慢呀，而且我們的教練的經驗比他們的豐富多了。

安德森：　是啊。本來咱們一直領先，可是後來人家把比分慢慢

第十三课　谈体育

一·课文

（一）对 话

　　张天明搬出学生宿舍已经好几个月了。他一个人住在校外比住在校内安静多了，有很多时间做功课。可是有的时候一个人也会觉得寂寞。这天晚上张天明做完了功课，闲着没事，就给安德森打了一个电话。

张天明：　喂，安德森吗？

安德森：　对，我是安德森。请问您是……

张天明：　怎么，你连我的声音都听不出来了？

安德森：　啊，天明，是你！看今天晚上的球赛了吗？

张天明：　球赛？今天晚上我根本没看电视。

安德森：　怎么，连这么重要的篮球比赛你都不看。

张天明：　谁跟谁比赛？

安德森：　咱们学校跟密西根。

张天明：　结果怎么样？

安德森：　唉，咱们输了。

张天明：　又输了？太让人失望了。

安德森：　可不是，密西根队个个身强体壮，特别是他们的五号，速度快极了……

张天明：　我听说咱们队的速度也不慢呀，而且我们的教练的经验比他们的丰富多了。

安德森：　是啊。本来咱们一直领先，可是后来人家把比分慢慢地追上來了。最緊張的是最後二十秒鐘，比分是八十比八十。這時候他們的五號又進一球，球剛一進籃，時間就到了。八十二比八十，人家贏了。

張天明：　輸一次也沒什麼，反正不是決賽。

安德森：　這倒也是。其實，咱們隊打得還是不錯的，就是比賽經驗沒有他們多。打得最好的是咱們的三號，他得了三十分。

張天明：　誰是三號？

安德森：　你連三號都不知道？就是女孩子都喜歡的那位 " 帥哥 "。

張天明：　哦，我想起來了。下次再有精彩的比賽，別忘了告訴我。

安德森：　好！

張天明：　再見。

地追上来了。最紧张的是最后二十秒钟，比分是八十比八十。这时候他们的五号又进一球，球刚一进篮，时间就到了。八十二比八十，人家赢了。

张天明：　输一次也没什么，反正不是决赛。

安德森：　这倒也是。其实，咱们队打得还是不错的，就是比赛经验没有他们多。打得最好的是咱们的三号，他得了三十分。

张天明：　谁是三号？

安德森：　你连三号都不知道？就是女孩子都喜欢的那位"帅哥"。

张天明：　哦，我想起来了。下次再有精彩的比赛，别忘了告诉我。

安德森：　好！

张天明：　再见。

（二）閱 讀

　　上個星期，張天明收到表哥從南京寄來的一封信，信中提到中國體育運動的情況。八十年代以來，中國的體育運動有了很大的發展，中國運動員在奧林匹克運動會上拿到了很多金牌和銀牌，不少人還打破了世界記錄。很多中國人為此感到很驕傲，覺得這是整個國家的光榮。每當中國運動員在國際比賽中取得好成績時，就有成千上萬的人上街慶祝。表哥談到這些事情時很激動。可是張天明認為，人們所以參加體育運動，是因為運動有益於身體健康，不是為了給國家爭榮譽。而且因為贏了一兩塊金牌就上街慶祝，實在沒有必要。

（二）阅　读

　　上个星期，张天明收到表哥从南京寄来的一封信，信中提到中国体育运动的情况。八十年代以来，中国的体育运动有了很大的发展，中国运动员在奥林匹克运动会上拿到了很多金牌和银牌，不少人还打破了世界记录。很多中国人为此感到很骄傲，觉得这是整个国家的光荣。每当中国运动员在国际比赛中取得好成绩时，就有成千上万的人上街庆祝。表哥谈到这些事情时很激动。可是张天明认为，人们所以参加体育运动，是因为运动有益于身体健康，不是为了给国家争荣誉。而且因为赢了一两块金牌就上街庆祝，实在没有必要。

二・生詞表

寂寞		adj	jímò	lonely
聲音	声音	n	shēngyīn	voice
球賽	球赛	n	qiúsài	ball game (match)
重要*		adj	zhòngyào	important

想贏球，找一個好教練很重要。

我今天有重要的事要做。

結果	结果	adv	jiéguǒ	as a result
輸	输	v	shū	(in competition) lose
失望		v	shīwàng	be disappointed

他對這場球賽的比分很失望。

妹妹失望地說：「他今天不來了。」

可不是			kě bú shì	isn't that the truth?
隊	队	n	duì	team
身體*	身体	n	shēntǐ	body
強壯	强壮	adj	qiángzhuàng	strong
速度		n	sùdù	speed
教練	教练	n	jiàoliàn	coach
豐富	丰富	adj	fēngfù	rich; abundant

經驗豐富，商品豐富，節目豐富

本來	本来		běnlái	at first; originally
領先	领先	v	lǐngxiān	(in ball games) lead
人家		pn	rénjia	others; they

比分		n	bǐfēn	score (of a basketball match, etc.)
追		v	zhuī	catch up
緊張*	紧张	adj	jǐnzhāng	tense
秒鐘	秒钟	n	miǎozhōng	second
籃	篮	n	lán	basket
贏		v	yíng	win (a prize, a game, etc.)
反正		conJ	fǎnzhèng	anyway
決賽	决赛	n	juésài	final (match)
倒也是			dào ye shì	That's true (indicating concession)
得		v	dé	get
帥(哥)	帅(哥)	adj	shuàigē	(colloq.) handsome (guy)
精彩		adj	jīngcǎi	spectacular; exciting

奧林匹克運動會的比賽都很精彩。

明天有場精彩的籃球決賽。

表哥*		n	biǎogē	(elder male) cousin
封*		m	fēng	measure word (for lctters)
發展	发展	v	fāzhǎn	develop
運動員	运动员	n	yùndòng yuán	athlete
運動會	运动会	n	yùndòng huì	sports meet
金牌		n	jīnpái	gold medal
銀牌	银牌	n	yínpái	silver medal
世界記錄	世界记录	n	shìjiè jìlù	world record
為此	为此		wèi cǐ	of this; for this
感到		v	gǎndào	feel

236

驕傲	骄傲	adj	jiāo'ào	proud
整個	整个		zhěnggè	entire
國家	国家	n	guójiā	country
光榮	光荣	adj	guāngróng	glorious; proud
每當...時	每当...时		měi dāng...shí	whenever
國際*	国际*	n	guójì	international
取得		v	qǔdé	obtain
成績	成绩	n	chéngjī	achievement
成千上萬	成千上万		chéng qiān shàng wàn	tens of thousands
慶祝*	庆祝	v	qìngzhù	celebrate
參加	参加	v	cānjiā	attend; take part in
有益於	有益于	vc	yǒuyì yú	good for
爭	争	v	zhēng	fight for
榮譽	荣誉	n	róngyù	honor
實在	實在	adv	shízài	indeed; really
必要		v	bìyào	necessary

專名 Proper Nouns

| 密西根 | | Mìxīgēn | Michigan |
| 奧林匹克 | | Aòlínpǐkè | Olympics |

難寫的字：

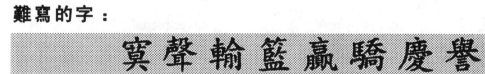

三· 語法註釋

1. "連...也/都..." :

"連 ...也/都..." introduces an extreme case. The following sentence denotes a conclusion arising from it. For instance,

(1) A：他會說中文嗎？

他会说中文吗？

Can he speak Chinese?

B：中文他連聽都沒聽過，怎麼會說呢？

中文他连听都没听过，怎么会说呢？

He's never even heard Chinese spoken. How could he speak it?

(2) 我連這個人的名字都沒聽說過，怎麼會認識他呢？

我连这个人的名字都没听说过，怎么会认识他呢？

I've never even heard of his name. How would I know him?

(3) 我姐姐會很多種語言，連阿拉伯文都會。

我姐姐会很多种语言，连阿拉伯文都会。

My sister knows many languages, even Arabic.

(4) 這兒天氣很冷，連夏天都得穿毛衣。

这儿天气很冷，连夏天都得穿毛衣。

The weather is really cold here. Even in the summer [you] have to wear a sweater.

In (1), "聽過中文" is the minimum condition for the ability to speak Chinese. From that, one can draw the conclusion that he cannot speak Chinese. In (3), one can deduce from the fact that the "my sister" knows Arabic, one of the most difficult languages to learn, that she knows many languages. In (4), one can conclude that the weather here is very cold based upon the fact that many people are wearing sweaters even in summer.

2. "反正"：

The adverb "反正" has two meanings:

A: It can emphasize that the result or conclusion would not change under any circumstances. "反正" generally appears in the second clause, which is usually preceded by a clause denoting two or more situations. For example,

(1) 這間房子你想住就住，反正我不住。

这间房子你想住就住，反正我不住。

If you want to live in the room, go ahead. I am not going to live here.

(2) 那個電影，你們誰想看誰看，反正我不看。

那个电影，你们谁想看谁看，反正我不看。

If you want to see that movie, go ahead. I am not going to see it.

(3) 不管你信不信，反正我不信。

不管你信不信，反正我不信。

I don't care if you believe it or not. I don't.

B: "反正" can also explain a situation or offer a reason. The circumstance or reason is often already known, or obvious. For example,

(1) 圖書館反正也不遠，咱們走著去吧。

图书馆反正也不远，咱们走着去吧。

Anyway, the library is not far away. Let's walk.

(2) 這道題你別做了，反正也不會考。

这道题你别做了，反正也不会考。

Don't bother with that question. It won't be on the exam anyway.

(3) 我送你回去吧，反正是順路。

我送你回去吧，反正是顺路。

Let me give you a ride. I'm going that way anyway.

In this lesson we are learning about the second usage.

3. "（成千）上（萬）"：

"上" here means "reach." For instance,

(1) 上百個中學生參加了這次考試。

上百个中学生参加了这次考试。

Hundreds of secondary school students took part in the examination.

(2) 這件衣服上千塊錢，你買得起嗎？

这件衣服上千块钱，你买得起吗？

This jacket is worth [as many as] a thousand dollars. Can you afford it?

(3) 他賺的錢都上百萬了。

他赚的钱都上百万了。

He made [as many as] a million dollars.

(4) 這場決賽有成千上萬的人排隊買票。

这场决赛有成千上万的人排队买票。

There are tens of thousands of people lining up to buy tickets for the final game.

4. "（有益）於"：

The preposition "於" is generally used in written language. It can be used before or after a verb. In "有益於" "於" is equivalent to "對." "體育運動有益於身體健康" is the same as "體育運動對身體健康有益."

5. Ways of making comparisons:

There are several ways to make comparisons:
A: When the result of the comparison is identical, we can use the pattern:

A 跟/和 B...一樣

(1) 這本書和那本書的價錢一樣。

这本书和那本书的价钱一样。

The price of this book is the same as that one.

(2) 姐姐跟妹妹一樣高。

姐姐跟妹妹一样高。

The elder sister is as tall as the younger sister.

(3) 這兩個房間一樣大。

这两个房间一样大。

The two rooms are equally big.

B: When the result is not identical, we can use one of the following forms of comparison:

a. A 比 B + Adj

(1) 這本書比那本書貴。

这本书比那本书贵。

This book is more expensive than that one.

(2) 今天比昨天冷一點。

今天比昨天冷一点。

Today is a bit colder than yesterday.

(3) 南方比北方暖和多了。

南方比北方暖和多了。

The south is much warmer than the north.

NB: If there is a phrase denoting degree or quantity, it must be placed after the adjective. See (2) and (3). More examples,

(4) 上海的人比北京多得多。

上海的人比北京多得多。

There many more people in Shanghai than in Beijing.

(5) 這個教室比那個教室大多了。

这个教室比那个教室大多了。

This classroom is much bigger than that one.

(6) 他姑媽比他父親大八歲。

他姑妈比他父亲大八岁。

His aunt is eight years older than his father.

b. A 沒有 B ＋ Adj

(1) 日文語法沒有中文的好學。

日文语法没有中文的好学。

Japanese grammar is not as easy to learn as Chinese grammar.

(2) 紐約沒有華盛頓遠。

纽约没有华盛顿远。

New York is not as far away as Washington.

(3) 今天沒有昨天那麼冷。

今天没有昨天那么冷。

Today is not as cold as yesterday.

It should be noted that we seldom use "沒有" with these adjectives: "小, 短, 壞, 細, 醜, 難看," but rather with their opposites: "大、長、好、高、粗、漂亮、好看." But if we add the word "那麼" before the adjective, then this restriction no longer applies.

When making comparisons, the structures and the phrases being compared in A and B are basically the same. Some identical components of A and B can be omitted as long as the meaning of the sentence remains intact. A(1), Ba(4), and Bb(1) are some of the examples.

c. A 不如 B ＋ Adj *(see Lesson Sixteen)*

6. Written Style:

There are substantial differences between written Chinese and spoken colloquial Chinese. The former is characterized by

a. longer sentences, more modifiers such as attributives and adverbials.

b. vestiges of classical Chinese, e.g. 於 as in 有益於 , 此 as in 爲此 .
Compare: 有益於健康(written style) and 對健康有好處 (spoken style); 爲此 (written style) and 因爲這個 (spoken style).

c. more connectives. Notice the following underlined words:

> 每當中國運動員在國際比賽中取得好成績時，就有成千上萬的人上街慶祝。表哥談到這些事情時很激動。<u>可是</u>張天明認爲，人們<u>所以</u>參加體育運動，<u>是因爲</u>運動有益於身體健康，<u>不是爲了</u>給國家爭榮譽。<u>而且</u><u>因爲</u>贏了一兩塊金牌就上街慶祝，實在沒有必要。

> 每当中国运动员在国际比赛中取得好成绩时，就有成千上万的人上街庆祝。表哥谈到这些事情时很激动。<u>可是</u>张天明认为，人们<u>所以</u>参加体育运动，<u>是因为</u>运动有益于身体健康，<u>不是为了</u>给国家争荣誉。<u>而且</u><u>因为</u>赢了一两块金牌就上街庆祝，实在没有必要。

四 · 詞語練習

1. " **本來** " (originally; at first) :

　　Example: 本來咱們一直領先。

　　　　　　本来咱们一直领先。

(1) 他＿＿＿＿＿＿＿＿，經常生病，後來他經常運動，現在身體很好了。(身體不好)

他＿＿＿＿＿＿，经常生病，后来他经常运动，现在身体很好了。(身体不好)

(2) 張天明本來想去加州上大學，後來決定＿＿＿＿＿＿＿了。
　　（東部的學校）

张天明本来想去加州上大学，后来决定＿＿＿＿＿＿＿了。
　　（東部的學校）

(3) 柯林本來想夏天去台灣學中文，後來＿＿＿＿＿＿＿＿了。
　　（北京）

　　柯林本来想夏天去台湾学中文，后来＿＿＿＿＿＿＿＿了。
　　（北京）

(4) ＿＿＿＿＿＿＿＿＿＿，後來改學商了。（醫學）
　　＿＿＿＿＿＿＿＿＿＿，后来改学商了。（医学）

2. " 倒也是 " (That is true)：

　　Example: 張天明： 輸一次也沒什麼，反正不是決賽。

　　　　　　張天明： 输一次也没什么，反正不是决赛。

　　　　　　安德森： 這倒也是。

　　　　　　安德森： 这倒也是。

(1) A： 我的錢包丟了，裏邊有現金還有信用卡。急死我了。

　　　 我的钱包丢了，里边有现金还有信用卡。急死我了。

　　B： 你別著急，再說著急也沒用。

　　　 你别着急，再说着急也没用。

　　A： ＿＿＿＿＿＿＿＿ 。
　　　 ＿＿＿＿＿＿＿＿ 。

(2) A： 我反對他們兩個交往。文化背景太不一樣了。

　　　 我反对他们两个交往。文化背景太不一样了。

　　B： 別急，他們只是男女朋友，＿＿＿＿＿＿。（結婚）

　　　 别急，他们只是男女朋友，＿＿＿＿＿＿。（结婚）

　　A： 這倒也是。

　　　 这倒也是。

(3) A： 我真不喜歡小明的女朋友。

　　　 我真不喜欢小明的女朋友。

B：_____，跟你沒關係。(他喜歡)

　　_____，跟你没关系。(他喜欢)

A：倒也是。

　　倒也是。

3. "還是...的，就是..." (...it's just)：

Example: A：這兒的天氣不錯吧？

　　　　　　　这儿的天气不错吧？

B：這兒天氣還是挺好的，就是常常颱風。

　　　这儿天气还是挺好的，就是常常刮风。

(1) 小張的男朋友人還是不錯的，就是_____。(脾氣)

　　小张的男朋友人还是不错的，就是_____。(脾气)

(2) 當醫生賺的錢還是挺多的，就是_____。(累)

　　当医生赚的钱还是挺多的，就是_____。(累)

(3) 這個學校的老師和設備還是不錯的，就是_____。(學費)

　　这个学校的老师和设备还是不错的，就是_____。(学费)

4. "每當...時/ 的時候，就..." (whenever)：

Example: 每當中國運動員在國際比賽中取得好成績時，
就有成千上萬的人上街慶祝。

　　每当中国运动员在国际比赛中取得好成绩时，
就有成千上万的人上街庆祝。

(1) 每當過年過節的時候，他_____。(想家)

　　每当过年过节的时候，他_____。(想家)

(2) _____，他就到外面走走。(學習很累)

　　_____，他就到外面走走。(学习很累)

(3) 每當學生在學習上有問題的時候，_____。

　　　　　　　　　　　　　　　　　　　　　　(老師幫助)

245

每当学生在学习上有问题的时候，＿＿＿＿＿＿＿＿。

（老师都助）

5. "所以...，是因為..."：

Example: 張天明認爲人們所以參加體育運動，是因爲運動有益於
身體健康。

張天明认为人们所以参加体育运动，是因为运动有益于
身体健康。

(1) 你媽媽所以叫你學醫，＿＿＿＿＿＿＿＿＿。（賺錢多）

你妈妈所以叫你学医，＿＿＿＿＿＿＿＿＿。（賺钱多）

(2) 他所以不讓他的孩子看電視，＿＿＿＿＿＿＿。

（影響不好）

他所以不让他的孩子看电视，＿＿＿＿＿＿＿。

（影响不好）

(3) 老師所以給你們很多功課，＿＿＿＿＿＿。（需要多練習）

老师所以给你们很多功课，＿＿＿＿＿＿。（需要多练习）

五·看圖說話

第十四課　家　庭

一·課　文

（一）對　話

　　過幾天就是感恩節了，學校放一個星期假。張天明回家去看爸爸媽媽，他坐飛機到了波士頓，他的父親開車來機場接他。在車上，父子倆聊了起來。

張　父：　天明，這個學期忙不忙？

張天明：　還好。只是有時候中文課的功課多一點。

張　父：　那電腦課呢？

張天明：　我沒選電腦課。

張　父：　爲什麼？你知道，靠你的中文課和歷史課，以後是賺不了多少錢的。要想找個鐵飯碗，就得學工程技術。要不然，聽你媽的，學醫也行。

張天明：　可是我的興趣不在那個方面。

張　父：　你要知道，過日子靠的是錢，而不是興趣。

張天明：　可是有些東西有錢也買不到。

張　父：　好了，好了，不說這些了，反正再過幾年，你就得獨立了。... 對了，天明，還記得惠敏嗎？

張天明：　當然記得，不就是李叔叔的女兒嗎？

張　父：　是的。你這次回來，去看看她，最好把你們的關係定下來。

張天明：　爸爸...

第十四课 家 庭

一·课文

（一）对 话

过几天就是感恩节了，学校放一个星期假。张天明回家去看爸爸妈妈，他坐飞机到了波士顿，他的父亲开车来机场接他。在车上，父子俩聊了起来。

张　父：天明，这个学期忙不忙？

张天明：还好。只是有时候中文课的功课多一点。

张　父：那电脑课呢？

张天明：我没选电脑课。

张　父：为什么？你知道，靠你的中文课和历史课，以后是赚不了多少钱的。要想找个铁饭碗，就得学工程技术。要不然，听你妈的，学医也行。

张天明：可是我的兴趣不在那个方面。

张　父：你要知道，过日子靠的是钱，而不是兴趣。

张天明：可是有些东西有钱也买不到。

张　父：好了，好了，不说这些了，反正再过几年，你就得独立了。… 对了，天明，还记得惠敏吗？

张天明：当然记得，不就是李叔叔的女儿吗？

张　父：是的。你这次回来，去看看她，最好把你们的关系定下来。

张天明：爸爸…

張　父：　我知道你在學校裏有個女朋友。可是人家是美國人
　　　　　……

張天明：　我也是美國人啊！

張　父：　可你首先是中國人啊。中國人還是跟中國人結婚嘛。
　　　　　東方人和西方人生活習慣不一樣。你看，天華和湯姆
　　　　　就是因為文化背景不同分手的。

張天明：　爸爸，他們分手是因為湯姆喝酒，不是因為文化背景
　　　　　的關係。再說，我不是小孩子了，我的事情我自己知
　　　　　道該怎麼辦。您別操心了。

张　　父：　我知道你在学校里有个女朋友。可是人家是美国人
　　　　　　……

张天明：　我也是美国人啊！

张　　父：　可你首先是中国人啊。中国人还是跟中国人结婚嘛。
　　　　　　东方人和西方人生活习惯不一样。你看，天华和汤姆
　　　　　　就是因为文化背景不同分手的。

张天明：　爸爸，他们分手是因为汤姆喝酒，不是因为文化背景
　　　　　　的关系。再说，我不是小孩子了，我的事情我自己知
　　　　　　道该怎么办。您别操心了。

（二）閱　讀

　　張天明的姑父幾年前去世了。姑媽今年六十歲，剛從一家工廠退休。這幾年姑媽一直覺得很寂寞，工廠裏的老朋友想幫她找個老伴兒。可是表嫂覺得姑媽找老伴兒是一件很丟人的事。姑媽覺得表嫂管得太多，說話太衝，所以婆媳關係變得緊張起來。他們本來住在一起，後來表哥和表嫂就帶著女兒玲玲搬出去住了。

　　玲玲今年八歲，很聰明，在學校裏成績不錯。可是她一放學回家，她媽媽不是要她去學鋼琴，就是要她去學畫畫。有時候玲玲想玩一會兒，她媽媽就罵她太懶。玲玲常常哭著跑到奶奶那兒去告狀。

　　張天明的表哥工作很忙，抽不出多少時間來管女兒的事。表嫂因此常和表哥吵架。要不是表嫂覺得單親家庭對小孩的影響不好，說不定早就鬧離婚了。張天明沒想到中國的家庭居然也有這麼多問題。

（二）阅 读

　　张天明的姑父几年前去世了。姑妈今年六十岁，刚从一家工厂退休。这几年姑妈一直觉得很寂寞，工厂里的老朋友想都她找个老伴儿。可是表嫂觉得姑妈找老伴儿是一件很丢人的事。姑妈觉得表嫂管得太多，说话太冲，所以婆媳关系变得紧张起来。他们本来住在一起，后来表哥和表嫂就带着女儿玲玲搬出去住了。

　　玲玲今年八岁，很聪明，在学校里成绩不错。可是她一放学回家，她妈妈不是要她去学钢琴，就是要她去学画画。有时候玲玲想玩一会儿，她妈妈就骂她太懒。玲玲常常哭着跑到奶奶那儿去告状。

　　张天明的表哥工作很忙，抽不出多少时间来管女儿的事。表嫂因此常和表哥吵架。要不是表嫂觉得单亲家庭对小孩的影响不好，说不定早就闹离婚了。张天明没想到中国的家庭居然也有这么多问题。

二 · 生 詞 表

家庭		n	jiātíng	family
感恩節	感恩节	n	Gǎn'ēnjié	Thanksgiving
父子		n	fùzǐ	father and son
歷史	历史	n	lìshǐ	history
賺(錢)*	赚(钱)	v(o)	zhuàn (qián)	make (money)
鐵飯碗	铁饭碗	n	tiě fànwǎn	iron rice bowl (metaphor: secure job)
工程		n	gōngchéng	engineering
技術	技术	n	jìshù	technology
方面		n	fāngmiàn	aspect
過日子	过日子	col	guò rìzi	live
而		conj	ér	and, but
獨立	独立	adj	dúlì	independent
叔叔		n	shūshu	爸爸的弟弟
定下來		vc	dìng xialai	fix; clarify (the relationship)
首先		adj	shǒuxiān	first and foremost
結婚	结婚	v	jié hūn	get married

他姐姐明年結婚。

她哥哥跟一個英國人結婚了。

嘛			ma	particle (indicating evident and clear reasoning)
分手		v	fēn shǒu	part company

天華跟湯姆分手了。

他們分手以後就再也沒說過話。

操心		v	cāo xīn	trouble about
				父母常常為子女操心。
				這件事你別操心。
姑父		n	gūfu	姑媽的先生
去世		v	qùshì	pass away
工廠	工厂	n	gōngchǎng	factory
退休		v	tuìxiū	retire
老伴兒	老伴儿	col	lǎobànr	(of an old married couple) husband or wife
表嫂		n	biǎosǎo	表哥的太太
丟人		v	diū rén	lose face; be disgraced
				偷東西很丟人。
				大學念了七年還畢不了業是一件丟人的事。
衝	冲	adj	chòng	abrupt; blunt
				弟弟說話很衝。
				你說話別那麼衝。
婆媳			pó xí	mother-in-law and daughter-in-law
聰明*	聪明	adj	cōngming	bright; intelligent
成績*	成绩	n	chéngjī	grades
放學	放学	v	fàng xué	after school
鋼琴*	钢琴	n	gāngqín	piano
畫畫	画画	vo	huà huàr	paint; draw
罵	骂	v	mà	scold
懶	懒	adj	lǎn	lazy
奶奶*		n	nǎinai	(paternal) grandmother

告狀	告狀	v	gào zhuàng	bring a lawsuit against sb.; lodge a complaint against sb. with his superior
抽		v	chōu	take out
				你抽時間給媽媽打個電話吧。
				我很忙，抽不出時間。
因此		conj	yīncǐ	because of this; therefore
吵架		v	chǎo jià	quarrel
要不是		conj	yàobúshì	were it not for the fact that
單親	单亲		dānqīn	single parent
離婚	离婚	v	lí hūn	divorce
居然		adv	jūrán	to one's surprise

專名 Proper Nouns

| 惠敏 | | | Huìmǐn | a feminine name |
| 玲玲 | | | Língling | a feminine name |

難寫的字：

鐵　嘛　衝　聰　鋼　畫　離

三‧語法註釋 Grammar Notes

1. Directional complement(III): indicating state

Directional complements can indicate a change in state. There are several kinds of directional complements:

A: Indicating a change from inaction to action, the initiation of an action and its continuation (上, 起, 起來, 開)

(1) 他...就打起電話來。（起來，第五課）

他...就打起电话来。（起来，第五课）

He began to make phone calls. (***Lesson Five***)

(2) 汽車開得快起來了。

汽车开得快起来了。

The car began to accelerate.

(3) 打開燈，房間一下子亮起來了。

打开灯，房间一下子亮起来了。

After the light was on, the room brightened up.

(4) 孩子從學校一回家就彈起鋼琴來。

孩子从学校一回家就弹起钢琴来。

The kid began to play the piano as soon as he got home.

(5) 兩個老朋友坐下以後，聊起天來了。

两个老朋友坐下以后，聊起天来了。

The two old friends sat down and began to chat.

"起來" can also indicate a change in speed, light, temperature, weight, etc. For instance,

(1) 天氣慢慢暖和起來了。

天气慢慢暖和起来了。

The weather began to warm up.

(2) 這幾年學中文的學生多起來了。

这几年学中文的学生多起来了。

In the last couple of years the number of students taking Chinese has begun to increase.

NB: If there is an object, it should be between "起" and "來."

"上, 開" can also indicate the start of an action or state. However, while "起來" can be combined with many adjectives, "上" and "開" can only be combined with a limited number of adjectives.

(1) 我們在上課，你怎麼唱上了？

我们在上课，你怎么唱上了？

我們在上課，你怎麼唱開了？

我们在上课，你怎么唱开了？

We are having a class. How come you're beginning to sing?

(2) 她剛才還很高興，現在怎麼哭上了？

她刚才还很高兴，现在怎么哭上了？

她剛才還很高興，現在怎麼哭開了？

她刚才还很高兴，现在怎么哭开了？

She was very happy just a moment ago. How come she's crying now?

(3) 他一回家就唱上了。

他一回家就唱上了。

The minute he got home he started to sing.

(4) 他聽了我的話以後就笑開了。

他听了我的话以后就笑开了。

After he listened to what I said, he started to laugh.

B: "下來" indicates a change from a dynamic to a static state.

(4) 汽車停下來了。

汽车停下来了。

The car slowed down.

(5) 關上燈，房間一下子暗下來了。

关上灯，房间一下子暗下来了。

After the light was off, the room began to darken.

(6) 最近他瘦下來了。

最近他瘦下来了。

He has started to lose weight lately.

"下去" indicates the continuation of an action or state:

(1) 張天明不好意思不聽下去。（第五課）

张天明不好意思不听下去。（第五课）

Zhang Tianming could not bring himself to stop listening.

(2) 說下去！

说下去！

Keep on talking!

(3) 天再熱下去，我就受不了了。

天再热下去，我就受不了了。

If the temperature keeps on rising, I won't be able to bear it.

2. Potential Complements "(V) + 不/得 + 了" (pronounced "liǎo"):

Potential complements "(V) + 不/得 + 了" can be construed as the equivalent of "不能/能." For instance,

(1) 外面在下雨，比賽不了了。

外面在下雨，比赛不了了。

It's raining outside. The game can't take place.

(2) 孩子病了，上不了學了。

孩子病了，上不了学了。

The kid is sick and can't go to school.

(3) 一百塊錢買不了幾本書。

一百块钱买不了几本书。

A hundred bucks can only buy a few books.

This kind of complement is used mainly in negative sentences, and is interchangeable with this pattern, "能/不能."

NB: "V+不/得+了" can also mean "不能/能+(V)+完." For instance, "吃不了" (cannot eat it all up). Compare the following:

(4) 水果壞了，吃不了了。

水果坏了，吃不了了。

The fruit is spoiled. You shouldn't eat it.

(5) 飯給得太多了，我吃不了。

饭给得太多了，我吃不了。

You've given me too much rice. I can't finish it.

3. "要"（應該）：

"要" can mean "should" or "must." For instance,

(1) 中國人認爲孩子要聽父母的話，幫忙帶弟弟妹妹。

中国人认为孩子要听父母的话，帮忙带弟弟妹妹。

The Chinese believe that children should be filial to their parents, and help take care of their younger brothers and sisters.

(2) 明天早上有考試，你們要早一點起來。

明天早上有考试，你们要早一点起来。

There will be an exam tomorrow morning. You should get up a bit earlier (than usual).

(3) 你跟他借的錢要還給他。

你跟他借的钱要还给他。

You must pay back the money you borrowed from him.

Use "不用/不必" to negate:

> (4) 你跟我借的錢，不必還了。
>
> 　　你跟我借的钱，不必还了。
>
> You don't have to pay back the money you borrowed from me.
>
> (5) 明天是週末，不用早起。
>
> 　　明天是周末，不用早起。
>
> Tomorrow is the weekend. There is no need to get up early.

4. "下來" : indicating result

"下來" denotes separation or consolidation. For instance, 撕下來 (tear off), 摘下來 (pull down), 揭下來 (pull off), 拿下來 (take down); 住下來 (settle down), 待下來 (stay), 決定下來 (decide on), 定下來 (decide).

5. Topics II:

In a sentence, if the noun signifies something that is already known, while the adjective to describe it conveys something new, then we should place the noun at the beginning of the sentence, i.e., treat it as a topic, and put the adjective after the noun. Compare the following examples and pay particular attention to the difference between Chinese and English:

> (1) 只是有時候中文課的功課多一點。
>
> 　　只是有时候中文课的功课多一点。
>
> It is just that sometimes there is rather too much homework for the Chinese class. (*Lesson Fourteen*)

We don't say,

> (1)* 只是有時候中文有比較多的功課。
>
> 　　只是有时候中文有比较多的功课。
>
> It's just that sometimes there is too much homework for the Chinese class.

(2) 東方人和西方人生活習慣不一樣。

东方人和西方人生活习惯不一样。

Orientals and westerners, (their) life styles/customs are different.

We don't say,

(2)*東方人和西方人有不同的生活習慣。

东方人和西方人有不同的生活习惯。

Orientals and westerners have different life styles/customs.

(3) 你看，天華和湯姆就是因爲文化背景不同分手的。

你看，天华和汤姆就是因为文化背景不同分手的。

See, Tianhua and Tom broke up precisely because of their differences in cultural background.

We don't say,

(3)*你看，天華和湯姆就是因爲有不同的文化背景而分手的。

你看，天华和汤姆就是因为有不同的文化背景而分手的。

See, Tianhua and Tom broke up precisely because they had different cultural backgrounds.

四·詞語練習

1. "**而**" (a conjuction to show contrast between the 1st & 2nd clause) :

　　Example: 過日子靠的是錢，而不是興趣。

　　　　　　过日子靠的是钱，而不是兴趣。

　　(1) 他們分手是因爲＿＿＿＿＿＿，而不是因爲

　　　　＿＿＿＿＿＿。

　　　　他们分手是因为＿＿＿＿＿＿，而不是因为

　　　　＿＿＿＿＿＿。

(2) 小林畢業以後想＿＿＿＿＿＿而不想＿＿＿＿＿＿。

　　小林毕业以后想＿＿＿＿＿＿而不想＿＿＿＿＿＿。

(3) 過端午節應該吃＿＿＿＿，而不應該吃＿＿＿＿。

　　过端午节应该吃＿＿＿＿，而不应该吃＿＿＿＿。

2. " 最好 " (had better; it's best) :

　　Example:你這次回來，去看看她，最好把你們的關係定下來。

　　　　　　　你这次回来，去看看她，最好把你们的关系定下来。

(1) 吃完飯後，＿＿＿＿＿＿＿＿＿＿＿。（馬上運動）

　　吃完饭后，＿＿＿＿＿＿＿＿＿＿＿。（马上运动）

(2) 要是這個包裹很重要，＿＿＿＿＿＿＿。（掛號）

　　要是这个包裹很重要，＿＿＿＿＿＿＿。（挂号）

(3) 這部電影很吸引人，＿＿＿＿＿＿＿＿。（早點買票）

　　这部电影很吸引人，＿＿＿＿＿＿＿＿。（早点买票）

3. " 要不是 " (if it were not for):

　　Example: 要不是表嫂覺得單親家庭對小孩的影響不好，説不定早就鬧離婚了。

　　　　　　要不是表嫂觉得单亲家庭对小孩的影响不好，说不定早就闹离婚了。

(1) 要不是＿＿＿＿＿＿，我們很可能迷路。

　　要不是＿＿＿＿＿＿，我们很可能迷路。

(2) 要不是＿＿＿＿＿，他＿＿＿＿＿＿。

　　　　　（我催他早點出門，肯定來不及）

　　要不是＿＿＿＿＿，他＿＿＿＿＿＿。

　　　　　（我催他早点出门，肯定来不及）

262

(3)要不是＿＿＿＿＿＿＿＿＿＿，＿＿＿＿＿＿＿＿＿＿。

　　　　（昨天下了雨，今天會更熱）

　　要不是＿＿＿＿＿＿＿＿＿＿，＿＿＿＿＿＿＿＿＿＿。

　　　　（昨天下了雨，今天会更热）

4. " 說不定 " (probably)：

Example: 要不是表嫂覺得單親家庭對小孩的影響不好，說不定早就鬧離婚了。

　　　　要不是表嫂觉得单亲家庭对小孩的影响不好，说不定早就闹离婚了。

(1) 感恩節坐飛機的人多，機票＿＿＿＿＿＿＿＿＿＿。

　　感恩节坐飞机的人多，机票＿＿＿＿＿＿＿＿＿＿。

(2) ＿＿＿＿＿＿＿＿＿，你不用告訴他了。（他知道了）

　　＿＿＿＿＿＿＿＿＿，你不用告诉他了。（他知道了）

(3) 我們隊越打越好，＿＿＿＿＿＿＿＿。（能贏他們）

　　我们队越打越好，＿＿＿＿＿＿＿＿。（能赢他们）

5. " 沒想到 " (didn't expect)：

Example: 張天明沒想到中國的家庭居然也有這麼多問題。

　　　　张天明没想到中国的家庭居然也有这么多问题。

(1) 他們結婚才兩個月，＿＿＿＿＿＿＿＿＿＿。（鬧離婚）

　　他们结婚才两个月，＿＿＿＿＿＿＿＿＿。（闹离婚）

(2) 她才三歲，＿＿＿＿＿＿＿＿＿＿。

　　　　　　（畫兒就畫得那麼好）

　　她才三岁，＿＿＿＿＿＿＿＿＿＿。

　　　　　　（画儿就画得那么好）

(3) 沒想到＿＿＿＿＿＿＿＿＿＿。（這個學校的學費，貴）

　　没想到＿＿＿＿＿＿＿＿＿。（这个学校的学费，贵）

五·看圖說話

第十五課 男女平等

一‧課文

（一）對 話

麗　　莎：　天明，昨天晚上我高中的一個女同學來電話，說她懷
　　　　　　了孕，快生孩子了。她已經把工作辭了，待在家裏做
　　　　　　起家庭主婦來了。

張天明：　這不很好嗎？

麗　　莎：　好什麼？她是護士，才工作一年。真不公平，生孩子
　　　　　　是整個社會的事，為什麼擔子都在女人身上？

張天明：　麗莎，你這麼說，我看有點沒道理。難道讓我們男人
　　　　　　生孩子嗎？

麗　　莎：　誰讓你們生孩子了？我的意思是，一個女人生了孩子
　　　　　　以後，不管她願意不願意，都得辭了工作在家裏帶孩
　　　　　　子。這不是太不公平了嗎？為什麼不讓丈夫在家裏帶
　　　　　　孩子呢？

張天明：　你真的這麼想嗎？讓女的辭職，待在家裏當然不好；
　　　　　　可是反過來，讓男的在家裏帶孩子，也不見得公平。
　　　　　　應該想一個更好的辦法來解決這個問題。

麗　　莎：　等你想出好辦法以後，恐怕我都老了。實際上，男女
　　　　　　不平等的現象還有很多。比如，做同樣的工作，女的
　　　　　　薪水往往比男的少。

張天明：　這倒是。

麗　　莎：　還有，在美國當主管的，有幾個是女的？職位越高，
　　　　　　婦女越少，這不是歧視婦女嗎？

第十五课　男女平等

一·课文

（一）对　话

丽　　莎：　天明，昨天晚上我高中的一个女同学来电话，说她怀
　　　　　了孕，快生孩子了。她已经把工作辞了，待在家里做
　　　　　起家庭主妇来了。

张天明：　这不很好吗？

丽　　莎：　好什么？她是护士，才工作一年。真不公平，生孩子
　　　　　是整个社会的事，为什么担子都在女人身上？

张天明：　丽莎，你这么说，我看有点没道理。难道让我们男人
　　　　　生孩子吗？

丽　　莎：　谁让你们生孩子了？我的意思是，一个女人生了孩子
　　　　　以后，不管她愿意不愿意，都得辞了工作在家里带孩
　　　　　子。这不是太不公平了吗？为什么不让丈夫在家里带
　　　　　孩子呢？

张天明：　你真的这么想吗？让女的辞职，待在家里当然不好；
　　　　　可是反过来，让男的在家里带孩子，也不见得公平。
　　　　　应该想一个更好的办法来解决这个问题。

丽　　莎：　等你想出好办法以后，恐怕我都老了。实际上，男女
　　　　　不平等的现象还有很多。比如，做同样的工作，女的
　　　　　薪水往往比男的少。

张天明：　这倒是。

丽　　莎：　还有，在美国当主管的，有几个是女的？职位越高，
　　　　　妇女越少，这不是歧视妇女吗？

張天明：　你說的有道理。不過，我想隨著社會的發展，婦女的
　　　　　地位會不斷得到提高的。

麗　莎：　我不像你那麼樂觀。

張天明：　哎，麗莎，我覺得在家庭裏，男女已經很平等了。就
　　　　　拿我家來說吧，我爸爸跟媽媽分擔家務，教育孩子也
　　　　　主要是爸爸。親戚朋友都說我爸爸是一個模範丈夫。

麗　莎：　我看你姐夫對你姐姐也很體貼。

張天明：　我姐夫比我爸爸更＂模範＂，見了姐姐，就像老鼠見
　　　　　了貓。我很看不慣。

麗　莎：　男女平等這個問題，大概是很難討論清楚的。

张天明：　你说的有道理。不过，我想随着社会的发展，妇女的
　　　　　地位会不断得到提高的。

丽　莎：　我不像你那么乐观。

张天明：　哎，丽莎，我觉得在家庭里，男女已经很平等了。就
　　　　　拿我家来说吧，我爸爸跟妈妈分担家务，教育孩子也
　　　　　主要是爸爸。亲戚朋友都说我爸爸是一个模范丈夫。

丽　莎：　我看你姐夫对你姐姐也很体贴。

张天明：　我姐夫比我爸爸更"模范"，见了姐姐，就像老鼠见
　　　　　了猫。我很看不惯。

丽　莎：　男女平等这个问题，大概是很难讨论清楚的。

（二）閱　讀

　　在歷史上，特別是從宋朝開始，中國就是一個重男輕女的社會。在家裏，女子出嫁以前要服從父親，出嫁以後要服從丈夫，丈夫死了還要服從兒子。那個時候，婚姻完全由父母做主，有的還指腹為婚。有的地方，如果女孩還沒長大，未婚夫就死了，就不讓這個女孩跟別人結婚，甚至叫死了未婚夫的女孩跟一個木刻的“男人”結婚。

　　五十年代開始，中國婦女的情況有了很大的變化。特別是在城市裏，女孩子和男孩子一樣有受教育的機會；在工作方面，同工同酬；婦女的社會地位也有很大的提高。

　　但是，改革開放以來，男女不平等的問題又突出起來。比如，升學或找工作的時候，女生都比男生難得多；在一些工廠和公司又出現了同工不同酬的現象；職位高的婦女人數明顯減少了。不過，在一般年輕的夫婦中，大部份丈夫十分體貼、照顧妻子。所以，也許家庭是男女平等體現得最多的地方。

（二）阅 读

　　在历史上，特别是从宋朝开始，中国就是一个重男轻女的社会。在家里，女子出嫁以前要服从父亲，出嫁以后要服从丈夫，丈夫死了还要服从儿子。那个时候，婚姻完全由父母做主，有的还指腹为婚。有的地方，如果女孩还没长大，未婚夫就死了，就不让这个女孩跟别人结婚，甚至叫死了未婚夫的女孩跟一个木刻的"男人"结婚。

　　五十年代开始，中国妇女的情况有了很大的变化。特别是在城市里，女孩子和男孩子一样有受教育的机会；在工作方面，同工同酬；妇女的社会地位也有很大的提高。

　　但是，改革开放以来，男女不平等的问题又突出起来。比如，升学或找工作的时候，女生都比男生难得多；在一些工厂和公司又出现了同工不同酬的现象；职位高的妇女人数明显减少了。不过，在一般年轻的夫妇中，大部份丈夫十分体贴、照顾妻子。所以，也许家庭是男女平等体现得最多的地方。

二 · 生 詞 表

男女			nánnǚ	male and female; men and women
平等		adj	píngděng	equal; equality
懷孕	怀孕	v	huái yùn	become pregnant
辭	辞	v	cí	resign
家庭主婦	家庭主妇	n	jiātíng zhǔfù	housewife
護士	护士	n	hùshi	nurse
公平		adj	gōngpíng	fair

你們的老師對大家很公平。

不公平的事大家都會反對。

社會	社会	n	shèhuì	society
擔子	担子	n	dànzi	burden
女人		n	nǚrén	(colloq.) woman
不管		conj	bùguǎn	no matter how
帶	带	v	dài	(colloq.) raise

很多人不喜歡帶孩子。

丈夫		n	zhàngfu	husband
辭職	辞职	vo	cí zhí	resign from a position
反過來	反过来		fǎn guolai	conversely
辦法	办法	n	bànfǎ	method; wherewithal
解決	解决	v	jiějué	resolve

他們兩個人的矛盾已經解決了。

我學習上有很多困難，你能幫助我解決嗎？

現象	現象	n	xiànxiàng	phenomenon
薪水		n	xīnshui	salary
往往		adv	wǎngwǎng	often (indicating tendency rather than frequency)
主管		n	zhǔguǎn	person-in-charge
職位	职位	n	zhíwèi	(professional) position
婦女	妇女	n	fùnǚ	woman
歧視	歧视	v	qíshì	discriminate
隨著	随着	conj	suí zhe	along with
地位		n	dìwèi	status
不斷	不断	adv	búduàn	constantly

電話不斷地響，真吵。
上課時，他總是不斷地跟老師問問題。

| 得到 | | v | dédào | obtain |
| 提高 | | v | tí gāo | lift; improve |

去中國學習了一年，我的中文水平明顯提高了。
為了提高婦女的社會地位，國家想了很多辦法。

樂觀	乐观	v	lèguān	optimistic
分擔	分担	v	fēndān	share (burden; responsibilities)
家務	家务	n	jiāwù	household duties

主要		adj	zhǔyào	main; chief
				我主要在學校上學，周末出去工作。
				他這次去中國主要目的是參加體育比賽。
親戚	亲戚	n	qīnqi	relatives
模範	模范	n/adj	mófàn	model
姐夫		n	jiěfu	姐姐的丈夫
體貼	体贴	v	tǐtiē	considerate
老鼠		n	lǎoshǔ	mouse
貓	猫	n	māo	cat
看不慣	看不惯	vc	kàn bu guàn	cannot bear the sight of; frown upon
大概		adv	dàgài	probably
				會已經開完了，他大概不會來了。
				你大概不認識他吧，他是我哥哥。
重男輕女	重男轻女		zhòng nán qīng nǚ	privilege men over women
女子		n	nǚzǐ	(formal) woman
出嫁		v	chū jià	(of a woman) get married
服從	服从	v	fúcóng	obey
婚姻		n	hūnyīn	marriage
由		pr	yóu	preposition indicating agent
做主		v	zuò zhǔ	decide
指腹為婚	指腹为婚		zhǐ fù wéi hūn	pointing to the stomach (of the pregnant mother) to arrange a marriage (for the child)
未婚夫		n	wèihūn fū	fiance

甚至			shènzhì	even
木刻			mùkè	carved in wood; wood carving
變化	变化	v	biànhua	change
城市*		n	chéngshì	city
機會	机会	n	jīhuì	opportunity

你最近有機會去歐洲嗎？

去中國工作是提高中文水平的好機會。

同工同酬			tóng gōng tóng chóu	equal pay for equal work
改革開放		v	gǎigé kāifàng	reform
突出		v	tūchū	prominent
升學	升学	v	shēng xué	go to school of a higher level
女生		n	nǚshēng	female student
男生		n	nánshēng	male student
出現	出现	v	chūxiàn	appear

最近這兒出現了一些奇怪的現象。

最近他們倆在生活中出現了一些矛盾。

人數	人数	n	rénshù	number of people
明顯	明显	adj	míngxiǎn	obvious
減少	减少	v	jiǎnshǎo	decrease
年輕	年轻	adj	niánqīng	young
夫婦	夫妇	n	fūfù	husband and wife
大部份	大部分		dà bùfen	majority
照顧	照顾	v	zhàogu	take care of; look after
妻子		n	qīzi	wife

| 體現 | 体现 | v | tǐxiàn | embody; manifest |

專名 Proper Noun

| 宋朝 | | | Sòngcháo | the Song dynasty (960-1279) |

難寫的字：

懷辭護擔職隨斷範鼠酬顯顧

三・語法註釋 Grammar Notes

1. "同樣" and "一樣"：

"同樣" is a pre-nominal modifier, i.e., it always appears before the nouns that it modifiers whereas "一樣" is used as a predicate or complement. For instance,

(1) A：這本字典的價錢跟那本一樣。

这本字典的价钱跟那本一样。

The price of this dictionary is the same as that one.

B：我想用同樣的價錢，也買一本你這樣的字典。

我想用同样的价钱，也买一本你这样的字典。

I'd like to pay the same amount for a dictionary like yours.

(2) A：我們兩個人的看法一樣。

我们两个人的看法一样。

The two of us, our opinions are the same.

B：你們常常看同樣的書，有同樣的看法一點也不奇怪。

你们常常看同样的书，有同样的看法一点也不奇怪。

You often read the same books. No wonder you have the same opinions.

(3) 姐姐跟妹妹長得一樣。

姐姐跟妹妹长得一样。

The elder sister looks exactly like the younger one.

(4) 哥哥和弟弟在一個班，上同樣的課。

哥哥和弟弟在一个班，上同样的课。

The brothers are in the same class, and take the same courses.

2. "隨著......" ：

"隨著" is used in the first clause to indicate a changed circumstance. The second clause introduces a concomittant change. For example,

(1) 隨著經濟的發展，人民的生活水平也得到提高。

随着经济的发展，人民的生活水平也得到提高。

With economic development, people's living standards are improving.

(2) 隨著交往時間的增加，兩個人相處得越好。

随着交往时间的增加，两个人相处得越好。

The longer they are together, the better they get along with each other.

(3) 隨著他中文水平的提高，他看中文報的速度越來越快了。

随着他中文水平的提高，他看中文报的速度越来越快了。

As his proficiency in Chinese improves, he can read Chinese newspapers much more quickly.

3. "在...方面" ：

"在...方面" mainly denotes an area or scope. Verbs and some dissyllabic abstract nouns can be inserted in the construction:

(1) 在男女平等方面，這個國家還存在很大的問題。

在男女平等方面，这个国家还存在很大的问题。

In the area of gender equity, there is still a big problem in this country.

(2) 在穿的方面，他不太在乎，可是在吃的方面，他非常挑剔。

在穿的方面，他不太在乎，可是在吃的方面，他非常挑剔。

He's not too particular about clothes, but he is very finicky about food.

(3) 在體育運動方面，中國最近幾年發展很快。

在体育运动方面，中国最近几年发展很快。

China has advanced a great deal in sports in recent years.

(4) MIT可以說是在工程技術方面最有名的大學了。

MIT可以说是在工程技术方面最有名的大学了。

MIT is the most famous university in the area of engineering and technology.

4. "甚至"：

The conjunction "甚至" is used for emphasis or to stress the speaker's point of view:

(1) 弟弟很聰明，才五歲，不但能看書，甚至能寫詩。

弟弟很聪明，才五岁，不但能看书，甚至能写诗。

My brother is really bright. He's only five, but he can read, and even write poetry.
(Using "writing poetry" to show how smart the kid is.)

(2) 他是個中國通，甚至連氣功都懂。

他是个中国通，甚至连气功都懂。

He is a China expert. He even knows *qigong*.
(Using "understanding *qigong*" to show he is a real China expert.)

(3) A：你看過電影《白毛女》嗎？

你看过电影《白毛女》吗？

Have you seen the movie, "The White-Haired Girl"?

B：沒有，什麼《白毛女》，我甚至都沒聽說過。

沒有，什么《白毛女》，我甚至都没听说过。

No, what "White-Haired Girl"? I haven't even heard of it.
(Using "never heard of" to emphasize that B truly hasn't seen the movie.)

(4) 他對中國的節日一點都不清楚，甚至連春節都不知道。

他对中国的节日一点都不清楚，甚至连春节都不知道。

He doesn't know anything about Chinese holidays. He hasn't even heard of the Spring Festival.

(Using "not knowing the Spring Festival" to show how little he knows about Chinese holidays.)

"甚至" is often used together with "連...也/都...."

5. Word Order in Chinese (III)

We've already talked about word order in Chinese. In this lesson we will summarize what we have learned. The normal word order in Chinese is:

(attributive) subj. -- time + place + other adverbials -- verb—complement -- (attributive) obj.

Here, by complement we mean resultative complements and directional complements (for the position of directional complements and objects, see the relevant grammar notes). When there is a complement introduced by "得" and an object at the same time, one must repeat the verb. Similarly, if there is a phrase after a verb indicating the duration of the action or the number of its occurrence, one must also repeat the verb. For instance,

(1) 我昨天在電影院看了一個新電影。

我昨天在电影院看了一个新电影。

I saw a new movie at a cinema yesterday.

(2) 明天我上完課就去圖書館。

明天我上完课就去图书馆。

Tomorrow I'll go to the library as soon as the classes are over.

(3) 他學中文學了三年多了。

他学中文学了三年多了。

He has been studying Chinese for more than three years now.

(4) 我寫字寫得很慢。

我写字写得很慢。

I write (characters) very slowly.

If somebody or something has already been mentioned, under normal circumstances we should treat the noun denoting that person or thing as a topic, and put it at the beginning of the sentence, or after "把." For example,

(5) 你告訴我的那件事情我已經知道了。

你告诉我的那件事情我已经知道了。

The thing that you told me about, I had already known.

(6) 請你把桌子上的地圖給我。

请你把桌子上的地图给我。

Please give me the map on the table.

四 · 詞語練習

1. " 反過來 " (conversely):

Example: 可是反過來，讓男的在家裏帶孩子，也不見得公平。

可是反过来，让男的在家里带孩子，也不见得公平。

(1) 小明，妹妹罵你當然不對，_____。（你打她）

小明，妹妹骂你当然不对，_____。（你打她）

(2) 丈夫不做家務事當然不好，可是，_____。

（妻子不體貼丈夫）

丈夫不做家务事当然不好，可是，_____。

（妻子不体贴丈夫）

(3) 我認為大國不應該打小國，＿＿＿＿＿＿＿＿＿＿。

（小國不講道理）

我认为大国不应该打小国，＿＿＿＿＿＿＿＿＿＿。

（小国不讲道理）

2. "**實際上**" (in actual fact)：

Example: 實際上，男女不平等的現象還有很多。比如，做同樣的工作，女的薪水往往比男的少。

实际上，男女不平等的现象还有很多。比如，做同样的工作，女的薪水往往比男的少。

(1) 這個學校雖然很有名，＿＿＿＿＿＿＿＿＿＿。

（不怎麼樣）

这个学校虽然很有名，＿＿＿＿＿＿＿＿＿＿。

（不怎么样）

(2) 有人說中國菜太油，＿＿＿＿＿＿＿＿。

（要看你怎麼做了）

有人说中国菜太油，＿＿＿＿＿＿＿＿。

（要看你怎么做了）

(3) 大家都以為那家購物中心的東西便宜，＿＿＿＿＿＿。

（並不便宜）

大家都以为那家购物中心的东西便宜，＿＿＿＿＿＿。

（並不便宜）

3. "**就拿...來說**" (take somebody or something for example)：

Example: 就拿我家來說吧，我爸爸跟媽媽分擔家務。

就拿我家来说吧，我爸爸跟妈妈分担家务。

(1) 那家飯館的菜貴得不得了。＿＿＿＿＿＿＿＿＿。

（青菜一盤居然十五塊錢）

　　那家饭馆的菜贵得不得了。＿＿＿＿＿＿＿＿＿＿。

　　　　　　　　　　　　　（青菜一盘居然十五块钱）

(2) 這個班的學生學習都很努力，＿＿＿＿＿＿＿＿＿＿。

　　　　　　　　　　　（小李每天都要學習六七個鐘頭）

　　这个班的学生学习都很努力，＿＿＿＿＿＿＿＿＿＿。

　　　　　　　　　　　（小李每天都要学习六七个钟头）

(3) 他的三個女兒都會說好幾種外語，＿＿＿＿＿＿＿＿＿。

　　　　　　　　　　　（老二會說法文，日文和中文）

　　他的三个女儿都会说好几种外语，＿＿＿＿＿＿＿＿＿。

　　　　　　　　　　　（老二会说法文，日文和中文）

4. " 明顯 " (appreciably; obviously) :

　　Example: 職位高的婦女人數明顯減少了。

　　　　　　職位高的妇女人数明显减少了。

(1) 這幾年＿＿＿＿＿＿＿＿＿。（中國人的生活水平提高）

　　这几年＿＿＿＿＿＿＿＿＿。（中国人的生活水平提高）

(2) 最近十幾年來，＿＿＿＿＿＿＿＿＿＿＿＿＿。

　　　　　　　　　　（很多國家婦女的地位提高了）

　　最近十几年来，＿＿＿＿＿＿＿＿＿＿＿＿＿。

　　　　　　　　　　（很多国家妇女的地位提高了）

(3) 那個孩子最近電視看得太多，＿＿＿＿＿＿＿。

　　　　　　　　　　　　　（學習受影響）

　　那个孩子最近电视看得太多，＿＿＿＿＿＿＿。

　　　　　　　　　　　　　（学习受影响）

5. Compare "...以後" and "...以來":

"...以後" (after a certain point in time), e.g.,

(1) 上大學以後，我們一直沒有見過她。

上大學以后，我們一直沒有見過她。

(2) 她跟我吵架以後，我就不喜歡她了。

她跟我吵架以后，我就不喜欢她了。

(3) 一上大學我們就住在一個宿舍，一年以後我搬走了。

一上大学我们就住在一个宿舍，一年以后我搬走了。

"...以來" (from a certain point in the past to the present), e.g.,

(1) 我跟他認識以來，從來沒有見他吸過煙。

我跟他认识以来，从来没有见他吸过烟。

(2) 上大學以來，我一直沒有見過她。

上大学以来，我一直没有见过她。

(3) 畢業以來，他已經換了五個工作了。

毕业以来，他已经换了五个工作了。

五·看圖說話

第十六課 健康與保險

一・課文

（一）對 話

張天明： 麗莎，這個星期五我不能陪你去看電影了，我得去
　　　　 機場接我姑媽，她要來我們大學醫院看病。

麗　莎： 哪個姑媽？

張天明： 多倫多的那個。

麗　莎： 她為什麼不在加拿大看病？我聽說加拿大的醫療保
　　　　 險很好，醫院也不錯。她來這兒看病不是得自己花

第十六课 健康与保险

一·课文

（一）对 话

张天明：　丽莎，这个星期五我不能跟你去看电影了，我得去
　　　　　机场接我姑妈，她要来我们大学医院看病。

丽　莎：　哪个姑妈？

张天明：　多伦多的那个。

丽　莎：　她为什么不在加拿大看病？我听说加拿大的医疗保
　　　　　险很好，医院也不错。她来这儿看病不是得自己花

　　　　　　　錢嗎？

張天明：　加拿大的保險制度是不錯，人人都有保險。可是如果不是急病的話，看病得等很長時間。我姑媽的心臟病雖然不太嚴重，可是她不願意再等下去了。加上她聽說我們學校醫院的心臟科很有名，所以決定來這兒做手術。聽說很多加拿大人來美國看病。

麗　莎：　可是，如果你是個窮人的話，你就會覺得美國的醫療制度不如加拿大的好，因為在加拿大至少你不必擔心付不起醫療費。

張天明：　在美國，政府每年拿出很多錢照顧窮人。你沒有錢醫院也會給你看病。

麗　莎：　能得到政府幫助的人畢竟很少。很多人沒有買保險，有了病，受了傷，也不敢看醫生，等病重了才去看。有保險的人，保險費越來越高，實際上是替那些沒有保險的人付醫藥費。

張天明：　如果你有工作，工作單位會給你買保險，你自己只出一部份。

麗　莎：　可是不是所有的單位都給它的工作人員買保險。而且"羊毛出在羊身上"，公司會提高產品價格，再把錢賺回來，最後還是咱們自己出錢。這也正是美國藥比別的國家貴的原因。

張天明：　你說的不錯。可是你也得讓製藥公司有錢可賺哪！要不然美國怎麼會有世界上最好的藥呢？

麗　莎：　如果你沒有錢的話，藥無論多好，對你也是毫無意義的。反正我覺得美國的保險制度應該改革。對了，你姑媽什麼時候動手術？

張天明：　還不知道呢。你想不想見她？她以前在台灣還是個電影明星呢。聽我爸爸說，她拍了很多武打片。

　　　　　　　　钱吗？

张天明：　加拿大的保险制度是不错，人人都有保险。可是如果不是急病的话，看病得等很长时间。我姑妈的心脏病虽然不太严重，可是她不愿意再等下去了。加上她听说我们学校医院的心脏科很有名，所以决定来这儿做手术。听说很多加拿大人来美国看病。

丽　莎：　可是，如果你是个穷人的话，你就会觉得美国的医疗制度不如加拿大的好，因为在加拿大至少你不必担心付不起医疗费。

张天明：　在美国，政府每年拿出很多钱照顾穷人。你没有钱医院也会给你看病。

丽　莎：　能得到政府帮助的人毕竟很少。很多人没有买保险，有了病，受了伤，也不敢看医生，等病重了才去看。有保险的人，保险费越来越高，实际上是替那些没有保险的人付医药费。

张天明：　如果你有工作，工作单位会给你买保险，你自己只出一部分。

丽　莎：　可是不是所有的单位都给它的工作人员买保险。而且"羊毛出在羊身上"，公司会提高产品价格，再把钱赚回来，最后还是咱们自己出钱。这也正是美国药比别的国家贵的原因。

张天明：　你说的不错。可是你也得让制药公司有钱可赚哪！要不然美国怎么会有世界上最好的药呢？

丽　莎：　如果你没有钱的话，药无论多好，对你也是毫无意义的。反正我觉得美国的保险制度应该改革。对了，你姑妈什么时候动手术？

张天明：　还不知道呢。你想不想见她？她以前在台湾还是个电影明星呢。听我爸爸说，她拍了很多武打片。

麗　　莎：　是嗎？那我真想見見她，我們星期六請她吃飯怎麼
　　　　　　樣？

張天明：　好啊。就這麼說定了。

（二）閱　讀

　　在現在的世界上，當然還有人在爲吃飯發愁。可是對不少
人來說，他們擔心的已經不是營養不足，而是營養過剩的問
題。隨著生活水平的提高，人們越來越關心自己的健康與身
材。吃素的人越來越多，另外也有不少人減肥。可是有些人過
份節食，結果患上營養不良症。營養專家指出，應該注意攝取
多種營養，因爲只有營養均衡，才能保證身體健康。

丽　　莎：　是吗？那我真想见见她，我们星期六请她吃饭怎么
　　　　　　样？
张天明：　好啊。就这么说定了。

（二）阅读

　　在现在的世界上，当然还有人在为吃饭发愁。可是对不少
人来说，他们担心的已经不是营养不足，而是营养过剩的问
题。随着生活水平的提高，人们越来越关心自己的健康与身
材。吃素的人越来越多，另外也有不少人减肥。可是有些人过
分节食，结果患上营养不良症。营养专家指出，应该注意摄取
多种营养，因为只有营养均衡，才能保证身体健康。

二 · 生 詞

保險	保险	n/v	bǎoxiǎn	insurance
醫院	医院	n	yīyuàn	hospital
看病*		vo	kàn bìng	go see a doctor
醫療	医疗	n	yīliáo	medical treatment
花錢	花钱	vo	huā qián	spend money
制度		n	zhìdù	system
急病		n	jí bìng	serious illness; illness that needs immediate medical attention
心臟病	心脏病	n	xīnzàng bìng	heart disease

太太得了心臟病，他很著急。

那個國家很多孩子上不了學，情況很嚴重。

嚴重	严重	adj	yánzhòng	serious
加上		vc	jiā shàng	in addition
心臟科	心脏科	n	xīnzàng kē	cardiology department
有名		adj	yǒumíng	famous
決定		v/n	juédìng	decide; decision

他決定大學畢業以後上醫學院。

手術	手术	n	shǒushù	surgery
窮人	穷人	n	qióngrén	poor people
不如			bùrú	not as...
至少		adv	zhìshǎo	at least
不必			búbì	not necessary; no need to

老師病了，今天我們不必擔心。

擔心*	担心	v	dān xīn	worry
付*		v	fù	pay
費*	费	n	fèi	fee
政府		n	zhèngfǔ	government
畢竟	毕竟	adv	bìjìng	after all
受傷	受伤	v	shòu shāng	get wounded
所有			suǒyǒu	all
單位	单位	n	dānwèi	unit
一部份	一部分		(yí) bùfen	(one) part
人員	人员	n	rényuán	personnel; staff
羊毛		n	yángmáo	wool; fleece
出		v	chū	yield; come from
產品	产品	n	chǎnpǐn	product
價格	价格	n	jiàgé	price
藥*	药	n	yào	medicine
原因		n	yuányīn	cause; reason
製藥	制药		zhì yào	pharmaceutical
毫無	毫无		háo wú	not an iota; not in the least
意義	意义	n	yìyì	sense; meaning
動手術	动手术	vo	dòng shǒushù	perform an operation; have an operation
明星		n	míngxīng	bright star; star
拍		v	pāi	make (films)
武打片		n	wǔdǎ piān	martial arts movies

發愁	发愁	v	fā chóu	worry
				他畢業以後一直找不到工作，每天都在發愁。
				他發愁的不是工作，而是孩子的教育。
營養	营养	n	yíngyǎng	nutrition; nourishment
不足			bù zú	not sufficient; not enough
過剩	过剩	v	guòshèng	excess; surplus
水平		n	shuǐpíng	(water) level
關心	关心	v	guānxīn	be concerned with
與	与	conj	yǔ	(formal) and
身材		n	shēncái	figure
吃素*		adj	chī sù	eat vegetarian food
減肥	减肥	v	jiǎnféi	lose weight
過份	过分		guòfèn	excessive
節食	节食	v	jiéshí	restrict one's food intake
患		v	huàn	contract; suffer from (an illness)
營養不良	营养不良		yíngyǎng bùliáng	undernourishment; malnutrition
症		n	zhèng	disease
專家	专家	n	zhuānjiā	expert
指出		v	zhǐchū	point out
注意		v	zhùyì	pay attention to
				上課應該注意聽講，這樣可以節省很多時間。
攝取	摄取	v	shèqǔ	absorb
只有		conj	zhǐyǒu	only when

均衡		adj	jūnhéng	balanced; proportionate
保證	保证	v/n	bǎozhèng	guarantee

這本書我保證你喜歡。

專名 Proper Nouns

多倫多	多伦多	Duōlúnduō	Toronto
加拿大		Jiā'nádà	Canada
台灣	台湾	Táiwān	Taiwan

難寫的字：

醫療臟窮費製藥養攝衡

三·語法注釋 Grammar Notes

1. Multiple Attributives：

A noun can be preceded by several attributives. The order of the attributives follows certain rules. First, descriptive attributives must appear after those that denote possession or other non-descriptive attributives. Numerals and measure words, demonstrative pronouns + measure words are sandwiched between these two kinds of attributives. For instance,

(1) 在中國，我們遊覽了北京的幾個最大的公園，以及南京的那個有名的夫子廟。

在中国，我们游览了北京的几个最大的公园，以及南京的那个有名的夫子庙。

In China, we toured several of the biggest parks in Beijing and that famous Confucian Temple in Nanjing.

"北京" and "南京" indicate places; they are non-descriptive. They appear first. "最大" and "有名" are descriptive; they appear last. "幾個" and "那個" are inserted between these two kinds of attributives. More examples,

(2) 媽媽昨天給妹妹講了一個非常有意思的故事。

妈妈昨天给妹妹讲了一个非常有意思的故事。

Yesterday Mother told a very interesting story to my sister.

(3) 我給姐姐買的那件襯衫很漂亮。

我给姐姐买的那件衬衫很漂亮。

The shirt that I bought for my sister was very pretty.

(4) 我從來不看電視裏撥的那些無聊的新聞。

我从来不看电视里拨的那些无聊的新闻。

I never watch those boring news stories broadcasted on TV.

Among descriptive attributives, attributives that do not require "的" are the nearest to the nouns that they modify. For example, 好的中文老師 (a good Chinese teacher), 很新的木頭桌子 (a very new wooden table). When both attributives are adjectives, simple adjectives follow more complex ones, e.g. , 窄窄的小河 (a little narrow river), 胖胖的圓臉 (a chubby round face), 很大的紅蘋果 (a big red apple). When both attributives are adjectives, those that describe colors follow other kinds of adjectives, e.g., 大紅蘋果 (a big red apple), 小白兔 (a small white bunny).

2. "是" indicating emphasis or confirmation :

In Chinese when an adjective serves as the predicate of the sentence, the verb "是" is not required. Only when one wishes to emphasize a fact, does one use "是" before the adjective. When speaking, the verb "是" should be stressed. For instance,

(1) A：今天天氣不錯。

今天天气不错。

The weather today is rather nice.

B：今天天氣是不錯，咱們出去玩玩吧？

今天天气是不错，咱们出去玩玩吧？

The weather today *is* rather nice. Let's go out and play.

(2) 你剛才說現在男女不平等。對，現在男女是還不夠平等，可是已經比從前好多了。

你刚才说现在男女不平等。对，现在男女是还不够平等，可是已经比从前好多了。

You just said that men and women are not equal today. You're right. There *is* gender inequity today, but it's much better than before.

(3) A：這個女孩鋼琴彈得真好。

这个女孩钢琴弹得真好。

This girl plays the piano really well.

B：她鋼琴彈得是好，連我都被她吸引住了。

她钢琴弹得是好，连我都被她吸引住了。

She does play the piano well. Even I was captivated by her music.

3. "V＋不／得＋起"：

The pattern "V＋不／得＋起" is used to mean whether one can afford the money or time. For example,

(1) 戲票太貴，我買不起。

戏票太贵，我买不起。

The tickets to the play are too expensive. I can't afford them.

(2) 多穿點兒，別生病了。我們沒保險，看不起病。

多穿点儿，别生病了。我们没保险，看不起病。

Put on more clothes. Don't get sick. We don't have health insurance. We cannot afford to see the doctor.

(3) 那家飯館的菜貴得不得了，咱們吃不起。

那家饭馆的菜贵得不得了，咱们吃不起。

That restaurant is impossibly expensive. We can't afford to eat there.

(4) 我每天那麼忙，你讓我陪你去看電影，我可陪不起。

我每天那么忙，你让我陪你去看电影，我可陪不起。

I'm very busy everyday. I can't afford the time to go to the movies with you, even if you did ask me.

4. Modal Verb " 會 " :

The modal verb "會" has several meanings.　One common meaning is "to be able to do something after learning."　For instance, "我會說漢語" (I can speak Chinese.); "你會開車嗎？" (Can you drive?); "我妹妹不會游泳" (My sister doesn't know how to swim.)

In this lesson, "會" indicates future probability.　For example,

(1) A：我沒有錢了，你說我跟小王借，他會借給我嗎？

我没有钱了，你说我跟小王借，他会借给我吗？

I don't have any money left. Do you think Xiao Wang would lend some to me if I asked him?

B：我想他會借給你。

我想他会借给你。

I think he would.

(2) A：飛機是九點的，現在走會晚嗎？

飞机是九点的，现在走会晚吗？

The plane is scheduled for take-off at nine o'clock.　Is it too late to leave now?

B：別著急，不會晚。

别着急，不会晚。

Don't worry.　(We) won't be late.

5. " 畢竟 (到底、究竟) " :

The adverbs "畢竟" and "到底" are similar in usage. When they are used to mean "after all, in the final analysis" or to emphasize the cause or special characteristics of something, "究竟" and "到底" are interchangeable. For instance,

(1) 你畢竟在家裏常常聽父母說中文，學中文比我容易多了。

你毕竟在家里常常听父母说中文，学中文比我容易多了。

After all, you hear your parents speak Chinese at home. For you learning Chinese is much easier than it is for me.

(2) 媽媽畢竟是媽媽，永遠會愛自己的孩子的。

妈妈毕竟是妈妈，永远会爱自己的孩子的。

A mom is a mom, after all. She will always love her children.

(3) 現在畢竟是春天了，天氣無論多冷，也跟冬天不一樣。

现在毕竟是春天了，天气无论多冷，也跟冬天不一样。

After all, it's spring now. No matter how cold it is, it's not the same as winter.

6. Using "不如" to make comparisons:

"不如" can be used to compare. For example,

(1) 今天的天氣不如昨天。

今天的天气不如昨天。

Today's weather is not as good as yesterday's weather.

(2) 他覺得美國的健康保險制度不如加拿大好。

他觉得美国的健康保险制度不如加拿大好。

He feels that the American health insurance system is not as good as Canada's.

(3) 這部電影不如昨天看的那部有意思。

這部电影不如昨天看的那部有意思。

This film is not as interesting as the one we saw yesterday.

NB:

A: When using "不如," one can omit the adjective "好," as in (1).

B: The adjectives used in this kind of sentence are usually "positive," for instance, 好 (good), 大 (big), 長 (long), 厚 (thick), 重 (heavy), 亮 (bright), rather than their opposites, 壞 (bad), 小 (small), 短 (short), 薄 (thin), 輕 (light), and 暗 (dark).

(4) 我的功課不如他。

我的功课不如他。

My grades are not as good as his.

(5) 你的指導教授不如我的指導教授負責任。

你的指导教授不如我的指导教授负责任。

Your advisor is not as responsible as mine.

(6) 打字機不如電腦方便。

打字机不如电脑方便。

Typewriters are not as convenient as computers.

This form is similar to the "沒有" form, but "不如" is complete by itself. See (1). It means "not as good as..."

We can also use "不比" to make comparisons. We should note that:
First, when we use "不比," it is usually to contradict someone else's opinion. Usually, there is a previous use of "比." For example,

(7) **A**： 我姐姐比你高。

我姐姐比你高。

My sister is taller than you.

B： 不，你姐姐不比我高。

不，你姐姐不比我高。

No, your sister is no taller than I.

(8) A：日文比中文難。

日文比中文难。

Japanese is more difficult to learn than Chinese.

B：我覺得日文不比中文難。

我觉得日文不比中文难。

I don't think that Japanese is any more difficult to learn than Chinese.

Secondly, "沒有" and "不比" have slightly different meanings. For instance,

(9) 我姐姐沒有你高。

我姐姐没有你高。

My sister is not as tall as you.
(=You're taller than my sister.)

我姐姐不比你高。

我姐姐不比你高。

My sister is no taller than you.
(=You are taller than my sister or my sister is as tall as you.)

When making comparisons, we can often omit some words and phrases, such as (1), (2), (4), etc.

7. Reduplication of Measure Words:

Measure words can be reduplicated to suggest all-inclusiveness or the lack of exceptions to the rule. A few nouns like "人," "年," "天" can also be reduplicated. For instance,

(1) 今天過年，人人都很高興。

今天过年，人人都很高兴。

Today is New Year. Everybody is very happy.

(2) 我們班的學生，雖然個個都很聰明，可是都很懶。

我们班的学生，虽然个个都很聪明，可是都很懒。

Although every student in our class is smart, they are not very hardworking.

(3) 他頓頓都吃魚。

他顿顿都吃鱼。

He eats fish for every meal.

NB:

A: The word "每" differs from reduplicated measure words. "每" implies entirety, but also the individual members within it.

(4) 端午節的時候，家家都吃粽子。

端午节的时候，家家都吃粽子。

During the Dragon Boat Festival, every family eats dumplings.
[Entirety made up of individual members]

端午節的時候，每家都吃粽子。

端午节的时候，每家都吃粽子。

During the Dragon Boat Festival, every family eats dumplings.
[Entirety made up of individual members]

(5) 我們姐妹三人，每個人的興趣不同。

我们姐妹三人，每个人的兴趣不同。

Each one of us three sisters has her own interests.
[Individuals within a group]

Incorrect: 我們姐妹三人，人人的興趣不同。

我们姐妹三人，人人的兴趣不同。

B: Unlike "每," reduplicated measure words generally cannot modify the object or serve as the object. Compare,

(6) 你要把信寄給班上每一個人。

你要把信寄给班上每一个人。

You must send a letter to everyone in our class.

Incorrect：你要把信寄給班上人人。

你要把信寄给班上人人。

(7) 請你把信送到每一家的門口。

请你把信送到每一家的门口。

Please deliver the letter to each family's doorway.

Incorrect：請你把信送到家家的門口。

请你把信送到家家的门口。

四·詞語練習

1. " 加上 " (in addition)：

Example：她不願意等，加上她聽說我們學校醫院的心臟科很有名，所以決定來這兒做手術。

她不愿意等，加上她听说我们学校医院的心脏科很有名，所以决定来这儿做手术。

(1) 林先生跟林太太賺的錢都很多，＿＿＿＿＿＿＿＿＿。
兩個人日子過得很舒服。　　　　　（他們沒有孩子）

林先生跟林太太赚的钱都很多，＿＿＿＿＿＿＿＿＿。
两个人日子过得很舒服。　　　　　（他们没有孩子）

(2) 他平常營養過剩，又不運動，＿＿＿＿＿＿＿＿，大
家都很擔心他的身體健康。　　　（還有心臟病）

他平常营养过剩，又不运动，＿＿＿＿＿＿＿＿，大
家都很担心他的身体健康。　　　（还有心脏病）

(3) 張太太先生去世了，＿＿＿＿＿＿＿＿，一個人在家
實在太寂寞了。（孩子都出國了）

张太太先生去世了，＿＿＿＿＿＿＿＿，一个人在家
实在太寂寞了。（孩子都出国了）

2. " 至少 " (at least) :

    Example: 在加拿大至少你不必擔心付不起醫療費。

            在加拿大至少你不必担心付不起医疗费。

    (1)他做事雖然做得很慢，＿＿＿＿＿＿，比你只說不做好。

       （他在做）

      他做事虽然做得很慢，＿＿＿＿＿＿，比你只说不做好。

       （他在做）

    (2)雖然社會上還有許多男女不平等的現象，但是

      ＿＿＿＿＿＿＿＿。（比以前好多了）

      虽然社会上还有许多男女不平等的现象，但是

      ＿＿＿＿＿＿＿＿。（比以前好多了）

    (3)這次考試他雖然考得不太好，但是＿＿＿＿＿＿。

      （他復習了）

      这次考试他虽然考得不太好，但是＿＿＿＿＿＿。

      （他复习了）

3. " 毫無 " (none whatsoever) :

    Example: 如果你沒有錢的話，藥無論多好，對你也是毫無意義的。

            如果你没有钱的话，药无论多好，对你也是毫无意义的。

    (1)她的女兒不上學，也不工作，但是他＿＿＿＿。（辦法）

      她的女儿不上学，也不工作，但是他＿＿＿＿。（办法）

    (2)我們已經離婚了，他跟我之間＿＿＿＿＿＿。（關係）

      我们已经离婚了，他跟我之间＿＿＿＿＿＿。（关系）

    (3)他大學剛畢業，也沒實習過，＿＿＿＿＿＿。（工作經驗）

      他大学刚毕业，也没实习过，＿＿＿＿＿＿。（工作经验）

301

4. “(沒)有”＋N＋“可”＋V：

Example: 可是你也得讓製藥公司有錢可賺哪！

可是你也得让製药公司有钱可赚哪！

(1) 你不是閒著沒事嗎？咱們明天搬家，這樣就＿＿＿＿＿＿。

（有事）

你不是闲着没事吗？咱们明天搬家，这样就＿＿＿＿＿。

（有事）

(2) 他們的看法太不同了，坐在一起＿＿＿＿＿＿＿。

（沒有話）

他们的看法太不同了，坐在一起＿＿＿＿＿＿＿。

（没有话）

(3) 陳教授今天晚上請我們吃飯，這下子我們＿＿＿＿＿＿。

（有飯）

陈教授今天晚上请我们吃饭，这下子我们＿＿＿＿＿＿。

（有饭）

5. “只有...，才...”：

Example: 只有營養均衡，才能保證身體健康。

只有营养均衡，才能保证身体健康。

(1) 這個問題只有你的教授同意了，才能＿＿＿＿＿。

这个问题只有你的教授同意了，才能＿＿＿＿＿。

(2) 在美國只有買了保險才＿＿＿＿＿＿＿＿。

在美国只有买了保险才＿＿＿＿＿＿＿＿。

(3) 這幾年工作不容易找，只有念電腦或者工程技術才

＿＿＿＿＿＿＿＿＿。

这几年工作不容易找，只有念电脑或者工程技术才

＿＿＿＿＿＿＿＿＿。

五·看圖說話

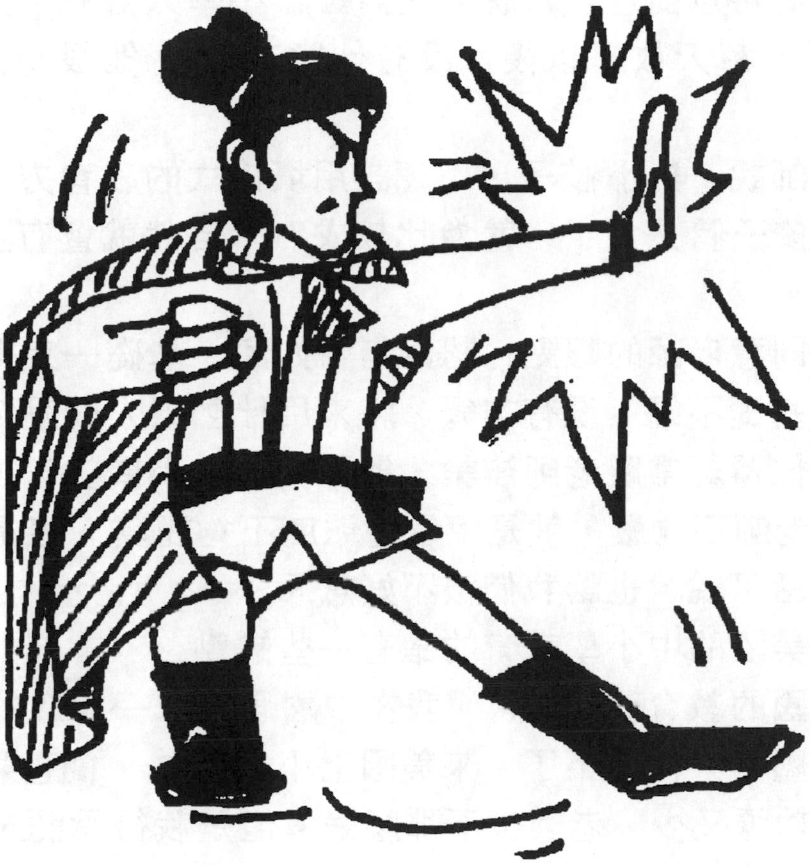

第十七課　教　育

一・課　文

（一）對　話

張天明：　姐姐，記得以前爸爸常說，在美國念小學太舒服，太輕鬆了，每天放學以後都沒有什麼功課，他很不以爲然。

張天星：　可是老師說，對小孩子，不應該用填鴨式的教育方式。等孩子們長大了，就會比較成熟，自然就會有上進心了。

張天明：　爸爸不同意老師的觀點，認爲無論如何，基礎一定得打好。基礎不好，沒有本領，將來用什麼跟人競爭？

張天星：　對了，他還經常跟老師辯論，批評美國的小學教育，不是說老師不夠嚴，就是說學生態度不夠認真。害得老師無話可說，也讓我們很不好意思。

張天明：　我覺得美國的中小學教育的確有一些缺點。

張天星：　但是中國的教育也有問題。我在中國念小學一年級的時候，壓力大得受不了。來美國上小學以後，簡直樂壞了，功課又少，老師也不那麼嚴。但是我得承認，要是沒有爸爸媽媽的督促，只靠在學校學的東西，我上學不會這麼順利。

張天明：　美國的教育重視讓孩子自由發展，發揮孩子的想像力。但是這樣的教育方式並不適合每個孩子。有的孩子不夠自覺，需要老師的指導，要不然很快就會被淘汰。

第十七课　教 育

一·课文

（一）对 话

张天明：　姐姐，记得以前爸爸常说，在美国念小学太舒服，太轻松了，每天放学以后都没有什么功课，他很不以为然。

张天星：　可是老师说，对小孩子，不应该用填鸭式的教育方式。等孩子们长大了，就会比较成熟，自然就会有上进心了。

张天明：　爸爸不同意老师的观点，认为无论如何，基础一定得打好。基础不好，没有本领，将来用什么跟人竞争？

张天星：　对了，他还经常跟老师辩论，批评美国的小学教育，不是说老师不够严，就是说学生态度不够认真。害得老师无话可说，也让我们很不好意思。

张天明：　我觉得美国的中小学教育的确有一些缺点。

张天星：　但是中国的教育也有问题。我在中国念小学一年级的时候，压力大得受不了。来美国上小学以后，简直乐坏了，功课又少，老师也不那么严。但是我得承认，要是没有爸爸妈妈的督促，只靠在学校学的东西，我上学不会这么顺利。

张天明：　美国的教育重视让孩子自由发展，发挥孩子的想像力。但是这样的教育方式并不适合每个孩子。有的孩子不够自觉，需要老师的指导，要不然很快就会被淘汰。

張天星：　可是中國的教育走另一個極端，從來不考慮學生的
　　　　　特點，對每個學生的要求都一樣，加上升學的壓
　　　　　力，使許多學生變成考試機器，只會死讀書。

張天明：　看來這兩種教育方式各有優缺點。

張天星：　以前我不懂，爲什麼爸爸媽媽每天都讓我們做那麼多
　　　　　的數學習題，現在才理解他們的苦心。

張天明：　中國人說，"望子成龍，望女成鳳"，咱們的父母爲
　　　　　了子女的教育，實在是用心良苦啊。

张天星： 可是中国的教育走另一个极端，从来不考虑学生
的特点，对每个学生的要求都一样，加上升学的压
力，使许多学生变成考试机器，只会死读书。

张天明： 看来这两种教育方式各有优缺点。

张天星： 以前我不懂，为什么爸爸妈妈每天都让我们做那么多
的数学习题，现在才理解他们的苦心。

张天明： 中国人说，"望子成龙，望女成凤"，咱们的父母为
了子女的教育，实在是用心良苦啊。

（二）閱　讀

　　在中國，學生負擔很重。白天上學，晚上還得上補習班或者請家庭教師，連週末都不能休息。中國的教育目標及方式與美國十分不同。在中國，"升學是教學的指揮棒"，教學總是隨著升學考試走。老師強調死記硬背。家庭作業更是壓得人喘不過氣來。但是學生"尊師重道"，即使有意見也不敢提。在美國，一般來說，老師重視自由發展。強調啟發式教育，鼓勵學生多思考，也很少留家庭作業。許多從中國移民到美國來的家長，以為美式教育能給孩子一個自由、快樂的童年。可是看著孩子放學回家沒什麼功課，他們就擔心孩子的基礎打不好，將來無法跟別人競爭。這時候，他們又想起中國的教育方式來了。

（二）阅 读

　　在中国，学生负担很重。白天上学，晚上还得上补习班或者请家庭教师，连周末都不能休息。中国的教育目标及方式与美国十分不同。在中国，"升学是教学的指挥棒"，教学总是随着升学考试走。老师强调死记硬背。家庭作业更是压得人喘不过气来。但是学生"尊师重道"，即使有意见也不敢提。在美国，一般来说，老师重视自由发展。强调启发式教育，鼓励学生多思考，也很少留家庭作业。许多从中国移民到美国来的家长，以为美式教育能给孩子一个自由、快乐的童年。可是看着孩子放学回家没什么功课，他们就担心孩子的基础打不好，将来无法跟别人竞争。这时候，他们又想起中国的教育方式来了。

二 · 生詞表

輕鬆	轻松	adj	qīngsōng	relaxed

他每天工作六小時，很輕鬆。

我妹妹很輕鬆地考上了理想的大學。

不以為然	不以为然		bù yǐ wéi rán	object to; disapprove
填鴨式	填鸭式		tiányāshì	cramming method (of teaching)
方式		n	fāngshì	method
成熟		adj	chéngshú	mature
自然		adj/adv	zìrán	naturally
上進心	上进心		shàngjìn xīn	the desire to be better
觀點	观点	n	guāndiǎn	point of view
無論如何	无论如何		wúlùn rúhé	under any circumstance
打基礎	打基础	vo	dǎ jīchǔ	establish foundation
本領	本领	n	běnlǐng	skill; capability
將來*	将来		jiānglái	in the future
競爭	竞争	v	jìngzhēng	compete

在這個學校裏，孩子競爭得很厲害。

一個人應該有競爭精神。

辯論	辩论	v	biànlùn	debate; argue

我們明天辯論男女平等的問題。

你說話沒有道理，我不跟你辯論了。

311

批評	批评	v	pīpíng	criticize
				今天老師批評我學習不認真。
嚴	严	adj	yán	strict
態度	态度	n	tàidù	attitude
				他做什麼事態度都很認真。
認真	认真	adj	rènzhēn	serious; earnest
害得		v	hàide	do harm to; cause trouble to
的確	的确	adv	díquè	indeed; really
缺點	缺点	n	quēdiǎn	shortcoming
小學	小学	n	xiǎoxué	elementary school
壓力	压力	n	yālì	pressure
簡直	简直	adv	jiǎnzhí	simply
樂壞了	乐坏了	vc	lè huài le	thrilled to pieces
承認	承认	v	chéngrèn	admit
				他跟父母承認自己錯了。
				你打了他，怎麼不承認？
督促		v	dūcù	supervise and urge
上學	上学	vo	shàngxué	go to school
重視	重视	v	zhòngshì	pay attention to; attach importance to
發揮	发挥	v	fāhuī	give free rein to
想像力	想象力	n	xiǎngxiànglì	imagination
適合	适合	v	shìhé	suit; fit
自覺	自觉	adj	zìjué	self-motivated
淘汰		v	táotài	eliminate through selection or competition

極端	极端	n	jíduān	extreme
特點	特点	n	tèdiǎn	distinguishing feature
要求		v	yāoqiú	demand
變成	变成	vc	biàn	change into
機器	机器	n	jīqì	machine; machinery
讀書	读书	v	dú shū	study; read
看來	看来		kànlái	appear; seem
優點	优点	n	yōudiǎn	merit; advantage
數學	数学	n	shùxué	mathematics
習題	习题	n	xítí	exercises
理解		v	lǐjiě	understand; comprehend

你女朋友跟你吵架了，
你心情不好，我能理解。

這個孩子的理解力很強。

苦心		n	kǔxīn	painstaking efforts
望子成龍	望子成龙		wàng zǐ chéng lóng	(lit.) hope for one's son to become a dragon; hope for one's son to be very successful
望女成鳳	望女成凤		wang nǚ chéng fèng	(lit.) hope for one's daughter to become a phoenix; hope for one's daughter to be very successful
子女		n	zǐnǚ	(one's) children
用心良苦			yòngxīn liángkǔ	have really given much thought to the matter
負擔	负担	n	fùdān	burden; load
白天		n	báitian	daytime
補習班	补习班	n	bǔxí bān	"cram" school
家庭教師	家庭教师		jiātíng jiàoshī	private tutor

休息		v	xiūxi	rest
目標	目标	n	mùbiāo	goal
及		conj	jí	(formal) and
教學	教学	v	jiàoxué	teaching; education
指揮棒	指挥棒	n	zhǐhuī bàng	conductor's baton
強調	强调	v	qiángdiào	stress; emphasize
死記硬背	死记硬背		sǐ jì yìng bèi	mechanical memorizing
作業	作业	n	zuòyè	homework
喘氣	喘气	v	chuǎn qì	gasp
尊師重道	尊师重道		zūn shī zhòng dào	respect the teacher and attach importance to the Way
一般來説	一般来说		yìbān lái shuō	generally speaking
啓發	启发	v	qǐfā	enlighten; inspire
鼓勵	鼓励	v	gǔlì	encourage
思考		v	sīkǎo	think about; ponder
留		v	liú	leave (a note, homework, etc.)
童年		n	tóngnián	childhood
無法	无法		wúfǎ	沒有辦法

難寫的字：

鬆 礎 將 辯 嚴 壓 壞

優 數 望 龍 鳳 尊 勵

三 · 語法註釋　Grammar Notes

1. "很不以為然":

"不以爲然" means "do not approve." "很" modifies "不以爲然." "很不以爲然"
"do not approve at all." However, in mainland China "不以爲然" has acquired a new
meaning in recent years, i.e, "to shrugg off." For example, "his mother told him children
shouldn't smoke. He just shrugged off (her remark.)." In this lesson, the expression is
used in the first sense.

2. "簡直":

"簡直" is used to exaggerate. It means "almost" or "almost completely." For
instance,

(1) 他們結婚才半年就要離婚，我簡直不能相信。

他们结婚才半年就要离婚，我简直不能相信。

I simply couldn't believe that they wanted to get a divoice after having been
married for only six months.
(=I almost couldn't believe it, but did.)

(2) 他居然做這樣的事，簡直不是一個人。

他居然做这样的事，简直不是一个人。

I can't believe that he actually did this. He's not a human being at all.

(3) 他減肥以後，我簡直認不出他來了。

他减肥以后，我简直认不出他来了。

After he lost some weight, I could hardly recognize him.

3. "V + 壞 + 了" indicating degree:

"壞" can be used after verbs to indicate an extreme degree, for instance, "急壞了" (worried sick,) "餓壞了" (starved to death,) "累壞了" (utterly exhausted,) "氣壞了" (really mad,) "樂壞了" (tickled to death.)

4. "適合" and "合適" compared:

"適合" is a verb. It must be followed by an object. "合適," on the other hand, is an adjective. It cannot take an object.

(1) 這件衣服不適合你穿，你媽媽穿可能合適。

這件衣服不适合你穿，你妈妈穿可能合适。

This jacket does not suit you. It might be suitable for your mom.

(2) 這種家俱適合家裏用，放在辦公室不合適。

这种家具适合家里用，放在办公室不合适。

This kind of furniture suits homes [more]. It's not suitable to be put in offices.

(3) 你跟父母這樣説話很不合適，應該向他們道歉。

你跟父母这样说话很不合适，应该向他们道歉。

The way you talked to your parents was really inappropriate. You should apologize to them.

(4) 這個專業不適合你，你還是選別的專業吧。

这个专业不适合你，你还是选别的专业吧。

This major does not suit you. You'd better pick another major.

5. "被" structure：

In Chinese, one does not need to use any specific word to indicate passivity. For example,

(1) 水果都吃完了，該去買了。

水果都吃完了，该去买了。

There's no fruit left. [We] should get some more.

(2) 功課做錯了，他只好再做一次。

功课做错了，他只好再做一次。

He screwed up his homework. He had to do it again.

(3) 房子租好了，明天就可以搬家了。

房子租好了，明天就可以搬家了。

The apartment is already rented. [We, you] can move in tomorrow.

In the above sentences, "水果," "功課," and "房子" are all objects of the actions. In other words, these sentences all express the idea of passivity even though no words such as "被," "叫," and "讓" are used. In fact, one cannot use "被," "叫" or "讓" in these sentences.

Generally speaking, these prepositions are used to signify that something unpleasant happened to a person or that something was lost.

(1) 屈原被楚國國王趕到南方去了。

屈原被楚国国王赶到南方去了。

The Lord of Chu expelled Quyuan to the South.
(lit. Quyuan was expelled to the South by the Lord of Chu.)

(2) 書叫郵局寄丟了。

书叫邮局寄丢了。

The post office lost the book. (lit. The book was lost by the post office.)

(3) 他讓爸爸打了一頓。

他让爸爸打了一顿。

He got a beating from his dad. (lit. He was beaten by his father.)

But one can say:

(4) 王朋被同學選爲班長。

王朋被同学选为班长。

Wang Peng was elected the class president by his classmates.

(5) 哥哥被派到國外去了。

哥哥被派到国外去了。

[My] brother was sent abroad.

Only a limited number of verbs can be used in this way.

6. "從來":

"從來" means "unchanged from the past to the present." It is often used in negative sentences for emphasis:

(1) A：我的作業是不是你拿去了？

我的作业是不是你拿去了？

Did you take my homework?

B：沒有啊，我從來不拿你的東西。

没有啊，我从来不拿你的东西。

No, I didn't. I never touch your stuff.

(2) 這件事情我從來沒聽説過。

这件事情我从来没听说过。

I have never heard of this matter.

(3) 我跟我的哥哥從來沒有在一起打過球。

我跟我的哥哥从来没有在一起打过球。

I've never played ball with my brother.

"從來" can also be used in affirmative sentences, and is often followed by "都是," "是."

(1) 這個人從來都是這樣，見到人不愛打招呼。

这个人从来都是这样，见到人不爱打招呼。

This guy is always like this, rather offish.

(2) 他從來是看別人怎麼做，他就怎麼做。

他从来是看别人怎么做，他就怎么做。

He always watches what others do and follows suit.

四·詞語練習

1. “ 自然 ” (naturally)：

Example：等孩子們長大了，就會比較成熟，自然就會有上進心了。

等孩子们长大了，就会比较成熟，自然就会有上进心了。

(1) A：我學中文的時候很注意發音，可是還是說得不標準。我的發音怎麼才能進步呢？

我学中文的时候很注意发音，可是还是说得不标准。我的发音怎么才能进步呢？

B：你多聽錄音，說話的時候多注意，發音_____。

(好)

你多听录音，说话的时候多注意，发音_____。

(好)

(2) 有的人認為感冒不用上醫院，一個星期以後

_____。(好)

有的人认为感冒不用上医院，一个星期以后

_____。(好)

(3) 沒有孩子的人＿＿＿＿＿＿＿＿＿＿＿＿＿＿＿＿。

（不知道教育好一個孩子有多麼不容易）

沒有孩子的人＿＿＿＿＿＿＿＿＿＿＿＿＿＿＿＿。

（不知道教育好一个孩子有多么不容易）

2. "不是...，就是..." (if not A, then B) :

Example: 不是說老師不夠嚴，就是說學生態度不夠認真。

不是说老师不够严，就是说学生态度不够认真。

(1) 我週末不是＿＿＿＿，就是＿＿＿＿，一點也不能休息。

我周末不是＿＿＿＿，就是＿＿＿＿，一点也不能休息。

(2) 來參加晚會的不是＿＿＿＿＿，就是＿＿＿＿＿，他都認識。

来参加晚会的不是＿＿＿＿＿，就是＿＿＿＿＿，他都认识。

(3) A：你們常常去飯館吃飯嗎？

你们常常去饭馆吃饭吗？

B：不，我們不是＿＿＿＿＿，就是＿＿＿＿＿，不去飯館
吃飯。

不，我们不是＿＿＿＿＿，就是＿＿＿＿＿，不去饭馆
吃饭。

3. "害得" (make [used in a negative context]) :

Example: 他還常常跟老師辯論，批評美國的小學教育，不是
說老師不夠嚴，就是說學生不夠認真。害得老師無
話可說，也讓我們很不好意思。

他还常常跟老师辩论，批评美国的小学教育，不是
说老师不够严，就是说学生不够认真。害得老师无
话可说，也让我们很不好意思。

(1) 你昨天回來那麼晚也不打一個電話回來，

＿＿＿＿＿＿＿＿＿＿＿。

（我等你等到夜裏兩點都不能睡覺）

你昨天回来那么晚也不打一个电话回来，

_____。

（我等你等到夜裏兩点都不能睡觉）

(2)他老愛開玩笑，_____。

（別人不知道他什麼時候說的是真的，什麼時候說
的是假的）

他老愛开玩笑，_____。

（別人不知道他什么时候说的是真的，什么时候说
的是假的）

(3)張天明隔壁的同學看球賽的時候老大喊大叫，

_____。

（學習受影響）

张天明隔壁的同学看球赛的时候老大喊大叫，

_____。

（学习受影响）

4. "**的確**" (truly)：

Example:我覺得美國的中小學教育的確有一些缺點。

我觉得美国的中小学教育的确有一些缺点。

(1)學生：老師，這一課課文太難了，我看了好幾次還是
不懂。

学生：老师，这一课课文太难了，我看了好几次还是
不懂。

老師：這一課課文_____。不過你要是把那幾個長
句子看懂了，整個課文也就懂了。

老师：这一课课文_____。不过你要是把那几个长
句子看懂了，整个课文也就懂了。

(2) 人們都説南京的中山陵很壯觀，我去年去那兒旅行，
發現中山陵_____。

人们都说南京的中山陵很壮观，我去年去那儿旅行，
发现中山陵_____。

(3) 你説這本書很有意思，_____，我看得都不想吃
飯，不想睡覺了。

你说这本书很有意思，_____，我看得都不想吃
饭，不想睡觉了。

5. "**看來**" (seem)：

Example: 看来這兩種教育方式各有優缺點。

看来这两种教育方式各有优缺点。

(1) 外邊雨下得這麼大，_____。
(今天不能去公園看紅葉了)

外边雨下得这麼大，_____。
(今天不能去公园看红叶了)

(2) 你上課一點精神也沒有，_____。
(昨天你沒睡好覺)

你上课一点精神也没有，_____。
(昨天你没睡好觉)

(3) 這個學期都過去三分之二了，我們才學了六課，
_____。(這本書學不完了)

这个学期都过去三分之二了，我们才学了六课，
_____。(这本书学不完了)

6. " 即使...也 " (even if):

　　Example: 但是學生 " 尊師重道 " ，即使有意見也不敢提。

　　　　　　但是学生 " 尊师重道 " ，即使有意见也不敢提。

(1) 那個電影故事很簡單，＿＿＿＿＿＿＿＿＿＿＿＿＿＿＿。

　　　　　　　　　　　　（不會英文的人）

　　 那个电影故事很简单，＿＿＿＿＿＿＿＿＿＿＿＿＿＿。

　　　　　　　　　　　　（不会英文的人）

(2) 中國的名勝古蹟太多了，＿＿＿＿＿＿＿＿＿＿＿。（一年）

　　 中国的名胜古迹太多了，＿＿＿＿＿＿＿＿＿＿＿。（一年）

(3) 他明年要考大學，壓力很大，＿＿＿＿＿＿＿＿＿。（週末）

　　 他明年要考大学，压力很大，＿＿＿＿＿＿＿＿＿。（周末）

五·看圖說話

第十八課 槍枝與犯罪

一. 課文

（一）對 話

約　翰：　這枝槍是誰的？張天明，槍是你的嗎？

張天明：　對，是我的。這是我給我哥哥買的生日禮物。他喜歡打獵。

約　翰：　你把槍放好，別亂放，不然太危險了。我們這兒進進出出的人那麼多，萬一不小心，槍走了火怎麼辦？

第十八课 枪枝与犯罪

一. 课文

（一）对 话

约　翰：　这枝枪是谁的？张天明，枪是你的吗？

张天明：　对，是我的。这是我给我哥哥买的生日礼物。他喜欢打猎。

约　翰：　你把枪放好，别乱放，不然太危险了。我们这儿进进出出的人那么多，万一不小心，枪走了火怎么办？

張天明：　你緊張什麼！我馬上把槍收好，行了吧？

約　翰：　我只是讓你小心點兒。

張天明：　我知道。

約　翰：　你也會用槍嗎？

張天明：　會，我是跟我哥哥學的。你呢？

約　翰：　我不會。槍這東西我連碰都不想碰。我爸爸有三枝槍，我媽和我常為這件事跟我爸爸吵架。那麼多人有槍，買槍那麼容易，我們這個社會簡直快沒有理智了！我看世界上沒有哪個國家的人像美國人這麼愛舞刀弄槍的。

張天明：　正因為那麼多人有槍，你也得有槍保護自己啊。萬一出了什麼事，你還等著警察來救你的命？

約　翰：　如果警察不夠，我們可以要求政府多僱一些警察呀。你不是不知道，有很多罪犯，前腳出了監獄，後腳就進槍店，買了槍就到處殺人。槍店也不查買槍的是什麼人，不管他是不是殺過人放過火，腦子正常不正常，只要給錢，他們就賣。

張天明：　你別這麼說，已經有法律規定，賣槍的時候一定要調查買槍人的背景。

約　翰：　算了吧，有幾個槍店會認真執行這些法律？槍這種東西應該全面禁止，私人不應該有槍，電視上也應禁止播賣槍的廣告。

張天明：　美國人可以買槍來保護自己，這和言論自由、集會自由一樣，是憲法保障的權利，不應該受到限制。難道你願意像羔羊一樣任人宰割嗎？

张天明：你紧张什么！我马上把枪收好，行了吧？

约　翰：我只是让你小心点儿。

张天明：我知道。

约　翰：你也会用枪吗？

张天明：会，我是跟我哥哥学的。你呢？

约　翰：我不会。枪这东西我连碰都不想碰。我爸爸有三枝枪，我妈和我常为这件事跟我爸爸吵架。那么多人有枪，买枪那么容易，我们这个社会简直快没有理智了！我看世界上没有哪个国家的人像美国人这么爱舞刀弄枪的。

张天明：正因为那么多人有枪，你也得有枪保护自己啊。万一出了什么事，你还等着警察来救你的命？

约　翰：如果警察不够，我们可以要求政府多雇一些警察呀。你不是不知道，有很多罪犯，前脚出了监狱，后脚就进枪店，买了枪就到处杀人。枪店也不查买枪的是什么人，不管他是不是杀过人放过火，脑子正常不正常，只要给钱，他们就卖。

张天明：你别这么说，已经有法律规定，卖枪的时候一定要调查买枪人的背景。

约　翰：算了吧，有几个枪店会认真执行这些法律？枪这种东西应该全面禁止，私人不应该有枪，电视上也应禁止播卖枪的广告。

张天明：美国人可以买枪来保护自己，这和言论自由、集会自由一样，是宪法保障的权利，不应该受到限制。难道你愿意像羔羊一样任人宰割吗？

（二）閱　讀

　　一九四九年以後，中國禁止賭博和販賣毒品，並取締妓女，打擊偷竊搶劫。中國政府通過強制教育等各種手段，使毒品、妓女在中國消失了，賭博的現象也基本上消滅了，偷竊、搶劫等犯罪也大大減少了。但是改革開放後，尤其是九十年代以來，中國的經濟發展得很快，各種社會問題也隨之產生。如貧富不均、價值觀念紊亂、經濟法規不健全等等。各種犯罪現象也開始出現了。不過總的來說，中國仍然是世界上犯罪率比較低的國家之一，基本上還是比較安全的。

（二）阅 读

    一九四九年以后，中国禁止赌博和贩卖毒品，并取缔妓女，打击偷窃抢劫。中国政府通过强制教育等各种手段，使毒品、妓女在中国消失了，赌博的现象也基本上消灭了，偷窃、抢劫等犯罪也大大减少了。但是改革开放后，尤其是九十年代以来，中国的经济发展得很快，各种社会问题也随之产生。如贫富不均、价值观念紊乱、经济法规不健全等等。各种犯罪现象也开始出现了。不过总的来说，中国仍然是世界上犯罪率比较低的国家之一，基本上还是比较安全的。

二‧生詞表

槍枝	枪枝	n	qiāngzhī	firearms
犯罪		v	fàn zuì	commit a crime
枝		m	zhī	measure word (for rifles, etc.)
槍	枪	n	qiāng	gun
打獵	打猎	v	dǎ liè	go hunting
亂放	乱放		luàn fàng	put (things) all over the place
不然			bùrán	otherwise
危險*	危险	adj/n	wēixiǎn	dangerous
小心*		adj	xiǎoxīn	careful
走火		v	zǒu huǒ	(of firearms) discharge accidentally
收好		vc	shōu hǎo	put things away in their proper places
碰		v	pèng	touch
理智		n/adj	lǐzhì	senses; reason

這個人到處殺人，簡直沒有理智了。

你應該理智一點兒，不要太激動。

舞刀弄槍	舞刀弄枪		wǔ dāo nòng qiāng	brandish swords and spears
正			zhèng	just; precise; precisely
保護	保护	v	bǎohù	protect
出事		vo	chū shì	have an accident
警察		n	jǐngchá	police
救命		v	jiù mìng	save someone's life

僱	雇	v	gù	hire; employ
罪犯		n	zuìfàn	criminal
監獄	监狱	n	jiānyù	jail; prison
到處	到处	adv	dàochù	at all places; everywhere
殺人	杀人	vo	shā rén	kill someone
查		v	chá	investigate; check
放火		v	fàng huǒ	set fire
腦子	脑子	n	nǎozi	brains; mind
正常		adj	zhèngcháng	normal

他的腦子有點兒不正常。

我認爲正常的人都會喜歡旅行。

只要		conj	zhǐyào	so long as
法律		n	fǎlǜ	law
規定		v/n	guīdìng	stipulate; stipulation
調查	调查	v	diào chá	investigate; check

那件事情正在調查，還沒有結果。

請你把調查結果告訴我。

執行	执行	v	zhíxíng	implement; execute
全面		adj	quánmiàn	comprehensive
禁止		v	jìnzhǐ	prohibit

禁止吸煙。

在美國禁止學生帶槍上學。

私人			sīrén	private individual
言論	言论	n	yánlùn	opinion on public affairs; speech

集會	集会	v	jíhuì	assemble
憲法	宪法	n	xiànfǎ	constitution
保障		v	bǎozhàng	ensure; safeguard
權利	权利	n	quánlì	right
受到		v	shòudào	receive (influence, restriction, etc.)
限制		n/v	xiànzhì	limit; restrict

這個國家婦女工作受到
很多限制。

填鴨式的教育限制兒童
想像力的發揮。

羔羊		n	gāoyáng	lamb
任人宰割			rèn rén zǎigē	allow oneself to be slaughtered, trampled upon
賭博	赌博	v	dǔbó	gamble
販賣	贩卖	v	fànmài	(derog.) traffic; sell
毒品		n	dúpǐn	narcotic drugs
並*	并		bìng	and; furthermore
取締	取缔	v	qǔdì	ban; suppress
妓女		n	jìnǚ	prostitute
打擊	打击	v	dǎjī	strike; attack
偷竊	偷窃	v	tōuqiè	steal; pilfer
搶劫	抢劫	v	qiǎngjié	rob; loot
通過	通过		tōngguò	through (a method)
強制		v	qiángzhì	coerce; compel
手段		n	shǒuduàn	means; method
消失		v	xiāoshī	disappear

基本上			jīběn shang	basically; fundamentally
消滅	消灭	v	xiāomiè	perish; die out
尤其是			yóuqí shì	particularly
經濟	经济	n/v	jīngjì	economy
隨之	随之		suí zhī	along with; in the wake of; 之 is a pronoun
產生	产生	v	chǎnshēng	give rise to
如			rú	such as; like
貧富不均	贫富不均		pín fù bù jūn	unequal distribution of wealth
價值觀念	价值观念		jiàzhí guānniàn	values and concepts
紊亂	紊乱	adj	wěnluàn	disorderly; chaotic
法規	法规	n	fǎguī	laws and regulations
健全		adj	jiànquán	(of laws, institutions) developed
仍然		adv	réngrán	still
率		n	lǜ	rate; proportion
低		adj	dī	low

難寫的字：

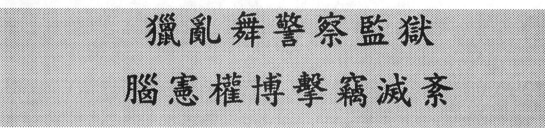

獵 亂 舞 警 察 監 獄
腦 憲 權 博 擊 竊 滅 紊

三·語法註釋 Grammar Notes

1. "槍走了火..." :

In colloquial Chinese, conjunctions are often omitted. The exact relationship between two clauses can only be determined from the context. For instance, in this sentence from the lesson, "我們這兒進進出出的人那麼多，萬一不小心，槍走了火怎麼辦," the conjunction "如果" or "要是" is left out. Therefore it is important to pay attention to this kind of sentence to figure out the relationship between the two clauses. Semantically, "走火" is one word. However, grammatically, it is two words. Words such as "了," "過," can be inserted in between. Similar words are "睡覺," "洗澡," "鞠躬," "跳舞," "唱歌," "見面" etc. Take care not to follow them up with an object or complement. For instance, it is incorrect to say, "我昨天見面他," or "今天晚上我要跳舞一會兒."

2. The Adverb "正" :

The adverb "正" can mean "it so happens, coincidentally, precisely." For instance,

(1) 學生： 老師，這個題我不會做，可以不做嗎？

學生： 老师，这个题我不会做，可以不做吗？

Laoshi, I don't know how to answer this question. Can I skip it?

老師： 正因為你不會做，才更應該做。不懂的地方可以問我。

老师： 正因为你不会做，才更应该做。不懂的地方可以问我。

Precisely because you don't know how to answer it, that's all the more reason that you should try. If there's something you don't understand, you can ask me.

(2) 今天正好我沒有事，我們出去看電影好嗎？

今天正好我没有事，我们出去看电影好吗？

I happen to be free today. Shall we go out and see a movie?

(3) A：這本書借我看看可以嗎？

　　　这本书借我看看可以吗？

　　　Could I borrow this book?

　 B：對不起，這本書我正在看，我看完了你再看吧。

　　　对不起，这本书我正在看，我看完了你再看吧。

　　　Sorry, I happen to be reading it. You can borrow it after I'm done.

3. Conjuction " 並 " :

The conjunction "並" means "in addition, furthermore." It is synonymous with "並且," and can connect two verbs or verbal phrases or two clauses. It is used primarily in written language. For instance,

(1) 昨天上課，老師帶我們念課文並講解了語法。

　　 昨天上课，老师带我们念课文并讲解了语法。

　　 Yesterday in class our teacher made us read aloud along with him. Moreover, he clarified the grammar.

(2) 最近報上報導中國的文章很多，其中有一篇介紹了
　　 中國經濟發展很快的原因，並指出了現有的問題。

　　 最近报上报导中国的文章很多，其中有一篇介绍了
　　 中国经济发展很快的原因，并指出了现有的问题。

　　 Recently, there have been many newspaper articles on China's economy. One of these talked about the reasons for the rapid development of China's economy and, in addition, pointed out the existing problems.

(3) 學校昨天開會，聽取學生提出的意見，並研究了解決的
　　 辦法。

　　 学校昨天开会，听取学生提出的意见，并研究了解决的
　　 办法。

　　 Yesterday the school had a meeting and heard students' complaints; in addition, they discussed ways of solving (the problems).

NB: In the above sentences, one cannot use "和 ."

4. "等(等)"：

"等" is used at the end of enumerative phrases. For instance,

(1) 參加討論會的有中國、美國、法國等三個國家。

參加讨论会的有中国、美国、法国等三个国家。

The conference participants came from China, America, and France.

(2) 奧林匹克運動會今天的比賽有籃球、游泳、跳水等等。

奥林匹克运动会今天的比赛有篮球、游泳、跳水等等。

Competition events at the Olympics today include basketball, swimming, diving, etc.

(3) 上半年我去了北京、上海、南京等五個城市。

上半年我去了北京、上海、南京等五個城市。

In the first six months of this year I went to five cities: Beijing, Shanghai, Nanjing, and so on.

The enumeration can be complete as in (1) or partial as in (3). "等" and "等等" are used interchangeably.

四·詞語練習

1. "萬一" (in case)：

Example: 萬一出了什麼事，你還等著警察來救你的命？

萬一出了什么事，你还等著警察来救你的命？

(1) 快走吧，＿＿＿＿＿＿＿，就不能參加考試了。(晚)

快走吧，＿＿＿＿＿＿＿，就不能参加考试了。(晚)

(2) A：她明天過生日，你送什麼禮物給她？

她明天过生日，你送什么礼物给她？

B：我打算買些化妝品送她。

我打算买些化妆品送她。

A：_____？（不喜歡）

_____？（不喜欢）

(3) _____，可不是開玩笑的。（槍走火）

_____，可不是开玩笑的。（枪走火）

2. " 只要 " (so long as)：

Example: 槍店也不查買槍的是什麼人，不管他是不是殺過人放過火，腦子正常不正常，只要給錢他們就賣。

枪店也不查买枪的是什么人，不管他是不是杀过人放过火，脑子正常不正常，只要给钱他们就卖。

(1) 吸毒是一件壞事，_____。

　　　　　　　　　　　　（腦子清楚的人）

吸毒是一件坏事，_____。

　　　　　　　　　　　　（脑子清楚的人）

(2) A：你明天去不去看電影？

你明天去不去看电影？

B：_____，我就去。（你去）

_____，我就去。（你去）

(3) _____，你的發音一定會越來越好。

　　（念課文）

_____，你的发音一定会越来越好。

　　（念课文）

3. “ **難道** ” (introducing a rhetorical queston: "Do you mean to say....? ") :

　　Example: 難道你願意像羔羊一樣任人宰割嗎？

　　　　　　难道你愿意像羔羊一样任人宰割吗？

　　(1) 他說好八點準時來，現在都快十點了，＿＿＿＿＿＿＿＿？

　　　　　　　　　　　　　　　　　　　　（在路上出了什麼事）

　　　　他说好八点准时来，现在都快十点了，＿＿＿＿＿＿＿＿？

　　　　　　　　　　　　　　　　　　　　（在路上出了什么事）

　　(2) 後天就要大考了，你怎麼還不開始準備，

　　　　＿＿＿＿＿＿＿＿？　（等到最後一秒鐘）

　　　　后天就要大考了，你怎么还不开始准备，

　　　　＿＿＿＿＿＿＿＿？　（等到最后一秒钟）

　　(3) 你跟老師說話這麼不客氣，＿＿＿連＿＿＿＿＿＿？

　　　　　　　　　　　　　　　　（不懂，“尊師重道”的道理）

　　　　你跟老师说话这么不客气，＿＿＿连＿＿＿＿＿＿？

　　　　　　　　　　　　　　　　（不懂，“尊师重道”的道理）

4. “ **通過** ” (through) :

　　Example: 政府通過強制教育等各種手段，使毒品、妓女在
　　　　　　　中國消失了。

　　　　　　政府通过强制教育等各种手段，使毒品、妓女在
　　　　　　中国消失了。

　　(1) ＿＿＿＿＿＿，張天明的電腦總算修好了。

　　　　（柯林的幫助）

　　　　＿＿＿＿＿＿，张天明的电脑总算修好了。

　　　　（柯林的帮助）

　　(2) ＿＿＿＿＿＿，我們對中國的文化有了更深的認識。

　　　　（這次旅行）

　　　　＿＿＿＿＿＿，我们对中国的文化有了更深的认识。

　　　　（这次旅行）

(3) _____，我的哥哥順利地寫完了他的論文。

　　（他的教授的指導）

　　_____，我的哥哥順利地写完了他的论文。

　　（他的教授的指导）

五‧看圖說話

第十九課 動物與人

一‧課文

（一）對 話

張天明： 你今天下午去哪兒了？我找了你半天都沒找到。

柯　林： 我到生物系抗議去了。

張天明： 抗議什麼？

柯　林： 校報說，生物系的一個教授爲了研究老年痴呆症，解剖猴腦，很多猴子就這樣死了，實在太可憐了，因此我們組織大家去生物系抗議。幾天前我們還去了紐

第十九课 动物与人

一·课文

（一）对 话

张天明： 你今天下午去哪儿了？我找了你半天都没找到。

柯　林： 我到生物系抗议去了。

张天明： 抗议什么？

柯　林： 校报说，生物系的一个教授为了研究老年痴呆症，解剖猴脑，很多猴子就这样死了，实在太可怜了，因此我们组织大家去生物系抗议。几天前我们还去了纽約，在幾家大的裘皮服裝店門前抗議，向他們的顧客扔雞蛋，剪她們的裘皮大衣。對了，還有幾個電影明星也跟我們一起抗議。後天我們準備去包圍生物系的動物房，你想去嗎？

張天明：　我沒空兒。我好不容易弄到兩張票，想找你後天一起去看全國大學籃球決賽。

柯　林：　那糟了，我已經說好要去包圍動物房了，只能犧牲這場球了。算了，你去找別人吧。

張天明：　你可別後悔啊！哎，柯林，你不覺得你們扔雞蛋，剪人家的裘皮大衣，包圍動物房，有點太過份了嗎？我同意，我們人對動物也應該講人道，但我覺得動物實驗是很有用的。很多藥只有通過動物實驗，才能知道對人是不是安全。

柯　林：　你這種想法是錯誤的。現在已經可以不通過動物實驗來做研究了。都快二十一世紀了，這麼虐待動物，實在是太野蠻，太不人道了！

張天明：　你的想法也太極端了。你不覺得人比動物更重要嗎？科學家也不是有意要虐待動物。讓那麼多人死於癌症、艾滋病，也不見得就人道。

柯　林：　你憑什麼說人比動物更重要？正是因為我們有這種想法，才去破壞大自然。現在熱帶雨林一天比一天少，很多珍稀動物瀕臨滅絕，生態失去平衡，我們不是已經開始自食其果了嗎？

張天明：　我承認你說的有點道理。如果可以避免用動物做實驗，當然應該避免。實在避免不了的話，也應該儘量減少動物的痛苦。但為了虛榮而穿裘皮大衣，那就大可不必了。

约，在几家大的裘皮服装店门前抗议，向他们的顾客扔鸡蛋，剪她们的裘皮大衣。对了，还有几个电影明星也跟我们一起抗议。后天我们准备去包围生物系的动物房，你想去吗？

张天明：　我没空儿。我好不容易弄到两张票，想找你后天一起去看全国大学篮球决赛。

柯　林：　那糟了，我已经说好要去包围动物房了，只能牺牲这场球了。算了，你去找别人吧。

张天明：　你可别后悔啊！哎，柯林，你不觉得你们扔鸡蛋，剪人家的裘皮大衣，包围动物房，有点太过分了吗？我同意，我们人对动物也应该讲人道，但我觉得动物实验是很有用的。很多药只有通过动物实验，才能知道对人是不是安全。

柯　林：　你这种想法是错误的。现在已经可以不通过动物实验来做研究了。都快二十一世纪了，这么虐待动物，实在是太野蛮，太不人道了！

张天明：　你的想法也太极端了。你不觉得人比动物更重要吗？科学家也不是有意要虐待动物。让那么多人死于癌症、艾滋病，也不见得就人道。

柯　林：　你凭什么说人比动物更重要？正是因为我们有这种想法，才去破坏大自然。现在热带雨林一天比一天少，很多珍稀动物濒临灭绝，生态失去平衡，我们不是已经开始自食其果了吗？

张天明：　我承认你说的有点道理。如果可以避免用动物做实验，当然应该避免。实在避免不了的话，也应该尽量减少动物的痛苦。但为了虚荣而穿裘皮大衣，那就大可不必了。

柯　　林：　你這不是自相矛盾嗎？為了虛榮而殺動物和為了救我
　　　　　　們自己而犧牲動物，有甚麼區別呢？
張天明：　我覺得很多事情不像你想的那樣黑白分明。好了，好
　　　　　　了，我不跟你辯論了。既然你不去看球賽，我就去
　　　　　　找別人了。

（二）閱　讀

　　中國有許多稀有動物，其中有不少是十分珍貴的。但由於
人口不斷增加，動物生存的空間越來越小，有些動物，如華南
虎等已瀕臨滅絕。最近幾年中國採取了一些保護珍稀動物的措
施，並設立了許多動物保護區。中國的國寶大熊貓，也得到了
很好的保護。但大多數中國人的動物保護意識還很薄弱。很多
人常常為了發展經濟而忽略動物保護，甚至認為動物保護和發
展經濟是互相矛盾的。因此，在發展經濟的同時注意動物保
護，是中國政府面臨的一大難題。

柯　林：　你这不是自相矛盾吗？为了虚荣而杀动物和为了救我
　　　　　们自己而牺牲动物，有甚么区别呢？
张天明：　我觉得很多事情不像你想的那样黑白分明。好了，好
　　　　　了，我不跟你辩论了。既然你不去看球赛，我就去
　　　　　找别人了。

（二）阅　读

　　中国有许多稀有动物，其中有不少是十分珍贵的。但由于
人口不断增加，动物生存的空间越来越小，有些动物，如华南
虎等已濒临灭绝。最近几年中国采取了一些保护珍稀动物的措
施，并设立了许多动物保护区。中国的国宝大熊猫，也得到了
很好的保护。但大多数中国人的动物保护意识还很薄弱。很多
人常常为了发展经济而忽略动物保护，甚至认为动物保护和发
展经济是互相矛盾的。因此，在发展经济的同时注意动物保
护，是中国政府面临的一大难题。

二·生詞表

動物	动物	n	dòngwù	animal
生物		n	shēngwù	biology
抗議	抗议	v/n	kàngyì	protest

美國政府向日本政府提出抗議。

我們抗議你們虐待動物的行為。

研究		v	yánjiū	research
老年痴呆症		n	lǎonián chīdāi zhèng	senile dementia
解剖		v	jiěpōu	dissect
猴腦	猴脑	n	hóu nǎo	monkey brain
猴子		n	hóuzi	monkey
可憐	可怜	v	kělián	pitiable

那個孩子沒有父母，很可憐。

可憐的妹妹，功課壓得她喘不過氣來。

組織	组织	v/n	zǔzhī	organize; organization

她組織同學上街抗議。

紅十字會是一個很有名的組織。

裘皮		n	qiúpí	fur
服裝	服装	n	fúzhuāng	clothes
顧客	顾客	n	gùkè	customer
扔		v	rēng	throw
雞蛋	鸡蛋	n	jīdàn	chicken egg
剪		v	jiǎn	cut

大衣		n	dàyī	overcoat
包圍	包围	v	bāowéi	surround; encircle
弄		v	nòng	(colloq.) get
糟了			zāo le	(colloq.) oh no; shoot
犧牲	牺牲	v	xīshēng	sacrifice
講	讲	v	jiǎng	(colloq.) stress; pay attention to
人道		n	réndào	humane
實驗	实验	v	shíyàn	experiment; test
錯誤	错误	n	cuòwù	mistake
世紀	世纪	n	shìjì	century
虐待		v	nüèdài	abuse
野蠻	野蛮	adj	yěmán	uncivilized; barbarous
科學家	科学家	n	kēxuéjiā	scientist
有意			yǒuyì	intentionally; on purpose

他有意叫女朋友不高興。
我做錯了，但不是有意的。

癌症		n	áizhèng	cancer
憑	凭		píng	lean on; base on
破壞	破坏	v	pòhuài	destroy
大自然		n	dà zìrán	(mother) nature
熱帶雨林	热带雨林	n	rèdài yǔlín	tropical rain forest
珍稀動物	珍稀动物	n	zhēnxī dòngwù	precious and rare animals
瀕臨	濒临	v	bīnlín	be on the verge of
滅絕	灭绝	v	mièjué	become extinct
生態	生态	n	shēngtài	ecology

平衡		v/adj	pínghéng	balance; equilibrium
				你賺錢少，花錢多，收支不平衡。
				看到別人考得比自己好，他心裏有點兒不平衡。
自食其果			zì shí qí guǒ	to suffer the consequences of one's own doing
避免		v	bìmiǎn	avoid
				爲了避免犯錯誤，他做事十分小心。
				他總是想辦法避免跟以前的女朋友見面。
儘量	尽量	adv	jǐnliàng	to the best of one's ability
痛苦		n	tòngkǔ	pain; suffering
虛榮	虚荣		xūróng	vanity
大可不必			dà kě búbì	no need whatsoever
區別	区别	v/n	qūbié	distinguish; distinction
				這兩個詞有什麼區別？
				你應該把“合適”和“適合”區別開。
黑白分明			hēibái fēnmíng	black and white; in sharp contrast; clear cut
稀有		adj	xīyǒu	rare
珍貴	珍贵	adj	zhēnguì	valuable; precious
由於	由于	prep	yóuyú	due to; owing to
增加		v	zēngjiā	increase
生存		v	shēngcún	exist; survive
空間	空间	n	kōngjiān	space
採取	采取	v	cǎiqǔ	adopt (measures, methods, etc. as opposed to children)

措施		n	cuòshī	measure
設立	设立	v	shèlì	establish; set up
保護區	保护区	n	bǎohù qū	protected area; conservation area
國寶	国宝	n	guóbǎo	national treasure
熊貓	熊猫	n	xióngmāo	panda
大多數	大多数		dà duōshù	most
意識	意识	n	yìshi	consciousness
薄弱		adj	bóruò	weak; frail
忽略		v	hūlüè	overlook; neglect
互相矛盾			hùxiāng máodùn	contradict each other
在...同時	在...同时		zài...tóngshí	at the same time as
面臨	面临	v	miànlín	face; on the verge of
難題	难题	n	nántí	difficult problem

專名 Proper Nouns

紐約	纽约		Niǔyuē	New York
艾滋病			Aìzībìng	AIDS
華南虎	华南虎		Huánán Hǔ	the Southern Chinese Tiger

難寫的字：

解 憐 圍 犧 蠻 瀕 寶 薄

三·語法註釋　Grammar Notes

1. "為了"" and "因為"：

"為了" denotes purpose; "因為" denotes cause:

(1) 為了學習中文，我明年要去中國。

為了学习中文，我明年要去中国。

In order to study Chinese, I'm going to China next year.

(2) 為了解決人口問題，中國政府只讓每個家庭生一個孩子。

为了解决人口问题，中国政府只让每个家庭生一个孩子。

In order to solve the problem of (over)population, China only allows every family to have one child.

(3) 我買槍是為了保護自己。

我买枪是为了保护自己。

I bought the gun to protect myself.

(4) 因為在美國學中文太貴，所以我去中國學。

因为在美国学中文太贵，所以我去中国学。

I am going to China to study Chinese, because it is too expensive to study it in the United States.

(5) 因為中國的人口太多，所以中國政府只讓一家生一個孩子。

因为中国的人口太多，所以中国政府只让一家生一个孩子。

Because there are too many people in China, the Chinese government only allows every family to have one child.

(6) 因為這兒不安全，所以我買了一枝槍。

因为这儿不安全，所以我买了一枝枪。

I bought a gun because it's not safe here.

(7) 因為這個學校很有名，所以我申請。

因为这个学校很有名，所以我申请。

Because this school is very well known, I'm applying to it.

(8) 我申請這個學校，是為了能跟我的女朋友在一起。

我申请这个学校，是为了能跟我的女朋友在一起。

I'm applying to this school so that I can be with my girlfriend.

2. Adverb " 可 " in " 你可別後悔 " :

In imperative sentences, "可" denotes caution or admonition, and is often followed by such modal verbs as "要," "能," and "應該" and a particle of mood.

(1) 那兒很危險，你可要注意啊！

那儿很危险，你可要注意啊！

It is very dangerous there. Please be careful!

(2) 明天的會特別重要，你可不能忘了。

明天的会特别重要，你可不能忘了。

Tomorrow's meeting is extremely important. Don't forget to come!

(3) 這件事你答應了，可別後悔呀。

这件事你答应了，可别后悔呀。

You've agreed to this matter. Don't regret it!

3. " (死) 於 " :

Here the preposition "於" denotes cause. It is used in written or formal language. For instance,

(1) 每年不少人死於艾滋病。

每年不少人死于艾滋病。

Every year many people die of AIDS.

(2) 最近我忙於寫論文，沒有時間給你打電話。

最近我忙于写论文，没有时间给你打电话。

I've been busy writing my thesis. [That's why] I haven't had the time to call you.

4. "其中"：

"其中" means "in the midst." It generally refers to a scope. For example,

(1) 三年級有十五個學生，其中有三個是日本人，三個是韓國人，其他的是美國人。

三年级有十五个学生，其中有三个是日本人，三个是韩国人，其他的是美国人。

The third year (class) has fifteen students. Among those, three are Japanese, three are Korean, and the rest are American.

(2) 學校附近有很多中國餐館，其中有一家是從紐約搬來的。

学校附近有很多中国餐馆，其中有一家是从纽约搬来的。

There are many Chinese restaurants near the school; one of them moved here from New York.

(3) 老師問了我不少問題，其中只有一個很容易，我會回答，別的我都不會。

老师问了我不少问题，其中只有一个很容易，我会回答，别的我都不会。

The teacher asked me many questions. Only one of them was easy enough for me to answer. I didn't have a clue about the rest.

Note that when using "其中," there must be a preceding sentence, and in that sentence there must be a phrase denoting a multiplicity of people or things, e.g. "fifteen students" in (1), "many Chinese restaurants" in (2), and "many questions" in (3). "其中" is placed in the second clause to indicate "in the midst of" those "fifteen students," "many Chinese restaurants," and "many questions."

5. "而"：

"而" can connect a phrase denoting purpose or cause with a verb. It is usually preceded by such words as "由於," or "因為," and is used in written language.

(1) 我們為國家而工作。

我们为国家而工作。

We work for our country.
[The verb is "工作;" "為國家" denotes the purpose.]

(2) 他們因為贏得了金牌而驕傲起來。

他们因为赢得了金牌而骄傲起来。

They became arrogant because they had won a gold medal.
[The verb and outcome is "驕傲起來;" "贏得金牌" denotes the reason.]

四 · 詞語練習

1. "抗議" (protest)：

Example: 柯　林：我到生物系抗議去了。

柯　林：我到生物系抗议去了。

張天明：抗議什麼？

张天明：抗议什么？

(1) 六十年代，很多學生上街＿＿＿＿＿＿＿。

（美國　派兵去越南 (Vietnam)）

六十年代，很多学生上街＿＿＿＿＿＿＿。

（美国　派兵去越南 (Vietnam)）

(2) 學生們＿＿＿＿＿＿＿＿＿＿＿＿＿＿＿。

（向校長　學校又一次提高學費）

学生们＿＿＿＿＿＿＿＿＿＿＿＿＿＿＿。

（向校长　学校又一次提高学费）

(3) 市政府前圍著很多人，＿＿＿＿＿＿＿＿＿＿＿。

（市政府在他們的住家附近建飛機場）

市政府前围着很多人，＿＿＿＿＿＿＿＿＿＿＿。

（市政府在他们的住家附近建飞机场）

2. " 說好 " (to come to an agreement)：

　　Example：我已經說好要去包圍動物房了。

　　　　　　　我已经说好要去包围动物房了。

　　(1) 張天明＿＿＿＿＿＿＿＿＿＿＿＿＿＿＿＿＿＿。

　　　　　　　（同學　說好了下午打籃球）

　　　　　張天明＿＿＿＿＿＿＿＿＿＿＿＿＿＿＿＿＿＿。

　　　　　　　（同学　说好了下午打篮球）

　　(2) 張天明和麗莎從南京回來後，＿＿＿＿＿＿＿＿＿＿。

　　　　　　　　　　　　　　　（明年去台灣旅行）

　　　　　張天明和丽莎从南京回来后，＿＿＿＿＿＿＿＿＿＿。

　　　　　　　　　　　　　　　（明年去台湾旅行）

　　(3) 我們＿＿＿＿＿＿＿＿＿＿＿＿＿，你怎麼後悔了？

　　　　　　（今年夏天一塊兒去台灣學中文）

　　　　　我们＿＿＿＿＿＿＿＿＿＿＿＿＿，你怎么后悔了？

　　　　　　（今年夏天一块儿去台湾学中文）

3. " 憑什麼 " (why on earth; on what basis do you)：

　　Example：你憑什麼說人比動物更重要？

　　　　　　　你凭什么说人比动物更重要？

　　(1) 我們看球都要買票，＿＿＿＿＿＿＿＿？（他可以不買）

　　　　　我们看球都要买票，＿＿＿＿＿＿＿＿？（他可以不买）

　　(2) 我們停車都得付錢，＿＿＿＿＿＿＿＿＿＿？

　　　　　　　　　　　（國會議員 (Congressmen) 停車不用付錢）

　　　　　我们停车都得付钱，＿＿＿＿＿＿＿＿＿＿？

　　　　　　　　　　　（国会议员 (Congressmen) 停车不用付钱）

　　(3) 我和他合租一套公寓，我們的房間一樣大，＿＿＿＿＿？

　　　　　　　　　　　　　　　　　　　　（我要多付50塊）

355

我和他合租一套公寓，我们的房间一样大，_____？

（我要多付50块）

4. "**儘量**"(as much as possible)：

Example：如果可以避免用動物做實驗，當然應該避免。避免不了的話，應該儘量減少動物的痛苦。

如果可以避免用动物做实验，当然应该避免。避免不了的话，应该尽量减少动物的痛苦。

(1) 學中文_____。

（多聽，多説，多讀，多寫）

学中文_____。

（多听，多说，多读，多写）

(2) 我最不喜歡寫字，寫什麼東西，如果_____，我就_____。　　（能用電腦）

我最不喜欢写字，写什么东西，如果_____，我就_____。　　（能用电脑）

(3) 運動後要_____。（多喝水）

运动后要_____。（多喝水）

五 · 看圖說話

第二十課　環境保護

一‧課　文

（一）對　話

張天明：　這兩天你在忙些什麼呀，怎麼總見不到你？

李　哲：　我這學期在化學系參加了一項研究，是州政府給的錢，要幫助解決這裏的工業廢氣、廢水、廢渣問題。化學系僱了幾個學生做化學分析，這兩天我天天在實驗室裏做實驗、寫報告。

張天明：　難怪我連你的影子都見不到，打了幾次電話也沒人接。這兒的工業三廢問題嚴重嗎？這個小地方有什麼工業？不就是個大學城嗎？

李　哲：　這兒有一個很大的化工廠，工廠排出的三廢對我們這個地方造成了嚴重的污染。因為聯邦環境保護法越來

第二十课 环境保护

一·课文

（一）对 话

张天明： 这两天你在忙些什么呀，怎么总见不到你？

李 哲： 我这学期在化学系参加了一项研究，是州政府给的钱，要帮助解决这里的工业废气、废水、废渣问题。化学系雇了几个学生做化学分析，这两天我天天在实验室里做实验、写报告。

张天明： 难怪我连你的影子都见不到，打了几次电话也没人接。这儿的工业三废问题严重吗？这个小地方有什么工业？不就是个大学城吗？

李 哲： 这儿有一个很大的化工厂，工厂排出的三废对我们这个地方造成了严重的污染。因为联邦环境保护法越来越嚴，所以州政府讓工廠解決他們的三廢問題。可是工廠說他們沒有能力解決這個問題，因為解決這個問題會增加成本，產品就會競爭不過外國。工廠要求州政府幫助他們解決這個問題，還威脅說，要是州政府不幫他們解決，他們就搬到墨西哥去。後來，州政府申請到一筆錢，委托我們學校化學系幫助化工廠解決污染問題。

張天明：　噢，原來如此。怪不得這裏的松樹林死了一大片，我以為是有害蟲呢。

李　哲：　這兒比山下好多了，山下面的污染更厲害。山下那個湖裏不是有魚嗎？以前大家都不知道湖裏的魚有毒不能吃，結果有人吃了被毒死了。

張天明：　哎，環保這件事情真難辦。你不治理環境吧，不行，治理吧，往往得花很多錢，有時還會造成一些人失業。

李　哲：　可是如果我們現在不注意環保的話，將來可能就太晚了。像臭氧層、酸雨這些問題，如果現在不管，將來後果會不堪設想。

（二）閱　讀

　　中國是世界上的能源大國之一，煤產量居世界第一位。由於石油比煤貴，核電站造價高、週期長，所以中國的發電廠大多用煤發電。這些發電廠每年排放大量的二氧化硫，對環境造成很大的污染。在中國，除發電廠外，另一個污染源是很多城市居民使用的煤爐。這些大大小小的污染源，對人體健康造成很大的危害。隨著中國工業化速度的加快，對能源的需求量也與日俱增。如果不採取有效措施，中國的空氣污染將會日益加劇，自然，人民的健康也會受到更大的威脅。

越严，所以州政府让工厂解决他们的三废问题。可是工厂说他们没有能力解决这个问题，因为解决这个问题会增加成本，产品就会竞争不过外国。工厂要求州政府帮助他们解决这个问题，还威胁说，要是州政府不帮他们解决，他们就搬到墨西哥去。后来，州政府申请到一笔钱，委托我们学校化学系帮助化工厂解决污染问题。

张天明：噢，原来如此。怪不得这里的松树林死了一大片，我以为是有害虫呢。

李　哲：这儿比山下好多了，山下面的污染更厉害。山下那个湖里不是有鱼吗？以前大家都不知道湖里的鱼有毒不能吃，结果有人吃了被毒死了。

张天明：哎，环保这件事情真难办。你不治理环境吧，不行，治理吧，往往得花很多钱，有时还会造成一些人失业。

李　哲：可是如果我们现在不注意环保的话，将来可能就太晚了。像臭氧层、酸雨这些问题，如果现在不管，将来后果会不堪设想。

（二）阅　读

　　中国是世界上的能源大国之一，煤产量居世界第一位。由于石油比煤贵，核电站造价高、周期长，所以中国的发电厂大多用煤发电。这些发电厂每年排放大量的二氧化硫，对环境造成很大的污染。在中国，除发电厂外，另一个污染源是很多城市居民使用的煤炉。这些大大小小的污染源，对人体健康造成很大的危害。随着中国工业化速度的加快，对能源的需求量也与日俱增。如果不采取有效措施，中国的空气污染将会日益加剧，自然，人民的健康也会受到更大的威胁。

二·生詞表

環境	环境	n	huánjìng	environment
總	总	adv	zǒng	總是
化學	化学	n	huàxué	chemistry
項	项	m	xiàng	measure word
工業	工业	n	gōngyè	industry
廢氣	废气	n	fèiqì	waste gas or steam
廢水	废水	n	fèishuǐ	waste water
廢渣	废渣	n	fèizhā	waste residue
分析		v	fēnxī	analyze
實驗室	实验室	n	shíyànshì	laboratory
影子		n	yǐngzi	shadow
三廢	三废		sānfèi	廢氣、廢水、廢渣
化工		n	huàgōng	chemical industry
排出		vc	pái chū	discharge; let out
造成		v	zàochéng	cause

大雨下了五天,造成了嚴重的水災。

州政府不給我們學校錢了,造成了很大的困難。

污染		v/n	wūrǎn	pollute; pollution
聯邦	联邦	n	liánbāng	federal
能力		n	nénglì	ability; capacity
成本		n	chéngběn	production cost
委託		v	wěituō	entrust
原來如此	原来如此		yuánlái rúcǐ	so that's the reason
怪不得		adv	guài bu de	no wonder

松樹林		n	sōng shùlín	pine grove
害蟲	害虫	n	hàichóng	destructive insect
湖*		n	hú	lake
毒		n	dú	toxin; poison
環保	环保		huánbǎo	環境保護; environmental protection
難辦	难办		nán bàn	hard to handle

這件事真難辦。

這個人誰的話都不聽，很難辦。

治理		v	zhìlǐ	bring under control
有時	有时		yǒushí	sometimes
失業	失业	v	shī yè	be out of work
臭氧層	臭氧层	n	chòuyǎng céng	ozone layer; ozonosphere
酸雨		n	suānyǔ	acid rain
後果	后果	n	hòuguǒ	consequence; aftermath
不堪設想	不堪设想		bùkān shèxiǎng	dreadful to contemplate

小明天天喝醉酒，這樣下去學習成績將不堪設想。

能源		n	néngyuán	energy resources
煤	煤	n	méi	coal
產量	产量	n	chǎn liàng	output
居		v	jū	occupy (a certain position)
石油		n	shíyóu	petroleum; oil
核電站	核电站	n	hédiàn zhàn	nuclear power plant
造價	造价	n	zàojià	manufacturing cost
週期	周期	n	zhōuqī	cycle; period (of time)
發電廠	发电厂	n	fādiàn chǎng	power plant

大多		adv	dàduō	most
排放		v	páifàng	discharge; let out
大量			dàliàng	large quantity
二氧化硫		n	èryǎnghuàliú	sulphur dioxide
污染源		n	wūrǎn yuán	source of pollution
居民		n	jūmín	resident
使用		v	shǐyòng	use
煤爐	煤炉	n	méilú	coal stove
人體	人体	n	réntǐ	human body
危害		v	wēihài	harm
加快		v	jiākuài	quicken; speed up
需求量		n	xūqiú liàng	(quantity of) demand
與日俱增	与日俱增		yǔ rì jù zēng	grow with each passing day
有效		adj	yǒuxiào	effective
空氣	空气	n	kōngqì	air
將	将	adv	jiāng	will; shall
日益加劇	日益加剧		rìyì jiājù	become more aggravated day by day
人民		n	rénmín	people

難寫的字：

廢 實 驗 聯 蟲 層 酸 爐

三·語法註釋 Grammar Notes

1. "怎麼" and "為什麼":

　　"怎麼" is an interrogative pronoun used to inquire about the manner of an action, as in "How do you write that character?" "怎麼" can also be used to inquire about reasons. For instance, "How come I haven't seen you for the past couple of days?" How does "怎麼" differ from "為什麼?" "怎麼" generally implies surprise or bewilderment. For example,

(1) 三點了，他應該來了，怎麼還沒來？

　　三点了，他应该来了，怎么还没来？

　　It's three o'clock. He should have gotten here. How come he is not here?

(2) 明天考試？我怎麼不知道？

　　明天考试？我怎么不知道？

　　There's an exam tomorrow. How come I didn't know?

(3) 怎麼？他沒來上課？

　　怎么？他没来上课？

　　What? He didn't come to the class?

　　"為什麼," on the other hand, does not necessarily imply bewilderment. It is used primarily to inquire about reasons. In the first example, "為什麼" can be substituted for "怎麼." The tone will shift from one of puzzlement to reproach. In the second example, "怎麼" cannot be replaced without the meaning being substantially changed as well. "為什麼" would sound as if the speaker were complaining. Therefore use "為什麼" to inquire about reasons:

(4) 這麼重要的事情，你為什麼不告訴我？

　　这么重要的事情，你为什么不告诉我？

　　Why didn't you tell me about such an important thing?

(5) 飛機為什麼會飛？

　　飞机为什么会飞？

　　Why can airplanes fly?

(6) 他為什麼不來？為什麼？為什麼？

他为什么不来？为什么？为什么？

Why isn't he coming? Why? Why?

In (4) "怎麼" can be substituted for "為什麼." There would be a slight difference in meaning. "怎麼" would connote curiosity rather than reproach. In (5), "怎麼" cannot be substituted for "為什麼." The sentence could have been taken from a physics textbook. It is a pure question. The tone of voice is neutral. "怎麼" cannot be used at the end of a sentence, unlike "為什麼" in (6). "為什麼" cannot be used at the beginning of a sentence by itself, unlike "怎麼" in (3).

2. "（好）多了" and "（好）得多" :

When making a comparison, one can use "多了" or "得多" after the adjective to indicate an extreme degree. For example,

(1) 這兒的天氣比東岸熱多了。

这儿的天气比东岸热多了。

這兒的天氣比東岸熱得多。

这儿的天气比东岸热得多。

The weather here is much hotter than the East Coast.

(2) 中國的人口比美國多多了。

中国的人口比美国多多了。

中國的人口比美國多得多。

中国的人口比美国多得多。

China's population is much larger than that of the U.S.

(3) A：你姐姐的病好一點了嗎？

你姐姐的病好一点了吗？

Is your sister (her illness) a little better? (meaning, "is it better than before?")

B：好多了。

好多了。

Much better.

It is incorrect to say, "好得多."

NB:

A: In these comparative sentences the adjectives cannot be preceded by modifiers. For example, one cannot say, "他比我很好", etc. One can put "一點兒, 得很, 得多, 多了, 很多," etc. after the adjectives. However, one cannot put modifiers both before and after the adjectives in these comparative sentences. For instance, one cannot say, "他比我好得多了."

B: If there are no words that indicate comparison such as "比," the adjectives can only be followed by "一點兒, 多了." Cf (3).

3. "...吧, ...吧...," :

This construction suggests two alternative hypotheses, and is used to indicate that the speaker is in a dilemna and unable to make a decision. For instance,

(1) 我的車買了好幾年了，最近老有問題。修理吧，得花不少錢，不修理吧，不能開，買新的吧，又沒有錢，真難辦。

我的车买了好几年了，最近老有问题。修理吧，得花不少钱，不修理吧，不能开，买新的吧，又没有钱，真难办。

I bought my car a few years ago; lately it's been having many problems. I could have it fixed, but then I'd have to spend a lot of money. If I don't fix it, I can't drive it. I could buy a new one, but I don't have any money. I don't know what to do.

(2) 晚上有一個電影，聽說不錯，可是今天作業很多。去看電影吧，怕回來作業做不完，不看吧，又覺得很可惜。

晚上有一个电影，听说不错，可是今天作业很多。去看电影吧，怕回来作业做不完，不看吧，又觉得很可惜。

There is a movie tonight. I hear it's pretty good, but I have a lot of homework tonight. If I go to the movie, I'm afraid when I come back I won't have the time to finish my homework, but if I don't see it, it will be such a pity.

(3) 他的女朋友的妹妹明天舉行生日晚會。他想，去吧，沒有錢買禮物，不去吧，又怕女朋友生氣。怎麼辦呢？

他的女朋友的妹妹明天举行生日晚会。他想，去吧，没有钱买礼物，不去吧，又怕女朋友生气。怎么办呢？

His girlfriend's sister is having a birthday party tomorrow. He thinks if he goes, he won't have the money to buy a present, but he's afraid if he doesn't go his girlfriend will be mad. What should he do?

4. "往往" and "常常":

Both "往往" and "常常" indicate high frequency, but they differ in degree:

A: "往往" usually indicates a higher frequency than "常常."

B: "往往" is used of predictable situations, and cannot be used with verbs that denote subjective desire. "常常" is placed in front of the verb and indicates constant recurrence which is not necessarily predictable. It can be used with verbs that denote subjective desire. For instance,

(1) 過去我常常希望他來，現在怕他來。

过去我常常希望他来，现在怕他来。

In the past I often hoped he would come; now I dread the prospect of his coming.

Incorrect: *過去我往往希望他來，現在怕他來。

*过去我往往希望他来，现在怕他来。

(2) 我希望你以後常常來。

我希望你以后常常来。

I hope you'll come often.

Incorrect: *我希望你以後往往來。

*我希望你以后往往来。

(3) 週末他往往不在家。

周末他往往不在家。

On weekends more often than not he's not at home.

週末他常常不在家。

周末他常常不在家。

On weekends he's often not at home.

These two sentences are different.

C: "往往" can only be used of the past or of situations in which time is not a factor. This restriction does not apply to "常常." For instance,

我以後星期六會常常來。

我以后星期六会常常来。

From now on I will come often on Saturdays.

Incorrect: *我以後星期六會往往來。

　　　　　*我以后星期六会往往来。

四 · 詞語練習

1. **" (競爭) 不過 "** (cannot compete with; be no match for) :

Example: 產品將競爭不過外國。

　　　　　产品将竞争不过外国。

(1) 我妹妹很會說話，每次和人辯論，別人＿＿＿＿＿＿＿＿。
　　　　　　　　　　　　　　　　　　　　　　（說）

　　我妹妹很会说话，每次和人辩论，别人＿＿＿＿＿＿＿＿。
　　　　　　　　　　　　　　　　　　　　　　（说）

(2) 他每天都練長跑，你讓我跟他比賽，我肯定＿＿＿＿＿＿。
　　　　　　　　　　　　　　　　　　　　　（跑）

　　他每天都练长跑，你让我跟他比赛，我肯定＿＿＿＿＿＿。
　　　　　　　　　　　　　　　　　　　　　（跑）

(3) 她在中國待了三年，能說不少中文，而我從來沒去過
　　中國，所以在聽說方面，＿＿＿＿＿＿＿＿＿＿。
　　　　　　　　　　　　　　　（比）

她在中国待了三年，能说不少中文，而我从来没去过
中国，所以在听说方面，＿＿＿＿＿＿＿＿＿＿。

（比）

2. **"委托"** (entrust; ask)：

Example: 州政府···委托我們學校化學系幫助化工廠解決
污染問題。

州政府···委托我们学校化学系帮助化工厂解决
污染问题。

(1) 校長不能參加今年的畢業典禮，所以他

＿＿＿＿＿＿＿＿＿。　　　（張教授，講話）

校长不能参加今年的毕业典礼，所以他

＿＿＿＿＿＿＿＿＿。　　　（张教授，讲话）

(2) 美國的電視公司常常＿＿＿＿＿＿＿＿＿＿＿＿。

（蓋洛普 Gallup公司，做民意調查）

美国的电视公司常常＿＿＿＿＿＿＿＿＿＿＿＿。

（盖洛普 Gallup公司，做民意调查）

(3) 美國政府＿＿＿＿＿＿＿＿＿＿＿＿＿＿。

（她，參加世界環境保護大會）

美国政府＿＿＿＿＿＿＿＿＿＿＿＿＿＿。

（她，参加世界环境保护大会）

3. **"原來如此"** (So that's how it is; so that's why)：

Example: ...噢，原來如此。怪不得這裏的松樹林死了一
大片。

...噢，原来如此。怪不得这里的松树林死了一
大片。

(1) A：他過生日的時候，我送了他一個鐘，他好像有些不
高興。

他过生日的时候，我送了他一个钟，他好像有些不
高兴。

　　B：在中國，你是不能送鐘的。

　　　　在中国，你是不能送钟的。

　　A：為什麼？

　　　　为什么？

　　B：因為 " 送鐘 " 和 " 送終 " (bury a parent or a senior member of the family) 發音一樣，所以中國人覺得送鐘非常不合適。

　　　　因为 " 送钟 " 和 " 送终 " (bury a parent or a senior member of the family) 发音一样，所以中国人觉得送钟非常不合适。

　　A：噢，_____，我應該跟他說聲對不起 。

　　　　噢，_____，我应该跟他说声对不起 。

(2) A：他為什麼這兩天沒來上課？

　　　　他为什么这两天没来上课？

　　B：他的奶奶病了，他去波士頓看奶奶去了。

　　　　他的奶奶病了，他去波士顿看奶奶去了。

　　A：噢，_____。

　　　　噢，_____。

4. " 不就是 " (meaning "只是" or "只有" and introducing a rhetorical question)：

Example：這個小地方有什麼工業？不就是一個大學城嗎？

　　　　　这个小地方有什么工业？不就是一个大学城吗？

(1) 他不就是個研究生嗎？他的論文為什麼_____？

　　　　　　　　　　　　　　　　　　　　　　　　（有影響）

　　他不就是个研究生吗？他的论文为什么_____？

　　　　　　　　　　　　　　　　　　　　　　　　（有影响）

(2) 今天的考試_____？你不要那麼緊張。

　　　　　　（生詞小考）

　　今天的考试_____？你不要那么紧张。

　　　　　　（生词小考）

(3) 他們_____？你別那麼激動。

　　　　（贏了場球）

　　他们_____？你别那么激动。

　　　　（赢了场球）

五·看圖說話

Index to Vocabulary

A

Ādídási	阿迪達斯	4
āiyā	哎呀	4
áizhèng	癌症	19
Aìzībìng	艾滋病	19
àiguó	愛國	12
ānhǎo	安好	11
ānquán	安全	1
Aòlínpǐkè	奧林匹克	13

B

báitian	白天	17
bǎifēn zhī	百分之	4
bǎi	擺	2
bài nián	拜年	12
bān jiā	搬家	1
bànfǎ	辦法	15
bàn gōng	辦公	10
bāo	包	6
bāoguǒ	包裹	10
bāowéi	包圍	19
bǎohù	保護	18
bǎohùqū	保護區	19
bǎoxiǎn	保險	16
bǎozhàng	保障	18
bǎozhèng	保證	16
bēizi	杯子	4
bèijǐng	背景	7
bèizi	被子	2
běnlái	本來	13
běnlǐng	本領	17
bǐfēn	比分	13
bǐrú	比如	15

bǐsài	比賽	6
bìjìng	畢竟	16
bìyè	畢業	5
bìyào	必要	13
bìmiǎn	避免	19
biānpào	鞭炮	12
biàn	變	17
biànhua	變化	15
biànlùn	辯論	17
biāozhǔn	標準	4
biǎomiàn shang		
	表面上	12
biǎosǎo	表嫂	14
biǎoxiàn	表現	12
biē sǐ	憋死	7
bié jù fēnggé	別具風格	11
bīnlín	瀕臨	19
bǐnggān	餅乾	10
bìng	並	18
bō	播	8
bōcài	菠菜	3
Bōshìdùn	波士頓	1
bóruò	薄弱	19
bǔxíbān	補習班	17
búbì	不必	16
búduàn	不斷	15
búguò	不過	5
bùguǎn	不管	15
bújiàndé	不見得	1
bù kān shè xiǎng		
	不堪設想	20
bùrán	不然	18
bùrú	不如	16
bùtóng	不同	7
bù yǐ wéi rán	不以爲然	17
bùzú	不足	16
bùqiāng	步槍	18
bù	部	7

C

cāi duì le	猜對了	2
cǎiqǔ	採取	19
càidān	菜單	3
cānguǎn	餐館	2
cānjiā	參加	13
cāoxīn	操心	14
céng	層	2
céngjīng	曾經	9
chá	查	18
chǎnliàng	產量	20
chǎnpǐn	產品	16
chǎnshēng	產生	18
chángkè	常客	3
chángduǎn	長短	4
chángtú	長途	10
chǎo jià	吵架	7
chèn	趁	10
chēng	稱	10
chéngběn	成本	20
chéngjī	成績	13
chéng qiān	成千上萬	13
shàng wàn		13
chéngshú	成熟	17
chéngwéi	成爲	11
chéngdù	程度	11
chéngrèn	承認	17
chī cù	吃醋	9
chòng	衝	14
chōu	抽	14
chòuyǎng céng	臭氧層	20
chū	出	16
chū chāi	出差	10
chū guó	出國	9
chūjià	出嫁	15
chūshēng	出生	1
chū shì	出事	18
chūxiàn	出現	15
chúfēi	除非	9

chuántǒng	傳統	12
chuǎnqì	喘氣	17
chuānghu	窗户	2
chuáng	床	2
chuī	吹	7
Chūn Jié	春節	12
chúnmián de	純棉的	4
cí	辭	15
cí zhí	辭職	15
cónglái	從來	7
cuī	催	11
cuòshī	措施	19
cuòwù	錯誤	19

D

dǎjī	打擊	18
dǎ jīchǔ	打基礎	17
dǎ jiāodào	(跟...)打交道	5
dǎ liè	打獵	18
dǎ pò	打破	7
dǎsuàn	打算	5
dǎtīng	打聽	9
dǎ tōng	打通	10
dǎ zhāohu	打招呼	6
dǎ zhé	打折	4
dà bàn	大半	5
dà bùfen	大部份	15
dàduō	大多	20
dà duōshù	大多數	19
dàgài	大概	15
dà guān	大官	12
dà hǎn dà jiào	大喊大叫	6
dà kě búbì	大可不必	19
dàliàng	大量	20
dàlóu	大樓	10
dàlù	大陸	9
dàrén	大人	8
dàrénwù	大人物	11

dàshēng	大聲	6
dàxiǎo	大小	4
dàyī	大衣	19
dàzìrán	大自然	19
dāi	待	9
dài	帶	2
dài	帶	6
dài	帶	15
dài	戴	12
dānqīn	單親	14
dānwèi	單位	16
dànzi	擔子	15
dāngnián	當年	11
dāngshí	當時	12
dàolǐ	道理	1
dàochù	到處	18
dào ye shì	倒也是	13
dé	得	13
dédào	得到	15
de huà	的話	16
dēng	燈	12
Dēng Jié	燈節	12
děngděng	等等	4
dèng	瞪	11
dī	低	18
díquè	的確	17
dìdào	地道	2
dìtǎn	地毯	6
dìwèi	地位	15
dìzhǐ	地址	9
diànbào	電報	10
diànyǐngyuàn	電影院	7
diàochá	調查	18
dìng xialai	定下來	14
diūrén	丟人	14
dōng'àn	東岸	9
dōngfāng	東方	9
dōngyà shǐ	東亞史	5
dòng	棟	2
dòngrén	動人	12

dòng shǒushù	動手術	16
dòngwù	動物	19
dòufu	豆腐	3
dūcù	督促	17
dú shū	讀書	17
dú	毒	20
dúpǐn	毒品	18
dúlì	獨立	14
dǔbó	賭博	18
duān	端	12
Duānwǔ Jié	端午節	12
duì...lái shuō	對...來說	5
duìmiàn	對面	10
duì	隊	13
duōbàn	多半	8
Duōlúnduō	多倫多	16

E

ér	而	14
értóng	兒童	8
èryǎnghuàliú	二氧化硫	20

F

fā chóu	發愁	16
fā diàn chǎng	發電廠	20
fāhuī	發揮	17
fāzhǎn	發展	13
fǎguī	法規	18
fǎlǜ	法律	18
fān dào	翻到	6
fǎnduì	反對	8
fǎn'ér	反而	8
fǎnfù	反復	5
fǎn guolai	反過來	15
fǎnzhèng	反正	13
fànmài	販賣	18

fàn zuì	犯罪	18
fànqián	飯錢	5
fāngmiàn	方面	14
fāngshì	方式	17
fàng huǒ	放火	18
fàngxīn	放心	10
fàng xué	放學	14
fèiqì	廢氣	20
fèishuǐ	廢水	20
fèizhā	廢渣	20
fēndān	分擔	15
fēn shǒu	分手	14
fēnxī	分析	20
fènzǐ	份子	18
fēngfù	豐富	13
fēngshèng	豐盛	12
fēngsú	風俗	12
fǒuzé	否則	9
fūfù	夫婦	15
Fūzǐ Miào	夫子廟	11
fúcóng	服從	15
fúzhuāng	服裝	19
fùdān	負擔	17
fù zérèn	負責任	8
fùnǚ	婦女	15
fù qián	付錢	4
fùzǐ	父子	14

G

gāi	該	9
gǎigé kāifàng	改革開放	15
gǎn	敢	8
gǎn	趕	12
gǎnjǐn	趕緊	6
gǎndào	感到	13
Gǎn'ēn Jié	感恩節	14
gāozhōng	高中	7
gāoyáng	羔羊	18

gào zhuàng	告狀	14
gébì	隔壁	6
gèrén	個人	17
gè zhǒng gè yàng	各種各樣	12
gēn	跟	3
gēnběn	根本	12
gōng	弓	1
gōngchǎng	工廠	14
gōngchéng	工程	14
gōngxuéyuàn	工學院	5
gōngyè	工業	20
gōngyè huà	工業化	20
gōngpíng	公平	15
gōngsī	公司	9
gòuwù zhōngxīn	購物中心	4
gūfu	姑父	14
gūmā	姑媽	9
gǔlì	鼓勵	17
gǔ chéngqiáng	古城牆	11
gǔdiǎn yīnyuè	古典音樂	7
gù	僱	18
gùkè	顧客	19
gùshì	故事	11
guà	掛	2
guà hào	掛號	10
guài	怪	8
guāndiǎn	觀點	17
guānniàn	觀念	18
guānxīn	關心	16
guǎn	管	5
guǎnlǐ xueyuàn	管理學院	5
guāngróng	光榮	13
guǎnggào lán	廣告欄	6
guīdìng	規定	18
guìzi	櫃子	2
guóbǎo	國寶	19
guójiā	國家	13
guówáng	國王	12

guòfèn	過分	16
guòfèn	過份	19
guò jǐ tiān	過幾天	2
guò jié	過節	12
guoqu	過去	10
guò rìzi	過日子	14
guòshèng	過剩	16

H

hāhā dà xiào	哈哈大笑	11
háizi	孩子	5
hǎiyán	海洋	11
hǎiyùn	海運	10
hàichóng	害蟲	20
hàide	害得	17
Hánguó	韓國	9
hángkōng gōngsī	航空公司	9
háo wú	毫無	16
hǎochù	好處	1
hǎokàn	好看	4
hǎowár	好玩兒	9
hàoqi	好奇	10
hē zuì jiǔ	喝醉酒	7
hébāo	荷包	12
hédiànzhàn	核電站	20
hēibái fēnmíng	黑白分明	19
hěnhěn de	狠狠地	11
hōnggānjī	烘乾機	2
hóunǎo	猴腦	19
hóuzi	猴子	19
hòuguǒ	後果	20
hòuhuǐ	後悔	7
hòumiàn	後面	6
hòutiān	後天	5
hòubó	厚薄	4
hūlüè	忽略	19
hú	湖	11

hùshi	護士	15
hùzhào	護照	9
hùxiāng máodùn	互相矛盾	19
huā qián	花錢	16
Huánán Hǔ	華南虎	19
Huáqīng Chí	華清池	11
Huáshèngdùn	華盛頓	2
huà huàr	畫畫	14
huá chuán	划船	11
huàgōng	化工	20
huàxué	化學	20
huàzhuāngpǐn	化妝品	4
huái yùn	懷孕	15
huánbǎo	環保	20
huánjìng	環境	6
huàn	患	16
Huìmǐn	惠敏	14
huìyuán	會員	18
hūnyīn	婚姻	15
huǒ	火	8
huǒchái	火柴	8
huǒchē	火車	9
huǒlú	火爐	9
huǒzāi	火災	8
huò	或	6

J

jī	雞	12
jīdàn	雞蛋	19
jīhuì	機會	15
jīqì	機器	17
jīběn shang	基本上	18
jīdòng	激動	6
jí	及	17
jíbìng	急病	16
jízào	急躁	7
jídà	極大	20

jíduān	極端	17
jíshǐ	即使	17
jíhuì	集會	18
jǐ xialai	擠下來	11
jǐhū	幾乎	8
jìnǚ	妓女	18
jì duī	寄丟	10
jìlù piàn	紀錄片	8
jìmò	寂寞	13
jìshù	技術	14
jìsì	祭祀	12
jìzhě	記者	3
jì zhù	記住	5
jiātíng	家庭	14
jiātíng jiàoshī	家庭教師	17
jiātíng zhǔfù	家庭主婦	15
jiāwù	家務	15
jiāzhǎng	家長	8
jiākuài	加快	20
Jiā'nádà	加拿大	16
jiā shàng	加上	16
jiàgé	價格	16
jiàqián	價錢	4
jiàzhí guānniàn	價值觀念	18
jiàqī	假期	9
jiān	間	6
jiānyù	監獄	18
jiǎn	剪	19
jiǎnféi	減肥	16
jiǎnjià	減價	4
jiǎnshǎo	減少	15
jiǎnzhí	簡直	17
jiàn	建	11
jiànzhù	建築	11
jiànyì	建議	5
jiàn miàn	見面	7
jiànquán	健全	18
jiāng	江	12
jiāng	將	20
jiǎng	講	19
jiāo'ào	驕傲	13
jiāotōng	交通	6
jiāowǎng	交往	7
jiào	叫	3
jiàoliàn	教練	13
jiàoshòu	教授	5
jiàoxué	教學	17
jiàoyù	教育	8
jiē	街	6
jiéguǒ	結果	8
jiéhūn	結婚	14
jiéshù	結束	1
jiémù	節目	7
jiérì	節日	12
jiéshí	節食	16
jiějué	解決	15
jiěpōu	解剖	19
jiěfu	姐夫	15
jièkǒu	藉口	8
jièlán	芥蘭	3
jīnpái	金牌	13
jǐnliàng	儘量	19
jìnzhǐ	禁止	18
jìn kěnéng	儘可能	12
jīngcǎi	精彩	13
jīngshen	精神	12
jīngcháng	經常	7
jīngjì	經濟	18
jīngyàn	經驗	5
jǐngchá	警察	18
jìngzhù	敬祝	11
jìngzhēng	競爭	17
jìngzi	鏡子	7
jiǔbā	酒吧	7
jiù	救	12
jiù mìng	救命	18
jiù	舊	2
jū	居	20
jūmín	居民	20

jūrán	居然	14
jùshuō	據説	8
juédìng	決定	16
juésài	決賽	13
jūnhéng	均衡	16

K

kǎlùlǐ	卡路里	3
kǎtōng	卡通	8
kāilǎng	開朗	7
kāi qiāng	開槍	8
kāi wánxiào	開玩笑	6
kāi xué	開學	1
kànfǎ	看法	3
kànlái	看來	17
kàngyì	抗議	19
kào	靠	1
kào	靠	2
Kēlín	柯林	21
kēxuéjiā	科學家	19
kě bú shì	可不是	13
kěkào	可靠	10
kělián	可憐	19
kěnéng	可能	6
kěpà	可怕	9
kè zhōng	刻鐘	3
kěn	肯	11
kěndìng	肯定	5
kōng	空	2
kōngjiān	空間	19
kōngqì	空氣	20
kōngtiáo	空調	2
kōngyùn	空運	10
kǒngpà	恐怕	2
kǔxīn	苦心	17

L

lái bù jí	來不及	9
lái duì le	來對了	10
lán	籃	13
lǎn	懶	14
lǎo	老	4
lǎobǎixìng	老百姓	12
lǎobǎn	老板	3
lǎobànr	老伴兒	14
lǎonián chīdān zhèng	老年痴呆症	19
lǎoshēng	老生	1
lǎoshǔ	老鼠	15
lè huài le	樂壞了	17
lèguān	樂觀	15
líhūn	離婚	14
líkāi	離開	1
lǐjiě	理解	17
lǐxiǎng	理想	6
lǐzhì	理智	18
Lǐ Zhé	李哲	5
lǐtáng	禮堂	8
Lìshā	麗莎	7
lìhài	厲害	7
lìshǐ	歷史	14
liánbāng	聯邦	20
liànliàn bu shě	戀戀不捨	11
liàng	亮	12
Lín Xuěméi	林雪梅	3
Língling	玲玲	14
língmù	陵墓	11
lǐngxiān	領先	13
lǐngshìguǎn	領事館	9
lìng	另	8
lóngzhōu	龍舟	12
lóutī	樓梯	6
lóu xià	樓下	2
lùshang	路上	10
lùxiàn	路線	9

lù kōng liányùn

      陸空聯運 10
lǚlì 履歷 5
lǜ 率 18
luàn fàng 亂放 18
luàn qī bā zāo 亂七八糟 8
lún dào 輪到 10

M

mǎlù 馬路 2
mǎshàng 馬上 3
mà 罵 14
ma 嘛 14
mán 瞞 6
māo 貓 15
máoyī 毛衣 4
méi 煤 20
méilú 煤爐 20
měidāng...shí 每當...時 13
mén 門 5
mǐ 米 12
mìmì 秘密 11
Mìxīgēn 密西根 13
miànlín 面臨 19
miǎozhōng 秒鐘 13
miàolíng 妙齡 11
mièjué 滅絕 19
míngxiǎn 明顯 15
míngxìnpiàn 明信片 10
míngxīng 明星 16
míngpái 名牌 4
míngshèng gǔjī

      名勝古蹟 11
mófàn 模範 15
mófǎng 模仿 8
Mòxīgē 墨西哥 9
mǔqin 母親 10
mùbēi 墓碑 11

mùbiāo 目標 17
mùkè 木刻 15

N

ng 嗯 6
náshǒu 拿手 3
nàyàng 那樣 8
nánfāng 南方 12
Nánjīng 南京 9
nánnǚ 男女 15
nánshēng 男生 15
nán bàn 難辦 20
nándào 難道 4
nánguài 難怪 7
nánmiǎn 難免 8
nántí 難題 19
nántīng 難聽 7
nǎozi 腦子 18
nào fān 鬧翻 7
nèn 嫩 3
nénglì 能力 20
néngyuán 能源 20
nì 膩 9
niándài 年代 9
niánqīng 年輕 15
niúròu 牛肉 3
niúzǎikù 牛仔褲 4
Niǔyuē 紐約 19
nónglì 農曆 12
nǚhái 女孩 3
nǚrén 女人 15
nǚsheng 女生 15
nǚzǐ 女子 15
nüèdài 虐待 19

O

| ǒu'ěr | 偶爾 | 8 |

P

pāi	拍	10
pāi	拍	16
pái	排	20
pái chū	排出	20
pái duì	排隊	10
páifàng	排放	20
páizi	牌子	4
péi	陪	4
pèng	碰	18
pīpíng	批評	17
píqi	脾氣	7
piànmiàn	片面	3
píndào	頻道	8
pín fù bù jūn	貧富不均	18
píng	憑	19
píngděng	平等	15
pínghéng	平衡	19
póxí	婆媳	14
pòhuài	破壞	19
pǔtong	普通	9

Q

qīzǐ	妻子	15
qíshí	其實	3
qíguài	奇怪	10
qíshì	歧視	15
qǐfā	啓發	17
qiānwàn	千萬	11
qiān zì	簽字	4
qiánbian	前邊	1
qiánkē	前科	18
qiántiān	前天	2

qiāng	槍	18
qiāngzhī	槍枝	18
qiángdiào	強調	17
qiángzhì	強制	18
qiángzhuàng	強壯	13
qiǎngjié	搶劫	18
qīn péng hǎo yǒu	親朋好友	12
qīnqi	親戚	15
Qínguó	秦國	12
Qínhuái Hé	秦淮河	11
qīngcài	青菜	3
qīngdàn	清淡	3
qīngzhēng	清蒸	3
qīngsōng	輕鬆	17
qíngkuàng	情況	7
qióngrén	窮人	16
qiúchǎng	球場	6
qiúmí	球迷	6
qiúsài	球賽	13
qiúpí	裘皮	19
qūbié	區別	19
Qū Yuán	屈原	12
qǔdé	取得	13
qǔdì	取締	10
qùshì	去世	14
quánlì	權利	18
quánmiàn	全面	18
quēdiǎn	缺點	17
què	卻	10
quèshí	確實	9

R

ránhòu	然後	9
rèdài yǔlín	熱帶雨林	19
réndào	人道	19
rénjia	人家	13
rénkǒu	人口	11

rén lǎo zhū huáng	人老珠黄	11
rénmen	人們	12
rénmín	人民	20
rén shān rén hǎi	人山人海	11
rénshù	人數	15
réntǐ	人體	20
rénwù	人物	8
rényuán	人員	16
rěn bú zhù	忍不住	11
rèn rén zǎigē	任人宰割	18
rènwéi	認為	3
rènzhēn	認真	17
rēng	扔	19
réngrán	仍然	18
rìchéng	日程	10
rìyì jiājù	日益加劇	20
rìyòngpǐn	日用品	2
rìzi	日子	12
róngyù	榮譽	13
rú	如	18

S

sài	賽	12
sānfèi	三廢	20
sàn bù	散步	9
sàngshī	喪失	18
shā rén	殺人	18
shāngdiàn	商店	2
shāngliang	商量	9
shāngyè piàn	商業片	8
shǎng yuè	賞月	12
shàng jiē	上街	12
shàngjìn xīn	上進心	17
shàngyǎn	上演	8
shāowēi	稍微	6
shāo sǐ	燒死	8

shǎo	少	3
shàonǚ	少女	11
shèqǔ	攝取	16
shèhuì	社會	15
shèbèi	設備	2
shèlì	設立	19
shēn	深	11
shēnqǐng	申請	5
shēncái	身材	16
shēnshang	身上	12
shénmeyàng	什麼樣	6
shènzhì	甚至	15
shēngyīn	聲音	13
shēngcún	生存	19
shēngqì	生氣	11
shēngtài	生態	19
shēngwù	生物	19
shēngyì	生意	9
shēng xué	升學	15
shěng xialai	省下來	5
shěng qián	省錢	1
shī	詩	12
shīrén	詩人	12
shīwàng	失望	13
shī yè	失業	20
shíjì shang	實際上	12
shíxí	實習	5
shíyàn	實驗	19
shíyànshì	實驗室	20
shízài	實在	13
shíyóu	石油	20
shǐyòng	使用	20
shìjì	世紀	19
shìjiè jìlù	世界記錄	13
shìhé	適合	17
shìyìng	適應	1
shì	室	6
shōu hǎo	收好	18
shōujù	收據	4
shǒuduàn	手段	18

shǒushù	手術	16
shǒuxiān	首先	14
shǒuxù	手續	1
shòu bu liǎo	受不了	5
shòudào	受到	18
shòu shāng	受傷	16
shòu yǐngxiǎng	受影響	6
shū	輸	13
shūshu	叔叔	14
shúxi	熟悉	2
shùhǎi	樹海	11
shùlín	樹林	6
shùxué	數學	17
shuàigē	帥哥	13
shuāng xuéwèi	雙學位	5
shuǐdiàn	水電	6
shuǐpíng	水平	16
shuì	稅	4
shùnbiàn	順便	9
shùnlì	順利	10
shuō dìng	說定	11
shuōfǎ	說法	3
Sīdìfū	斯蒂夫	9
sīkǎo	思考	17
sīrén	私人	18
sǐ	死	11
sǐ jì yìng bèi	死記硬背	17
sōng shùlín	松樹林	20
Sòng Cháo	宋朝	15
sùcài	素菜	3
sùdù	速度	13
suānyǔ	酸雨	20
suàn	算	6
suí zhī	隨之	18
suí zhe	隨著	15
Sūn Zhōngshān	孫中山	11
suǒyǒu	所有	16

T

tái	台	2
Táiwān	台灣	16
táibì	台幣	9
tàidù	態度	17
tǎnzi	毯子	2
tāng	湯	3
Tāngmǔ	湯姆	7
tángguǒ	糖果	10
tàng	趟	9
táotài	淘汰	17
tǎolùn	討論	5
tào	套	6
tèchǎn	特產	10
tèdì	特地	10
tèdiǎn	特點	17
tīxùshān	T恤衫	4
tí	提	5
tígāo	提高	15
tǐhuì	體會	11
tǐtiē	體貼	15
tǐxiàn	體現	15
tǐyù	體育	7
tǐyùchǎng	體育場	6
Tiānhuá	天華	7
tiányāshì	填鴨式	17
tiāoti	挑剔	4
tiě fànwǎn	鐵飯碗	14
tīng	廳	6
tǐng	挺	7
tōngguò	通過	18
tóng gōng tóng chóu	同工同酬	15
tóngwū	同屋	2
tóngyì	同意	3
tóngnián	童年	17
tǒngjìxué	統計學	5
tòngkǔ	痛苦	19

tōuqiè	偷竊	18
tóu	投	12
tóu jiāng	投江	12
tūchū	突出	15
tūrán	突然	11
tú	圖	4
tuányuán	團圓	12
tuìxiū	退休	14

W

wàichū	外出	4
wàimian	外面	12
wánquán	完全	8
wànyī	萬一	10
wǎngwǎng	往往	15
wàng nǚ chéng fèng	望女成鳳	17
wàng zǐ chéng lóng	望子成龍	17
wàng bu liǎo	忘不了	9
wēixié	威脅	8
wēihài	危害	20
wèi	爲	5
wèicǐ	爲此	13
wěituō	委托	20
wěidà	偉大	11
wèihūn fū	未婚夫	15
wèidao	味道	3
wèikǒu	胃口	2
wèishēngzhǐ	衛生紙	4
wénjù	文具	2
wénkē	文科	5
wénxué	文學	5
wénzhāng	文章	3
wěnluàn	紊亂	18
wūrǎn	污染	20
wūrǎn yuán	污染源	20
wūlǐ	屋裏	7

wúfǎ	無法	17
wúlùn	無論	4
wúlùn rúhé	無論如何	17
wǔdǎ piān	武打片	16
wǔ dāo nòng qiāng	舞刀弄槍	18
wùlǐ	物理	5
wù měi jià lián	物美價廉	4

X

Xī'ān	西安	10
xī'àn	西岸	9
xīfāng	西方	5
xīyān	吸煙	3
xīyǐn	吸引	11
xīshēng	犧牲	19
xīyǒu	稀有	19
xítí	習題	17
xífù	媳婦	11
xǐyīfěn	洗衣粉	4
xǐyījī	洗衣機	2
xǐ zǎo	洗澡	11
xì	系	5
xì	戲	7
xìmí	戲迷	7
xián zhe méi shì	閑著沒事	8
xiànfǎ	憲法	18
xiànxiàng	現象	15
xiànzhì	限制	18
xiāng	香	3
Xiānggǎng	香港	9
xiāngzào	香皂	4
xiāngchǔ	相處	7
xiángxì	詳細	7
xiǎngfǎ	想法	5
xiǎng qǐlai	想起來	4
xiǎngxiàng	想像	11

xiǎngxiànglì	想像力	17
xiàng	項	20
xiàng	向	8
xiàngzhēng	象徵	12
xiāomiè	消滅	18
xiāoshī	消失	18
xiǎo báicài	小白菜	3
xiǎo nánhái	小男孩	8
xiǎohái	小孩	8
xiǎoxué	小學	17
xiào nèi	校內	1
xiào wài	校外	1
xiàoyuán	校園	7
xiéhuì	協會	18
xīnqíng	心情	7
xīnshì	心事	7
xīnzàng bìng	心臟病	16
xīnzàng kē	心臟科	16
xīnshēng	新生	1
xīnwén	新聞	8
xīnshui	薪水	15
xíngwéi	行為	8
xíngxiōng	行凶	18
xìnggé	性格	7
xióngmāo	熊貓	19
xiūxi	休息	17
xūqiú liàng	需求量	20
xūyào	需要	4
xūróng	虛榮	19
xǔduō	許多	11
Xuánwǔ Hú	玄武湖	11
xuǎn	選	5
xuǎnhǎo	選好	5
xuǎn kè	選課	5
xué dào	學到	5
xuéfēn	學分	5

Y

yā	鴨	12
yālì	壓力	17
yāsuìqián	壓歲錢	12
yágāo	牙膏	4
yán	鹽	3
yán	嚴	17
yánzhòng	嚴重	16
yánjiū	研究	19
yánjiūsuǒ	研究所	5
yánlùn	言論	18
yángmáo	羊毛	16
yàngzi	樣子	4
yáogǔnyuè	搖滾樂	7
yàobúshì	要不是	14
yàome	要麼	5
yāoqiú	要求	17
yěmán	野蠻	19
yěxǔ	也許	3
yìbān	一般	2
yìbān lái shuō	一般來說	17
yì běn zhèngjǐng 一本正經		11
yí bùfēn	一部分	16
yí xiàzi	一下子	10
yíxiàng	一向	10
yīliáo	醫療	16
yīxuéyuàn	醫學院	5
yīyuàn	醫院	16
yīguì	衣櫃	2
yímín	移民	9
yǐjí	以及	4
yǐlái	以來	7
yìshùpiàn	藝術片	8
yìjiàn	意見	5
yìshi	意識	19
yìyì	意義	16
yīncǐ	因此	14
yínpái	銀牌	13
yǐnqǐ	引起	8
yíng	贏	13

yíngyǎng	營養	16
yíngyǎng bùliáng		
	營養不良	16
yǐngzi	影子	20
yòngchu	用處	12
yòngxīn liángkǔ		
	用心良苦	17
yōudiǎn	優點	17
yōu guó yōu mín		
	憂國憂民	12
yóu	油	3
yóu	由	15
yóuyǔ	由於	19
yóuqí shì	尤其是	18
yóudiànjú	郵電局	10
yóujiǎn	郵簡	10
yóujú	郵局	10
yóupiào	郵票	10
yóukè	遊客	11
yóulǎn	遊覽	11
yǒu kòngr	有空兒	7
yǒumíng	有名	16
yǒushí	有時	20
yǒuxiào	有效	20
yǒuyì	有意	19
yǒuyì yú	有益於	13
yú	魚	3
yúshì	於是	4
yǔ	與	16
yǔ rì jù zēng	與日俱增	20
yùjīn	浴巾	4
yùshì	浴室	2
yuán	圓	12
yuánlái	原來	3
yuánlái rúcǐ	原來如此	20
yuányīn	原因	16
yuánxiāo	元宵	12
Yuánxiāo Jié	元宵節	12
yuànyi	願意	5
yuànzi	院子	12

Yuēhàn	約翰	2
yuèbǐng	月餅	12
yuèliang	月亮	12
yuèzū	月租	6
yùndòng huì	運動會	13
yùndòng yuán	運動員	13

Z

zàihu	在乎	4
zài...tóngshí	在...同時	19
zàisān	再三	11
zàishuō	再說	1
zánmen	咱們	5
zàng	葬	11
zāo le	糟了	19
zǎochén	早晨	12
zǎowǎn	早晚	12
zàochéng	造成	20
zàojià	造價	20
zhà	炸	8
zhǎi	窄	11
Zhànguó	戰國	12
Zhāng Tiānmíng		
	張天明	1
zhǎngdà	長大	1
zhàngfu	丈夫	15
zhāojí	著急	2
zhǎo bu dào	找不到	6
zhàogù	照顧	15
zhào xiàng	照相	9
zhéxué	哲學	5
zhēnguì	珍貴	19
zhēnxī dòngwù		
	珍稀動物	19
zhēnde	真的	2
zhēng	爭	13
zhēnglùn	爭論	4

zhēng xiān kǒng hòu		
	爭先恐後	12
zhěnggè	整個	13
zhěngtiān	整天	5
zhèng	症	16
zhèng	正	18
zhèngcháng	正常	18
zhènghǎo	正好	3
zhēngyuè	正月	12
zhèngfǔ	政府	16
zhī	枝	1
Zhījiāgē	芝加哥	9
Zhīmájiē	芝蔴街	8
zhī yī	之一	12
zhíwèi	職位	15
zhíxíng	執行	18
zhǐchū	指出	16
zhǐdǎo	指導	5
zhǐ fù wéi hūn	指腹爲婚	15
zhǐhuībàng	指揮棒	17
zhǐwàng	指望	18
zhǐhǎo	只好	3
zhǐyào	只要	18
zhǐyǒu	只有	16
zhìdù	制度	16
zhìlǐ	治理	20
zhìliàng	質量	4
zhìshǎo	至少	16
zhìyú	至於	5
zhìyào	製藥	16
Zhōngqiū Jié	中秋節	12
Zhōngshān Lù	中山路	10
Zhōngshān Líng		
	中山陵	11
zhòng nán qīng nǚ		
	重男輕女	15
zhòngshì	重視	17
zhōu	州	4
zhōuqī	週期	20
zhútǒng	竹筒	12
zhǔguǎn	主管	15
zhǔyào	主要	15
zhùcè	註册	1
zhùyì	注意	16
zhuānjiā	專家	16
zhuānyè	專業	5
zhuàn qián	賺錢	5
zhuàngguān	壯觀	11
zhuī	追	13
zǐnǚ	子女	17
zìcóng	自從	6
zìjué	自覺	17
zìrán	自然	17
zìshā	自殺	12
zì shí qí guǒ	自食其果	19
zì xiāng máo dùn		
	自相矛盾	8
zìyóu	自由	1
zǒng	總	20
zǒng de lái shuō		
	總的来説	3
zǒngsuàn	總算	11
zòngzi	粽子	12
zǒu huǒ	走火	18
zǒuláng	走廊	6
zūjīn	租金	6
zǔjí	祖籍	1
zǔzhī	組織	19
zuì	醉	7
zuìfàn	罪犯	18
zūn shī zhòng dào		
	尊師重道	17
zuò shēngyì	做生意	9
zuò zhǔ	做主	15
zuòyè	作業	17